Date: 9/28/20

362.29 ADD
Addictions : elements,
history, treatments, and

ADDICTIONS

Recent Titles in Health and Psychology Sourcebooks

Personality Disorders: Elements, History, Examples, and Research
Vera Sonja Maass

ADDICTIONS

Elements, History, Treatments, and Research

FRANCES R. FRANKENBURG, MD, EDITOR

Health and Psychology
Sourcebooks

 PRAEGER®

An Imprint of ABC-CLIO, LLC
Santa Barbara, California • Denver, Colorado

Library of Congress Cataloging-in-Publication Data

Names: Frankenburg, Frances Rachel, editor.
Title: Addictions : elements, history, treatments, and research / Frances R. Frankenburg, editor.
Other titles: Addictions (Frankenburg)
Description: Santa Barbara, California : Praeger, an imprint of ABC-CLIO, LLC, [2019] | Series: Health and psychology sourcebooks | Includes bibliographical references and index.
Identifiers: LCCN 2019019810 (print) | LCCN 2019021765 (ebook) | ISBN 9781440863400 (eBook) | ISBN 9781440863394 (print : alk. paper)
Subjects: | MESH: Substance-Related Disorders | Behavior, Addictive | Case Reports | United States
Classification: LCC RC564 (ebook) | LCC RC564 (print) | NLM WM 270 | DDC 362.29—dc23

LC record available at https://lccn.loc.gov/2019019810

ISBN: 978-1-4408-6339-4 (print)
       978-1-4408-6340-0 (ebook)

23 22 21 20 19   1 2 3 4 5

This book is also available as an eBook.

Praeger
An Imprint of ABC-CLIO, LLC

ABC-CLIO, LLC
147 Castilian Drive
Santa Barbara, California 93117
www.abc-clio.com

This book is printed on acid-free paper ∞

Manufactured in the United States of America

Contents

Series Foreword

An understanding of both physical diseases and mental disorders is vital to each of us, as sickness of body and mind touch every one of our lives, personally, with family, friends, associates, and in our immediate and greater society. Yet the cacophony of existing information sources—from piecemeal and poorly sourced websites to dense academic tomes—can make acquiring accurate, accessible, and objective facts a complicated venture. This series is a solution to that dilemma.

The *Health and Psychology Sourcebooks* series addresses physical, psychological, and environmental conditions that threaten human health and well-being. These books are designed to accessibly and reliably fulfill the needs of students and researchers at community and undergraduate college levels, whether one is seeking vetted information needed for core or elective courses, papers and publications, or personal enlightenment.

Each volume presents a topic in health or psychology and explains the symptoms, diagnosis, incidence, development, causes, treatments, and related theory. "Up Close" vignettes illustrate how the disease or disorder and its associated difficulties present in varied people and scenarios. History and classic as well as emerging research are detailed. Where controversy is present, that is discussed. Each volume also offers a glossary of terms, references, and sources for further reading.

Introduction

One line (written most unwillingly) to ask you to forgive me if I am absent tomorrow night. My doctor is trying to break me of the habit of drinking laudanum. I am stabbed every night at ten with a sharp-pointed syringe which injects morphia under my skin—and gets me a night's rest without any of the drawbacks of taking opium internally. If I only persevere with this, I am told I shall be able, before long, gradually to diminish the quantity of morphia and the number of nightly stabbings—and so emancipate myself from opium altogether.

—Wilkie Collins (quoted in Gasson 2019)

Nineteenth-century British novelist Wilkie Collins may be best known for the Victorian-era mystery *The Woman in White*, but what casual readers might not know is that he was intractably addicted to laudanum, a cocktail of opium and alcohol, which he used to treat his gout pain. In 1869, he described his addiction to laudanum, opium dissolved in alcohol, in a letter to a friend from which the previous quotation comes. In an attempt to "emancipate" Collins from his addiction, Collins's doctor began injecting him with morphine, a derivative of opium. While such a treatment (an opioid for an opioid addiction) might seem surprising to contemporary readers, at the time it was thought that injected drugs were safer and less addictive than those consumed by mouth. Not surprisingly, the doctor's experiment failed, and Collins continued to drink laudanum, in increasingly large doses, for the rest of his life.

Collins's use of the word "emancipate" suggests that he felt shackled by his dependence on opium. Indeed, the word *addiction* comes from the Latin for "slavery," and addiction can tyrannize an individual. Substance use may temporarily relieve some of the more unpleasant aspects of the human condition, such as pain, anxiety, boredom, and insomnia, but these shortcuts to relief carry with them many dangers, one of them being addiction. At first, such use may have enjoyable, even euphoric, effects, but if the use develops into an addiction, the initial pleasure melts away.

The way many neuroscientists now understand addiction is not far from this slavery metaphor. According to this understanding, the *neurobiologic theory of addiction*, a person with an addiction is subject to the demands of an imperious set of brain structures. While people may initially choose to use a drug or engage in an activity like gambling, in certain individuals, *future* use or activity become almost obligatory, or enslaving, because of changes in the brain's reward system.

This volume is designed to provide students and interested readers with a concise, contemporary, and accessible introduction to the various forms of addiction. The contributors are each experts on their respective use disorders—alcohol, cannabis, gambling, hallucinogens, inhalants, opioids, sedative hypnotics, stimulants, opioids—and their work is informed by the latest understanding of the criteria for each of these disorders (including symptoms, diagnosis, and incidence). They each trace the history of use; bring us up-to-date with the research and theory; offer case studies for discussion; and highlight innovations in treatment, among other topics. In addition, they have ample first-hand clinical experience treating those with addiction.

Symptoms of addiction include craving, misuse or abuse, dependence, and withdrawal. *Craving* is a powerful desire for a substance or activity. *Misuse* or *abuse* means that the person uses the drug or activity in a way that was not originally intended (for example, taking larger amounts of the substance) and encounters problems as a result of this usage, such as difficulty holding down a job, spending a lot of time recovering from drug use, or family conflicts at home, among others. *Dependence* is the inability to stop taking a drug or doing an activity and the development of tolerance, such that the person needs to take more of the drug or do more of the activity to get the desired effect. If the person does stop taking the drug, he or she will experience unpleasant *withdrawal* symptoms—ranging from anxiety and insomnia to prolonged inability to find pleasure in other activities to seizures. Alcohol withdrawal is the most serious and can at times be fatal.

The terminology of addiction has changed. The widely used *Diagnostic and Statistical Manual of Mental Disorders (DSM)*, a manual prepared by the American Psychiatric Association (APA) containing descriptions, symptoms, and other criteria for diagnosing mental disorders, is frequently modified in response to new research and clinical findings. The fifth edition, *DSM-5*, published in 2013, eliminates the distinction found in earlier versions between the concepts of abuse and dependence, arguing that there is no clear difference between the two. The words *addict* and *addiction* are not used as often now because of their pejorative implications. Instead, the APA has replaced the words *abuse, dependence,* and *addiction* with the phrase *substance use disorder* (SUD). Because the former words have been used for so long, they continue to be used by many, including, at times, the authors in this book. Reflecting the lack of consensus about the terminology, the title of the *DSM-5* chapter about SUDs is "Substance-Related and Addictive Disorders."

For most disorders, the *DSM-5* outlines 11 criteria, and a person meeting any 2 of the 11 criteria during the same 12-month period receives a diagnosis of SUD. Craving is a criterion new to *DSM-5*. Some variation exists among the disorders. Gambling disorder, for example, has nine criteria. Withdrawal does not occur when a user stops hallucinogens, inhalants, or gambling and so is not included as a criterion for these disorders. The severity of the disorder is on a spectrum—mild, moderate, or severe—based on the number of criteria met. People who meet more than six criteria (for most of the disorders) have severe SUD, or what is still often termed an addiction.

Gambling is now considered a behavioral disorder related to SUDs, marking a change from *DSM-IV*, where it was seen as an impulse-control disorder. This change mystifies many. Gambling is a complex activity involving luck, occasionally skill, and/or competition and has nothing to do with the ingestion of substances (unless the casino plies the gambler with free or cheap alcohol). Psychologist Clemens France described the emotional and interpersonal elements of gambling that make it seem quite different from an SUD:

> Hope and fear, joy and sorrow—are especially predominant. It is significant to note that hope must at the moment of action predominate over fear—a necessary biological condition of all action in uncertainty . . . we find arising emulation, aggression, the instinct of domination, with the love of humiliating one's opponent, much allied to the bullying and teasing tendency, pugnacity . . . Jealousy and envy are especially strong in the mind of the loser. [In poker] . . . the battle element is especially predominant. It is here also that the "bluff" plays so great a role—the attempt to beat your opponent by sheer boldness and self-confidence . . . the psychic effects of the bluffer in every day life only need to be mentioned. (France 1902, 386)

Yet there are many similarities between gambling, a behavioral addiction, and SUDs, as Grant, Grubbs, and Kraus describe in their chapter.

Prevalence and Incidence of Addiction

Exposure is a necessary but not sufficient condition to developing a use disorder—otherwise, most of us would have one. Considering all the disorders, only about 10% of people who use drugs or indulge in behaviors with the potential for addiction become addicted (Volkow, Koob, and McLellan 2016, 368). The authors of this book review the genetic, social, and environmental factors that contribute to the development of each addiction.

Each chapter addresses both *incidence*, the risk of developing a disorder, or the number of new cases, and *prevalence*, the number of people with a disorder. These numbers are approximate at best, in part because not all populations are adequately represented in surveys. For example, two of the main surveys of substance use in the United States are the National Survey on Drug Use and Health (NSDUH) and the National Epidemiologic Survey on Alcohol and Related Conditions (NESARC). The NSDUH, sponsored by the Substance Abuse and Mental Health Services Administration (SAMHSA), is an annual survey of people over the age of 12, excluding prison inmates. The data is provided anonymously and collected by a private firm using software designed for collecting sensitive data. Respondents can answer questions in their own homes. NESARC, from the National Institute on Alcohol Abuse and Alcoholism, has had three waves of in-person and in-depth diagnostic interviews of civilians over the age of 18, excluding the military and those living in institutions. Because there is a high prevalence of SUDs in prisons, both surveys may lead to underestimates of drug misuse. The numbers produced by these surveys differ, perhaps because of the dissimilar methods—computer-assisted interviews and in-person interviews can yield quite different answers. People who are addicted to a substance or behavior may be unforthcoming or uncooperative when it comes to answering questions to an interviewer in person but more willing to be honest on a computer survey. Moreover, NESARC changed some of their interview methods between the different waves. The 2001–2002 survey was conducted by U.S. Census Bureau employees and did not offer any incentives to the participants. The 2012–2013 wave, however, was conducted by a private contractor. Participants provided samples of saliva (for DNA analysis) and were paid for participation.

Because the definitions of and criteria for the disorders have changed, it can be difficult to compare data collected using earlier versions of the *DSM*. It is important, however, to try to determine trends in incidence and prevalence because they contribute to our understanding of SUDs.

Costs of Addiction

Like the prevalence and incidence of SUDs, estimates of their health and financial costs are also difficult to establish. In 2017, the National Institute of Drug Abuse (NIDA) reported that abuse of tobacco, alcohol, and illicit drugs in the United States cost more than $740 billion annually because of costs related to crime, lost work productivity, and health care (National Institute of Drug Abuse 2017). Worldwide, of all the substances of misuse, tobacco and alcohol misuse cause the greatest disease burden, which presumably would also mean the greatest financial cost (Peacock et al. 2017). Grant, Grubbs, and Kraus outline the costs of gambling to society in their chapter.

Medical History of Addiction

A common theme in the history of addiction is the development of a substance as a useful medication, and then its transformation into a drug of abuse. The most obvious example is opioids. In 1910, the physician-author William Osler described the pain he suffered from kidney stones and the relief opioids provided:

> And then abruptly, of working out of the steady pain, come the paroxysm, like a twisting tearing hurricane, with its well-known radiation, followed by the vaso-vagal features, the pallor, cold extremities, feeble pulse, nausea, vomiting, and in two attacks, a final, not altogether unpleasant period, when unconsciousness and the pain seemed wrestling for a victory reached only with the help of God's own medicine—morphia. (Quoted in Golden 2009, 519)

Osler's description of morphine as "God's own medicine" is often cited as a phrase that captures the sense of the miraculous relief offered by opioids.

In their chapter on opioids, Arout and Sofuoglu describe how the overly generous prescription of these substances has led to the current opioid epidemic, a leading cause of death in the United States. Physicians are now urged to limit their use of this miraculous medicine. Opioids are appropriate short-term treatments for acute pain (such as Osler's kidney stones) or pain associated with cancer, but they are not useful for chronic pain, and indeed may be harmful. The current arguments against using opioids for pain relief are, however, irrelevant for much of the world's population who have little access to opioids for the relief of acute pain (Berterame et al. 2016).

Perhaps less well known is the medical history of stimulants, a category of drugs including cocaine, amphetamine, and its close relative, methamphetamine. In 1884, Carl Koller, a young ophthalmologist, used cocaine as a local anesthetic to assuage the horrors and agonies of cataract surgery, and it continues to be used, legally and effectively, as a topical anesthetic for some head and neck procedures. At the time of Koller's discovery, Sigmund Freud, the father of psychoanalysis, was using cocaine orally as an energy booster and antidepressant. He wrote about it enthusiastically until he saw addictions develop. Amphetamine was prescribed to treat nasal congestion, fatigue, depression, and obesity, but those uses are rare today. In her chapter, Yule outlines the well-accepted use of amphetamine and related substances in the treatment of attention deficit hyperactivity disorder (ADHD), a psychiatric disorder marked by impulsivity, hyperactivity, and difficulty sustaining attention, and often comorbid with depression. The nonmedical use (NMU) of amphetamines on college campuses is problematic as is misuse of amphetamines and cocaine.

Cannabis, or marijuana, has long been used as a medicine in China and India. The cannabis plant produces many molecules, including cannabinoids, the best known of which is the psychoactive delta-9-tetrahydrocannabinol (THC). In the 1800s, many proprietary medications in the United States contained some cannabis. There is now a revival of interest in its medical use as well as increasing acceptance of its recreational use. In June 2018, the U.S. Food and Drug Administration (FDA) approved the use of cannabidiol (CBD), a cannabinoid with no psychoactive properties, for the treatment of seizures in some rare cases of epilepsy. Dronabinol, synthetic THC, is used to decrease nausea and vomiting and to increase appetite in some illnesses. However, cannabis is not entirely safe; some people become addicted, and in vulnerable adolescents, it can lead to psychosis (D'Souza et al. 2017).

Sedatives and hypnotics, reviewed by von Horn and LaRose, are some of the most widely prescribed and useful medications in the United States. Nevertheless, as with opioids, they also can be misused and can lead to difficult-to-treat addictions. Overdoses of benzodiazepines, the most commonly prescribed sedatives or hypnotics, when taken alone, are rarely fatal. But overdoses of benzodiazepines combined with alcohol, or other drugs, especially opioids, are dangerous (National Institute of Drug Abuse 2018).

The history of inhalants forms part of the history of anesthesia. In the eighteenth and nineteenth centuries, people sniffed ether and nitrous oxide for their intoxicating effects and noticed that they became insensible to pain. Eventually, dentists and physicians realized that the administration of these substances at higher doses could dull consciousness and make dental work and surgery more tolerable. Some of the early discoverers of the benefits of these substances used them for their intoxicating effects and became addicted to them.

The exotic history of hallucinogens and dissociative drugs involves shamans and rituals from Siberia to the Amazonian forests. These substances are part of healing in some non-Western cultures. Today, in the West, there is interest in the use of hallucinogens as treatment for addictions, terminal illnesses, depression, and post–traumatic stress disorder. Two hallucinogens, phencyclidine (PCP) and ketamine, were developed as anesthetic drugs. Ketamine is one of the newest treatments for depression and suicidality, and some anecdotal evidence suggests that ayahuasca (a foul-tasting tealike concoction) can be useful for the treatment of addictions. MDMA (3,4-methylenedioxymethamphetamine)—a synthetic hallucinogen also known as ecstasy—and PCP have no approved medical uses and can be both dangerous and addictive.

Advances in Chemistry and Technology

Advances in chemistry and technology have led to the creation of more dangerous drugs. For example, after 19th-century German chemists isolated the alkaloid cocaine from the coca leaf, the relatively benign leaf was transformed into a drug with a rapid onset of action. Further chemical work led to the formation of free-base cocaine. When smoked, this kind of cocaine is more likely to lead to an addiction than drinking coca tea or even snorting powder cocaine.

In her chapter about tobacco, Kelly describes how the invention of the cigarette in the late 1800s made tobacco easier to smoke. In the 21st century, companies are selling electronic cigarettes, or e-cigarettes, containing free-base nicotine that can be vaporized, or "vaped." While the conventional cigarette relies on the combustion of tobacco, an e-cigarette has no flame, and the vaporizers are discreet in smell and appearance. Vaping is thought to produce fewer carcinogenic substances than burning tobacco does. Clever companies have now developed the e-cigarette even further into "pod mods," small rechargeable devices that contain *nicotine salts*, which allow the user to inhale higher concentrations of nicotine than is possible with other e-cigarettes (Barrington-Trimis and Leventhal 2018). Both types of e-cigarettes come in flavors, such as mango, cool mint, and bubble gum, designed to appeal to youth.

While e-cigarettes are marketed as "safer" and "healthier" than regular cigarettes, there is often a delay in recognizing the adverse health consequences to new products. Those familiar with the history of opioids will remember that heroin was developed as a safe alternative to morphine—the revelation of its dangerousness came later. Likewise, many sleeping pills were promoted as safe until reports of strange sleep events and addiction began to accumulate. The cynic will wonder if e-cigarettes will turn out to be as—or even more—addictive, harmful, and profitable than the combustible cigarette.

With regard to cannabinoids, botanists and horticulturalists are increasing the potency of cannabis by selecting high-THC strains and growing the plants in greenhouses with artificially controlled light and humidity. Chemists are synthesizing cannabinoid molecules in the laboratory. The illegal synthetic cannabinoids, such as K2 and spice, have a different chemical structure than the plant cannabinoids. Their psychoactive effects, not modified by the myriad other substances in the cannabis plant, are stronger, longer-lasting, and more unpredictable than those of plant-based cannabinoids.

The story of the synthesis of methamphetamine, from 19th-century discoveries in Japan to Nazi Germany to "mom-and-pop meth labs" in the Midwest to large cartels in Mexico, is told in the stimulant chapter. The story is another illustration of how people all over the world, with different methods, use chemical techniques to make money and destroy lives by developing addictive drugs.

In their chapter about gambling, Grant, Grubbs, and Kraus discuss several advances, including the casino, electronic gambling machines, and internet gambling, that have made gambling an increasingly enslaving activity.

Addiction to More Than One Substance or Activity

The division of this book into chapters may deceive the reader into thinking addictions are separate, but often several addictive substances or activities are indulged in together. Casinos offer gamblers cheap or free alcohol to encourage them to gamble higher amounts of money. As is apparent in the passage by Wilkie Collins, laudanum, the opium and alcohol mixture, was popular in the 1800s. A laudanum-like elixir, the Brompton cocktail, was used at the Royal Brompton Hospital and then other British hospitals to relieve discomfort at the end of life. Tailored to the patient's requests, it was a mixture of opioids and sometimes cocaine or chlorpromazine. Wine and cocaine were combined to form the popular drink Vin Mariani. An American pharmacist had the same idea but added caffeine and replaced the wine with sugar. (Both caffeine and sugar may be mildly addictive or habit forming.) The coca leaf remained, but the psychoactive active components of the coca were removed. He carbonated the beverage—and then the world had Coca-Cola.

People often combine drugs in idiosyncratic ways. In a 1970 paper, English physician John Todd described patients with what he called "polymorphous" drug addiction. A 35-year-old woman used amphetamine, barbiturates, Benadryl, and morphine while also smoking cannabis and drinking as much cough medicine as she could. A 32-year-old woman sniffed coal gas, floor polish, glue, nail varnish remover, paint cleaner, and petrol lighter fluid. A 22-year-old man consumed amphetamine, barbiturates, and LSD, and inhaled carbon tetrachloride vapor (Todd 1970).

The mixture of drugs and activities can potentiate the effects of each drug, helpfully in the case of the Brompton cocktail, commercially successfully in the case of Vin Mariani or Coca-Cola, but often unpredictably or dangerously. The mixture of benzodiazepines with opioids, cocaine with opioids, or many drugs with alcohol can be lethal. The combination of cocaine and opioids forms what is colloquially called a "speedball," which can be snorted or injected. Cocaine speeds the person up, and the opioid calms the person down. In the past, the opioid of choice in a speedball was often heroin; in 2019, it may be the more potent fentanyl or a fentanyl analogue. Speedball usage has been associated with many deaths. The combination of cocaine and alcohol appeals to many, but it leads to the formation of cocaethylene, a compound that is harmful to the heart.

Some people use drugs to treat the problems or side effects caused by other drugs. For example, they will take sedatives such as benzodiazepines to calm themselves, and then stimulants to counteract the soporific effect of the sedatives. Sometimes people use drugs to help them stop taking other drugs. Sigmund Freud gave a physician friend of his cocaine to help him withdraw from morphine. Physicians treating American surgeon William Halsted tried the opposite—using morphine to wean him off his addiction to cocaine. In each case, the physician-patients became addicted to both substances. However, the practice of using one drug to stop using another drug can sometimes succeed. Physicians routinely and safely use benzodiazepines to treat alcohol withdrawal. Much of the medical community now believes in the effectiveness of medication-assisted treatment (MAT)—drugs to battle drugs—to help people stop misusing substances.

Addictions and Profit

As a society, we disapprove of the drug cartels and the "drug pushers" who profit from addictions to illegal drugs; but legal corporations that sell alcohol, opioid medications, and tobacco and organize gambling also knowingly profit from those who use their products to excess. These companies are quick to see marketing opportunities. Pharmaceutical companies marketed sleeping pills to stressed and unhappy women in the 1950s and 1960s; the Rolling Stones mocked these drugs as "mother's little helper." Dexamyl, a popular drug at the same time, combined an amphetamine to help one feel more energetic and lose weight and a barbiturate to treat the stimulant-caused jitteriness. Both substances are addictive. Tobacco companies exploited the misery of soldiers who were often terrified, in pain, or exhausted by supplying them with cigarettes, which decreased their anxiety and distracted them. The cigarettes were free during war time. Veterans returned home as smokers but now needed to pay for their cigarettes.

Another opportunity to make money legally is to promote an addictive substance as healthy. Philip Morris International, the world's largest publicly traded tobacco company, is promoting and profiting from e-cigarettes, claiming that they help people stop using combustible tobacco. Sometimes these companies go too far. Five large liquor companies were interested in helping fund a National Institutes of Health research study to determine if moderate alcohol consumption protects against heart disease, as has long been suspected. Because other research has established that industry-sponsored research often favors the industry's interests, the study was eventually cancelled. Companies that manufacture and distribute opioids have claimed that the drugs were safe and effective treatments of pain; these same companies are now being sued for facilitating the overuse of opioids even when evidence of misuse was accumulating. Although the medical community supports the use of medications to battle addiction, it does seem ironic that some pharmaceutical companies benefit from the products that now exist to treat the problem of opioid addiction.

Governments are ambivalent about substances of misuse. Legal sales of alcohol and tobacco generate tax revenue, yet alcohol and tobacco lead to lost productivity, violence, and increased health-care costs. The attitude of government toward alcohol is discussed in the alcohol chapter with respect to Prohibition. Grant, Grubbs, and Kraus describe how problem gambling is clearly costly for society, but many governments tax gambling wins, profit from state lotteries, and cannot give up the immediate pleasure of tax revenue.

Addictions and Women

For most of the substances discussed in this book, male users outnumber female users, and more men gamble than women. Most addiction research and treatment programs have been focused on men, and much research on SUDs has been done in the Veterans Administration Medical Centers, which treat predominantly male patients. As is discussed in these chapters, addiction affects men and women differently. For example, women and men gamble in different ways; and once they start gambling, women will escalate their habit more quickly than men. Women absorb and metabolize alcohol differently than men, and perhaps because of these differences, suffer more health effects from alcohol than men. Women are also more likely to choose to use substances such as nicotine or amphetamines that may be associated with weight loss and are more likely to be prescribed sedative hypnotics.

Substance misuse in pregnancy is problematic. Alcohol, when drunk heavily by the pregnant woman, can harm the unborn. The multiple risks that smoking tobacco confers upon the developing baby are well known. Babies born to women using opioids—whether illegal or prescription—might shows signs of withdrawal after birth. SUDs in pregnant women often are associated with poor prenatal care, misuse of several substances, poor nutrition, and socioeconomic difficulties. Concern for the welfare of the woman and baby is also sometimes exploited for political purposes. For example, crack cocaine misuse in black pregnant women was used to great effect in the "War on Drugs" in the 1980s. Politicians and journalists railed against "irresponsible" women bearing "crack babies" who would never be normal. They used these concerns as an argument for harsher sentences for drug users. Research has shown that the reports about "crack babies" were sensationalistic and inaccurate and that harsher treatment of pregnant women misusing crack cocaine did not lead to better care for the babies or for their mothers. Some of the results of harsher sentencing for possession (with intent to distribute) of crack cocaine versus powder cocaine are discussed in the stimulant chapter.

Pregnant and breastfeeding women should try to avoid ingesting all drugs or substances that could be harmful. They would be well advised to review with their clinician any drugs or substances that they are exposed to. As for the clinician, it is probably not helpful if the caregiver admonishes a pregnant woman who is misusing substances and who often is already feeling afraid and ashamed. A disparaging attitude may drive the person away from getting help.

Some physicians see addiction as a man's problem and will be less likely to suspect it in a woman, particularly if she is middle class and white. But substance misuse by such women has been addressed by writers. Two 20th-century literary masterpieces depict addiction in white women in bleak detail. In his acclaimed play *Long Day's Journey into Night*, Eugene O'Neill (2002) describes the Tyrone family, closely modeled on his own. The men are alcoholics, and Mary Tyrone, the matriarch, has been addicted to morphine ever since it was prescribed to her after a painful childbirth. The family blames her addiction on the cavalier prescribing practices of her incompetent physician. She, in turn, blames her addiction on her son. (The labor and delivery of this son were what led to the prescription of morphine.) In *To Kill a Mockingbird*, Harper Lee (1960) details the agony Mrs. Dubose undergoes as she tries to withdraw from opioids before she dies. Atticus Finch describes her as a brave woman, but most readers will probably remember how horribly she behaves toward his children, Scout, and Jem.

Society's Understandings of Addictions

In the past, people with addictions were seen as evil or immoral, and they were exhorted to change their ways, punished, or sent to some kind of institution. As noted in the alcohol chapter, the language of Alcoholics Anonymous (AA) makes it clear that AA still has some residue of this view. For example, although AA believes that alcoholism is a disease, the Twelve Steps refer to "a searching and fearless moral inventory" and "defects of character" (Alcoholics Anonymous 2001, 59).

Freud, a gifted interpreter of the dreams, thoughts, and actions of others, attributed addiction to the personality of the user, and later psychiatrists have adopted this approach. For example, when people began to report that they were addicted to benzodiazepines, the first impulse of the doctors was to deny the addictive potential of the drugs and to say that the "real problem with dependence was that patients worried about it too much" (Medawar 1992, 122). In the 1980s, psychiatrists finally acknowledged the problem but attributed it to "dependence-prone" personalities (Medawar 1992, 134–135).

In a 2012 article in *The Atlantic,* the literary critic Alan Jacobs described the complicated attitude of poet W. H. Auden toward various substances. In a pattern of drug taking that was similar to that of some of Dr. Todd's patients, Auden took sedatives and stimulants. In the morning he took Benzedrine, known colloquially as "bennies," an amphetamine used in inhalers or as tablets. Then he took alcohol and barbiturates to ensure sleep:

> The poet W. H. Auden considered it a sign of weak character that he had to rely on artificial stimulants to maintain his workday

discipline, but rely on them he did. For many years he started his days with bennies and ended them with alcohol and barbiturates: he called this "the chemical life." He strongly disapproved of hallucinogenic drugs, of which he wrote, "One is inclined to suspect that habitual taking of this type of drug, even if it has no harmful physical effects, would lead to a selfish indifference towards the common world we live in and a withering of love and affection for others." But bennies did not alter one's personality or distort one's perceptions of reality; they were, in that sense at least, morally acceptable. (Jacobs 2012)

Auden referred to his own use of stimulants, alcohol, and barbiturates as a "sign of weak character," while seeming to think that the use of hallucinogens was worse and not, in Jacobs's words, presumably reflecting Auden's belief, "morally acceptable." Western society is more tolerant of medications that wake us up in the morning and put us to sleep at night than drugs that alter how we see the world. Coffee and wine are celebrated; LSD is feared. But that view may be changing. We are becoming alarmed about the use of opioids and sedatives and more interested in the use of hallucinogens to help lessen distress at the end of life and possibly to treat addictions. In any event, a judgmental approach to addictions through the lens of immorality or weakness of character has fallen out of favor.

It is often easier to analyze others' addictions than our own. Both Bill W., one of the cofounders of AA, and Sigmund Freud each had psychological theories about why people became addicted—and each was stymied by his own nicotine addiction. Freud could not stop smoking cigars despite warnings from his doctors that his habit was worsening his jaw cancer (Markel 2011, 172, 224). Bill W. developed severe lung disease and continued to smoke cigarettes even while using oxygen (Lattin 2012, 242).

Addiction as Brain Disease

Current medical thinking is that SUD is a disease of the brain. As early as 1956, the American Medical Association declared that alcoholism is an illness. In 1997, Alan Leshner, then director of NIDA, wrote in a widely cited article in *Science*, that "the addicted brain is distinctly different from the nonaddicted brain" and that "addiction . . . [is] . . . a chronic, relapsing disease of the brain" (Leshner 1997, 46). Now neuroscientists can describe the underlying brain pathways of the addicted brain.

In 2016, Nora Volkow, director of NIDA, together with coauthors Koob and McLellan, updated Leshner's article in another widely cited and influential review of the neurobiologic advances in understanding SUDs (Volkow, Koob, and McLellan 2016).

The neurobiologic theory of addiction is that the normal functioning of the brain has been "hijacked" by addictive drugs or activities because of their effects on the brain's limbic system, deep within the brain, where we experience pleasure and memory.

The limbic system contains the reward system that is intimately connected with addiction. The ventral tegmental area (VTA) is an area in the midbrain with a large supply of dopaminergic neurons that travel to the nucleus accumbens via the mesolimbic pathway. When dopamine, a brain neurotransmitter, surges in the nucleus accumbens, the result is pleasure and motivation. The evolutionary purpose of the reward system is to motivate the person to do whatever is necessary to stay alive or to reproduce, typically eating and sexual activity. Other neurotransmitters, such as glutamate, gamma-aminobutyric acid, noradrenaline, endocannabinoids, and endorphins, are also involved. Addictive activities light up the powerful and nonverbal limbic system more strongly than do other activities. Addictions take over dopaminergic and glutamatergic input into the brain's reward system, or motivational circuitry. The nonverbal limbic system acts as though the life of the person or his or her ability to have progeny depends on continuing the drug or activity.

The reward system is intertwined with learning. Pathways that link addictive activities to remembered pleasure are formed and strengthened. Finally, the person must continue the drug to keep dopamine levels normal. In its absence, dopamine levels drop, which can be unbearable. The person craves the drug and has become dependent. Withdrawal will be difficult and sometimes prolonged.

Another important pathway is the mesocortical pathway, which travels from the VTA to the prefrontal cortex, the part of the brain involved in executive functioning. These higher level brain activities involve: the inhibition of impulses; initiating, planning, and monitoring tasks; and being flexible. People with intact executive functioning can: assess, compare, and judge the importance of different activities; know when they have made a mistake; and change course. The prefrontal cortex is where we cogitate, ponder, and realize the importance of family, achievements, relationships, and the rule of law. Input from the VTA alters the normal functioning of the prefrontal cortex. The person who has an addiction not only craves the substance or activity but also may have poorer executive functioning, and thus difficulty making and carrying out sensible decisions. Even when the person "knows" that the substance is harmful, executive functioning has become oriented toward getting drugs and is sadly diminished and unable to ignore or debate imperatives from the reward system.

An SUD is thus difficult to vanquish, particularly so for the adolescent, whose prefrontal cortex has not yet fully developed and so is more vulnerable to the impact of addictions. The earlier the onset of the addiction or the substance use, the more serious the problems are likely to be.

As a consequence of this neurobiologic approach, addiction is now seen more akin to chronic illnesses, such as autoimmune disorders, heart disease, or cancer. The stigma surrounding addiction has decreased, and the role of medications and medical professionals in the treatment of these disorders has been legitimized. There is no need for a person with an illness to keep it secret and no shame in asking for help. On the other hand, smoking and drunk driving are currently stigmatized; indeed, this disapproval has helped reduce these activities.

However, the oft-made comparison between addiction and chronic diseases puzzles some people with those latter diseases who claim that they never chose to overindulge or to take illegal substances and that their illness does not harm others, while addiction can and often does. A person crippled with rheumatoid arthritis might not identify with a drunk driver who has had repeated driving accidents. Although less popular, there are other current explanations for addiction that do not rely on the disease model.

Addiction as Choice or Learning

Not everyone finds the disease model of addiction compelling. Some understand drug misuse not as an illness but as a choice. According to this understanding, people choose to use a drug or to gamble, and then make that choice repeatedly. These people are not ill but are impulsive and do not consider the consequences of their actions. Psychologist Gene Heyman (2010) develops this argument at length in his book *Addiction: A Disorder of Choice*. Heyman argues that people can stop substance use if they are worried enough about job security, health, or finances, or when they "grow up." He quotes large epidemiological surveys finding that people quit drugs, may relapse again, but "by about age 30 most have quit for good" (Heyman 2010, 77). People relinquish their addiction when, to use another term, they "mature out" of their disorder or find another more fulfilling activity—such as religion, marriage, or a satisfying job.

Those who believe that addiction is not an illness say that to call the persistent use of drugs an irresistible craving or compulsion or disease because of brain changes is incorrect. In his discussion of SUDs, neuroscientist Marc Lewis (2018) reminds us that the brain changes with all activities and learning. Neurocognitive changes can be related to learning or adaptation, not just pathology. Moreover, neuroimaging findings come from people who *already* have SUDs:

> Evidence of a functional and (in some studies) structural disconnection between the prefrontal cortex and striatum [part of the reward system] has been pivotal for defining addiction as a brain disease. Unfortunately, these findings come from cross-sectional, not longitudinal, research, so some cortical differences must precede rather than follow addiction, as acknowledged by the researchers. Yet even cortical changes that arise from (or with) addictive drug use need not be considered pathologic. (Lewis 2018, 1555)

Lewis also reviews the complex environmental influences that can be the background to addiction and how the addiction itself changes the environment of the person:

> From these beginnings [early psychosocial adversity], a narrowing spiral of ineffective coregulation emerges between developing children and their caregivers, leading eventually to entrainment between drug seeking and its environmental concomitants. . . . addiction emerges universally as a response to the disruption of normal social interactions. Therefore, models of addiction predicated on embodied cognition should focus on environments in which social stressors affect early neuropsychological development, as a gateway to ongoing reciprocal adjustments between disadvantageous organismic adaptations and narrowing environmental opportunities. (Lewis 2018, 1557–1558)

Those in AA and those who hew to the disease model would not entirely disagree with this last paragraph. Most addiction experts acknowledge the important and reciprocal relationships between addiction and environment. Perhaps some of the differences between the disease model and the more psychologically oriented choice-learning model are a question of emphasis rather than disagreement.

Public Policy

Can governments promote policies to diminish the harm so often caused by addiction? One obvious way is to make certain substances or activities illegal. In the early 20th century, Prohibition in the United States demonstrated the futility of making substances illegal without an accompanying public consensus. If people want a drug that they cannot purchase legally, they will seek out the substance from lawbreakers who often provide it efficiently and unhampered by regulations, taxes, or input from shareholders or boards of directors. But these criminals may not be concerned about the safety of their products, and they may not pay or treat their workers well. With respect to cocaine, the farmers in the Andes who grow coca stay poor and the couriers and street vendors risk jail or death, while the large-volume traffickers become wealthy.

If currently illicit drugs were legalized, profits would be taxed and perhaps used more equably. The substances would be regulated, and the workers would be paid better. Criminality would be less profitable, the violence between competing criminal gangs would be reduced, and the number of people in jails and prisons would drop. But there are down-sides to legalization. Consumption of the substances might increase as they become more available and as corporations begin to promote them. People and industries that depend on the large number of prisons in the United States might lose jobs and income.

Public policy concerning drugs often seems to be racist and/or anti-immigrant. The first laws criminalizing opium in the 1870s in the United States were directed against Chinese immigrants in California. In the chapters about cannabis and cocaine, Frankenburg describes how much of the uproar against cannabis in the 1930s was related to fears about Mexican immigrants while the laws against crack cocaine seem to have been aimed against African Americans (or at least had that effect) (Alexander 2012).

Another way of fighting addiction is by suing the industries responsible. In her chapter, Kelly describes how 46 state attorneys general, five U.S. territories, and Washington, D.C., successfully sued the tobacco industry. The resulting 1998 Tobacco Master Settlement Agreement (MSA) is the largest legal settlement in U.S. history and might have been one of the reasons for the substantial decrease in cigarette smoking in the United States (Healton 2018). (One of these attorneys has gone on to sue the pharmaceutical companies manufacturing opioids.)

Prevention is another approach. Rather than treat an SUD, it would be better to encourage people not to begin misusing substances. One such attempt was the American Drug Abuse Resistance Education (DARE) program. Law enforcement and school officials developed this program in 1983 as a way of educating youth about the perils of drug abuse, but it is thought to have been ineffective. Griffith Edwards, an English alcoholism expert, argued that education was not helpful with respect to decreasing alcohol abuse, but that increasing the prices of alcohol and limiting its availability were helpful (Edwards 2003). Social disapproval and stigmatization, perhaps more than education, have helped decrease incidences of smoking and drunk driving.

Harm reduction is a public policy approach in which the aim is to reduce the risk associated with the activity, not necessarily to reduce the activity itself. The campaign against drunk driving is an example of harm reduction. Another example is the practice in some cities of giving clean needles to people who inject drugs so that they will be less likely to develop AIDS and/or hepatitis B or C. Other government agencies provide first responders with naloxone, an opioid antagonist, so that those who overdose on opioids can be rescued. Some argue that the use of e-cigarettes is a form of harm reduction.

Yet another governmental response has been to control the medical prescriptions of addictive drugs. In 1970, the U.S. Drug Enforcement Administration (DEA) divided drugs into five categories, or schedules, based on each drug's potential for misuse and medical usefulness. Schedule I contains the most dangerous drugs, which are illegal, addictive, and have no medical use. Heroin, for example, is a Schedule I drug. Doctors can prescribe drugs in Schedules II through V, all of which are thought to have some medical usefulness, with some limitations. Schedule II contains drugs that have the most potential for addiction, and Schedule V contains drugs that have the least potential for addiction, with the drugs in Schedules III and IV having intermediate potential. For example, benzodiazepines are Schedule IV drugs, and cough syrup with small amounts of codeine is a Schedule V drug. The scheduling has some peculiarities. Alcohol and tobacco, the most harmful substances, are not scheduled, presumably because of the public's acceptance of them and their long history of being available without prescription. Cannabis and the hallucinogens dimethyltryptamine (DMT) and mescaline are Schedule I drugs and hence illegal federally. But cannabis can be prescribed and/or used recreationally in many states. Both ayahuasca tea that contains DMT and mescaline can be used legally in some religious ceremonies.

Treatment

All the chapters review treatment for addictions. The chapter about hallucinogens differs in that it reviews hallucinogens *themselves* as possible treatment for addictions to other substances. Whether one calls an addiction an SUD, a brain disease, a poor choice, or a learned pattern of behavior, most experts will still recommend treatment. Indeed, one of the strongest critics of the theory that addiction is an illness, psychologist Stanton Peele, has his own treatment program. The goal of addiction treatment is to help the person first go through detoxification (known colloquially as "detox"), if necessary, and then to stabilize, and finally to achieve sustained abstinence, or at least decreased consumption with good overall functioning.

Experts generally agree that treatment results are better if the staff are well trained, work in interdisciplinary teams, and provide continuing care (Weisheit and White 2009, 208–219). On the other hand, with respect to treatment for alcoholism, regular and structured meetings with a medical professional and placebo (rather than active medications) seem to be as or more effective than specialized treatment (Anton et al. 2006).

Most people with SUDs in the United States receive inadequate treatment or none at all for several reasons: not everyone recognizes the need for treatment or wants it; treatment can be expensive; those who do want treatment and can afford it often must wait because many programs have waiting lists. Finally, people who enter treatment might stay for only a short time or not return for follow-up care (Weisheit and White 2009, 209). The situation is better in other countries. For example, in Sweden, more than 70% of people with opioid use disorder receive treatment, while in the United States that figure may be as low as 15% to 20% (Molero et al. 2018). Opportunities for treatment might be particularly limited in rural areas in the United States.

Treatment programs in the United States can be inpatient, residential, or outpatient, and they often have counseling and rehabilitation components. Some programs are funded by health insurance; some are very expensive. There are many programs within the criminal justice system. While detoxification takes just a few days, inpatient and outpatient programs can last anywhere from a few weeks to months. Self-help or mutual-aid groups, the most famous being AA, can be helpful treatment options. Some people attribute their sobriety and its maintenance to AA and may be active in the group for many years.

One important part of treatment is teaching the person how internal or external triggers, or "cues," can cause relapse. In their description of the neurobiological underpinning of substance abuse, Volkow, Koob, and McLellan (2016) note that dopaminergic cells begin to fire in anticipation when a trigger is encountered (364–366). The trigger or cue "predicts" a reward. If the reward is not delivered, dopamine neurons may stop their usual firing. Thus, the trigger is a strong motivator to get the reward (Hyman, 2005).

Therefore, if someone always uses a drug or gambles when in certain locations or with certain people, that person should stay away from those places or people to avoid being "triggered." If someone has an urge to drink whenever people talk about alcohol, that person should avoid conversations about alcohol. This advice must be repeated often to people trying to maintain sobriety.

It is somewhat paradoxical then that treatment programs usually involve proximity to people who use drugs and talk about it. It is not unusual for a person to refuse to go to AA or other self-help groups or treatment programs saying, "Everyone talks about drugs, and it just makes me want to use."

Medications, combined with substantial psychological support, are sometimes used to treat addictions. The two main types of medications used in MAT are antagonists (substances that stop the action of another) and agonists (substances that mimic the action of another). The best-known antagonist, naltrexone (used either by mouth or by monthly injection), seems to block the desired effects of alcohol or opioids, as is described in those chapters, and therefore leads to the "extinction" of drug-taking and drug-seeking behavior. Naltrexone has also been studied in the treatment of gambling, as some people think of naltrexone as a "pan-addiction treatment" (Aboujaoude and Salame 2016). Agonists have the opposite effect. As replacement or substitute therapies, they share some pharmacological effects with the drug of abuse but have less abuse potential and are delivered in a safer way. For example, it is safer to use methadone or buprenorphine than heroin. Because heroin is illegal, it not regulated or standardized, can be contaminated by fentanyl or other substances, and can be administered with dirty needles. Those who use it also can become involved in a world of illegal activities and relationships with lawbreakers, leading to further harm. Methadone and buprenorphine allow some people who are dependent on opioids to stop using illicit drugs, stabilize physically and psychologically, attend counseling and rehabilitation programs, and resume (or begin) more "normal" or at least law-abiding lives. Nicotine patches, gum, or lozenges deliver nicotine in safer ways than combustible tobacco.

MAT can help people break the chains of dependency. Moreover, these medications may mitigate some of the harms associated with addictions. For example, researchers from Sweden have described how MAT for alcohol and opioid use disorders appears to be helpful in diminishing the suicidality and crime associated with these disorders. In other words, suicidality and crime are not independent of addiction. A person who drinks alcohol and makes suicide attempts or commits armed robberies will likely be troubled less by suicidality and have fewer lawbreaking incidents when receiving MAT. These new findings are not surprising (Molero et al. 2018). However, not all people are comfortable taking drugs to combat a drug addiction problem. When considering MAT, the possible problems of diversion or misuse of the agonist must be considered.

Acknowledgments

The following people are all busy but, nonetheless, cheerfully volunteered to contribute their support, knowledge, and good sense in the preparation of this book. They are not responsible for any errors.

Charles Drebing, Sarah Carnes, Debbie Carvalko, Alan Cole, Gary Cole, Lucy Cole, Robert Frankenburg, Lawrence Herz, D. C. Park, Heather Rodino, and Mary Zanarini.

Bibliography

Aboujaoude, Elias, and Wael O. Salame. "Naltrexone: A Pan-Addiction Treatment?" *CNS Drugs* 30, no. 8 (2016), 719–733. doi:10.1007/s40263-016-0373-0.

Alcoholics Anonymous. *Alcoholics Anonymous: The Story of How Many Thousands of Men and Women have Recovered from Alcoholism,* 4th ed. New York: Alcoholics Anonymous World Services, 2001.

Alexander, Michelle. *The New Jim Crow: Mass Incarceration in the Age of Colorblindness*. New York: The New Press, 2012.

American Psychiatric Association. *Diagnostic and Statistical Manual of Mental Disorders (DSM-5)*, 5th ed. Arlington, VA: American Psychiatric Association, 2013.

Anton, Raymond F., Stephanie S. O'Malley, Domenic A. Ciraulo, Ron A. Cisler, David Couper, Dennis M. Donovan, David R. Gastfriend, et al. "Combined Pharmacotherapies and Behavioral Interventions for Alcohol Dependence." *JAMA* 295, no. 17 (2006), 2003–2017. doi:10.1001/jama.295.17.2003.

Barrington-Trimis, Jessica L., and Adam M. Leventhal. "Adolescents' Use of 'Pod Mod' E-Cigarettes—Urgent Concerns." *New Engl J Med* 379, no. 12 (2018), 1099–1102. doi:10.1056/nejmp1805758.

Berterame, Stefano, Juliana Erthal, Johny Thomas, Sarah Fellner, Benjamin Vosse, Philip Clare, Wei Hao, et al. "Use of and Barriers to Access to Opioid Analgesics: A Worldwide, Regional, and National

Study." *Lancet* 387, no. 10028 (2016), 1644–1656. doi:10.1016/s0140-6736(16)00161-6.

D'Souza, Cyril D., Rajiv Radhakrishnan, Mohamed Sherif, Jose Cortes-Briones, John Cahill, Swapnil Gupta, Patrick D. Skosnik, and Mohini Ranganathan. "Cannabinoids and Psychosis." *Curr Pharm Des* 22, no. 42 (2017), 6380–6391.

Edwards, Griffith. *Alcohol: The World's Favorite Drug.* London: Thomas Dunne Books, 2003.

France, Clemens J. "The Gambling Impulse." *Am J Psychol* 13, no. 3 (1902), 364–407. doi:10.2307/1412559.

Gasson, Andrew. "Wilkie Collins and laudanum (opium), in WILKIE COLLINS INFORMATION PAGES." Copyright Andrew Gasson 1998–2010. Last modified February 2019. http://www.wilkie-collins.info/index.htm.

Golden, Richard L. "William Osler, Urolithiasis, and God's Own Medicine." *Urology* 74, no. 3 (2009), 517–521. doi:10.1016/j.urology.2009.02.041.

Healton, Cheryl. "The Tobacco Master Settlement Agreement—Strategic Lessons for Addressing Public Health Problems." *New Engl J Med* 379, no. 11 (2018), 997–1000. doi:10.1056/nejmp1802633.

Heyman, Gene M. *Addiction: A Disorder of Choice.* Cambridge: Harvard University Press, 2010.

Hyman, Steven E. "Addiction: A Disease of Learning and Memory." *Am J Psychiatry* 162 (2005), 1414–1422. doi:10.1176/appi.ajp.162.8.1414.

Jacobs, Alan. "The Lost World of Benzedrine." *Atlantic*, April 2012. Accessed July 29, 2019. https://www.theatlantic.com/health/archive/2012/04/the-lost-world-of-benzedrine/255904/.

Lattin, Don. *Distilled Spirits: Getting High, Then Sober, with a Famous Writer, a Forgotten Philosopher, and a Hopeless Drunk.* Oakland: University of California Press, 2012.

Lee, Harper. *To Kill a Mockingbird.* New York: HarperCollins, 1960.

Leshner, Alan I. "Addiction Is a Brain Disease, and It Matters." *Science* 278, no. 5335 (1997), 45–47.

Lewis, Marc. "Brain Change in Addiction as Learning, Not Disease." *New Engl J Med* 379, no. 16 (2018), 1551–1560. doi:10.1056/nejmra1602872.

Markel, Howard. *An Anatomy of Addiction: Sigmund Freud, William Halsted, and the Miracle Drug Cocaine.* New York: Vintage Books, 2011.

Medawar, Charles. *Power and Dependence: Social Audit on the Safety of Medicines*. London: Social Audit, 1992.

Molero, Yasmina, Johan Zetterqvist, Ingrid A. Binswanger, Clara Hellner, Henrik Larsson, and Seena Fazel. "Medications for Alcohol and Opioid Use Disorders and Risk of Suicidal Behavior, Accidental Overdoses, and Crime." *Am J Psychiatry* 175, no. 10 (2018), 970–978. doi:10.1176/appi.ajp.2018.17101112.

National Institute of Drug Abuse. *Benzodiazepines and Opioids*. National Institute of Health, Revised March 2018. Accessed July 29, 2019. www.drugabuse.gov/drugs-abuse/opioids/benzodiazepines -opioids.

National Institute of Drug Abuse. *Trends and Statistics*. National Institute of Health, 2017. Accessed October 27, 2018. https://www.drugabuse .gov/related-topics/trends-statistics.

O'Neill, Eugene. *Long Day's Journey into Night*. New Haven: Yale University Press, 2002.

Peacock, Amy, Janni Leung, Sarah Larney, Samantha Colledge, Matthew Hickman, Jürgen Rehm, Gary A. Giovino, et al. "Global Statistics on Alcohol, Tobacco and Illicit Drug Use: 2017 Status Report." *Addiction* 113, no. 10 (2018), 1905–1926. doi:10.1111/add.14234.

Todd, John. "Some Unusual Forms of Drug Addiction." *Yorkshire Faculty J* 11, no. 1 (1970), 1–5.

Volkow, Nora D., George F. Koob, and A. T. McLellan. "Neurobiologic Advances from the Brain Disease Model of Addiction." *New Engl J Med* 374, no. 4 (2016), 363–371.

Weisheit, Ralph A., and William L. White. *Methamphetamine: Its History, Pharmacology, and Treatment*. Center City, MN: Hazelden, 2009.

CHAPTER 1

Alcohol

Frances R. Frankenburg

Alcohol, also known as ethanol or ethyl alcohol, is a small molecule containing two carbon atoms, six hydrogen atoms, and one oxygen atom. The molecule is smaller and simpler than the other substances described in this book. Alcohol is legal and widely used in the United States, generating large amounts of tax revenue. It plays an important role in the rituals and ceremonies of religions, such as Roman Catholicism and Judaism. The liquor industry in the United States is a large and important part of the hospitality industry and sponsors sporting events, music festivals, and other cultural events. While many people enjoy drinking alcohol, people who drink heavily and/or steadily may develop an alcohol addiction. The terminology regarding problems with alcohol has changed in the last few years. *Addiction*, *alcoholism*, and *abuse* are used less often, and in their place people will often use the phrases *alcohol use disorder* (AUD) and *alcohol misuse*.

Symptoms, Diagnosis, and Incidence

Symptoms

People addicted to alcohol use the substance in a compulsive or out-of-control way that interferes with other activities. They drink heavily despite adverse consequences, crave alcohol, are preoccupied with it, and are dependent on or tolerant of it. A common component of alcohol addiction is denial or a refusal or inability to recognize the seriousness of the addiction. Over time, a person's alcohol use may increase until the individual is spending significant amounts of time getting alcohol, drinking it, and being intoxicated. Secrecy and dishonesty often accompany the addiction. People with an addiction to alcohol find it difficult to stop drinking, in part because of the withdrawal symptoms, which can be severe and even life threatening in some cases.

Diagnosis

There are several ways of diagnosing addiction to alcohol, one of which is to ask a set of four simple questions known as the CAGE test. Positive answers to questions about wanting or being advised to decrease drinking, feeling guilty about drinking, or needing a drink first thing in the morning should raise suspicion and lead to further questioning by the clinician (Ewing 1984).

Another way to diagnose alcohol addiction is to ask a longer and more quantitative set of questions, the Alcohol Use Disorders Identification Test (AUDIT), published by the World Health Organization (Saunders 1993).

In terms of diagnostic criteria, in the fifth version of the *Diagnostic and Statistical Manual of Mental Disorders (DSM-5)* (American Psychiatric Association 2013), a manual prepared by the American Psychiatric Association containing descriptions, symptoms, and other criteria for diagnosing mental disorders, AUD is described along a continuum. According to the *DSM-5*, someone with an AUD has a troubling pattern of use, including drinking alcohol in larger quantities and more often than the person planned to; the inability to lower the amount of drinking; spending a lot of time on alcohol-related activities; experiencing strong urges to drink alcohol; the inability to carry out tasks because of alcohol misuse and its related problems; continuing to drink even though it is causing problems with others, including violence against partners or family members; abandoning other activities because of a preference for alcohol and the predominant role of alcohol in one's life; drinking alcohol even when it is clearly risky, such as driving while under the influence of alcohol; continuing to drink alcohol despite it causing or worsening problems, such as liver disease or depression; the development of a tolerance to alcohol, meaning that the person is able to drink or wants to drink larger quantities of alcohol without obvious adverse effects; having withdrawal symptoms (which can be very dangerous) when not using alcohol.

Anyone meeting any two of the 11 criteria during the same 12-month period receives a diagnosis of AUD. The severity of AUD—mild, moderate, or severe—is based on the number of criteria met. A person with two or three symptoms has a mild AUD, and someone with four or five symptoms has a moderate AUD. Fifteen percent of those with an AUD have a "severe" disorder, meaning that they meet six or more symptoms of the disorder within one year and have an addiction to alcohol—an old-fashioned phrase still used by many.

Incidence

Most adults in the United States have drunk or do drink alcohol, and, for some people, alcohol causes difficulties. There are several surveys that estimate how many people have a problem with alcohol use based on different criteria. In the United States, the 2017 National Survey on Drug Use and Health (NSDUH) found that 5.3% of respondents over the age of 12, 10.0% of those between the ages of 18 and 25, and 5.0% of those aged 26 or older had an AUD as diagnosed by *DSM-IV*, an earlier edition of the *DSM* (Substance Abuse and Mental Health Services Administration 2018). Using a different survey and the *DSM-5* diagnostic criteria, National Epidemiologic Survey on Alcohol and Related Conditions (NESARC) researchers estimated the 12-month prevalence of *DSM-5* AUD in adults between 2012 and 2013 to be 14%, or 18% in men and 10% in women (Grant et al. 2015).

History

Fermentation of sugar is the source of most alcohol. In this natural process, enzymes in yeasts break down sugar (glucose, fructose, or sucrose) into alcohol and carbon dioxide. Sugars that can be fermented into alcohol are found in a variety of grains or products, such as barley (associated with beer), grapes (associated with wine), or molasses (associated with rum). Alcohol is found in all cultures and in all parts of the world except the Arctic. Beer was popular in ancient Egypt and Mesopotamia, and wine was valued in ancient Greece and Rome.

Distillation, which has been practiced since the time of the Babylonians, became more popular in 16th-century Europe, and both the number and types of alcoholic beverages increased during that period. Yeast fermentation stops when the alcohol content of the liquid reaches 14% or 15%, so to create even stronger alcoholic beverages, the liquid must be distilled. During distillation, a liquid containing alcohol and water is heated in an apparatus called a "still." Alcohol has a lower boiling point than water, so when the liquid is heated to a temperature between the two boiling points, the alcoholic vapor can be captured and condensed, leading to a beverage with a higher percentage of alcohol by volume than could be achieved through mere fermentation.

Because of their greater strength, distilled beverages, such as gin, whiskey, rum, and vodka, sometimes known as spirits, were often associated with addiction. The "gin craze" in 18th-century London took place at a time when the poor indulged in gin drinking, which was blamed for violence, family breakdown, and crime.

In the 1800s, reformers in many parts of the world became increasingly concerned about the ill effects of alcohol. It was linked with poverty, depravity, unemployment, the maltreatment of women, and dissolution of the family. Some communities banned alcohol, and anti-alcohol movements such as the Woman's Christian Temperance Union and the Anti-Saloon League gained strength. Susan B. Anthony, the famous suffragette, also campaigned to ban alcohol. By 1846, Maine passed the first laws in the United States outlawing the sale of alcohol except for "industrial and medicinal purposes." Then in 1851, the state went further, prohibiting both the production and sale of alcohol. The ban eventually went nationwide, and Prohibition (see Sidebar 1.1) was in force in the entire country from 1920 to 1933.

Some indigenous communities (for example, in Australia) and other countries have banned alcohol. Finland prohibited it between 1919 and 1932. In 1914, the tsar of Russia banned both the manufacture and sale of alcohol; this prohibition lasted for 11 years. Mikhail Gorbachev tried to ban alcohol in the USSR from 1985 to 1988. Canada briefly had prohibition laws in the World War I era. In most cases, prohibition is not successful because there is not enough public support.

Sidebar 1.1 Prohibition in the United States

The word *prohibition* means the banning of a substance or activity; when capitalized, it usually refers to the 18th Amendment of the U.S. Constitution.

Although movements to ban alcohol had long existed in the United States, and some cities, counties, or states individually voted themselves "dry" (i.e., alcohol-free), few predicted that prohibition would ever become a national or federal issue. Several factors coalesced to make this unexpected event happen. The powerful Anti-Saloon League was an early "single-issue" lobbying movement. It portrayed saloons (places where alcohol was sold and drunk) as dens of iniquity where prostitution, gambling, and other unsavory activities had a home. When the United States joined World War I, anti-German sentiment and hence anti-beer sentiment increased. (This is similar to the anti-Mexican and anti-marijuana feelings at about the same time.) People believed or hoped that if sobriety increased, productivity would increase. The 18th Amendment was ratified in 1919, making illegal the "the production, importation, transportation, and sale of alcoholic beverages." In 1920, the Volstead Act was passed to implement the amendment, and Prohibition was in effect from 1920 to 1933. People could still drink alcohol in their own homes and for religious purposes, unless they lived in one of the states where possession was banned.

At first, Prohibition seemed to be a success. Alcoholism and alcohol-related morbidity and mortality decreased (Blocker 2006, 233–243). But new problems emerged. Organized crime flourished, and tax revenues plummeted. Recognizing the opportunities Prohibition created, criminals smuggled alcohol into the United States from Canada and the Caribbean, stockpiled it, and then sold it for handsome profits.

Alcohol was still needed for a variety of industrial uses, and in order to stop industrial alcohol from being drunk, it was "denatured," meaning that substances designed to discourage consumption were added. The additive most commonly used was methanol. People who did drink alcohol with methanol sometimes became blind or died. Alcohol itself never disappeared, thanks in part to organized crime. The saloon itself vanished, but some have suggested that because of that, alcohol use became more domestic, and women also became more comfortable drinking it (Blocker 2006, 233–243).

Enforcement was never well funded, and Prohibition became increasingly impotent and widely mocked. The expected improvements in national civility, health, and productivity never transpired. The final and perhaps most significant blow against Prohibition was the loss of tax revenue from the legal sale of liquor.

In 1932, Franklin Delano Roosevelt ran for president and promised to repeal Prohibition. He was elected, and, in 1933, the 21st Amendment ended federal Prohibition. The ban on alcohol lingered in some states and areas. For example, Kansas was dry until 1948, and Mississippi, the last entirely dry state, only repealed Prohibition in 1966. Prohibition is now often used as an example of the futility of legislation in the control of undesirable behaviors.

Bibliography

Blocker, Jack S. "Did Prohibition Really Work? Alcohol Prohibition as a Public Health Innovation." *Am J Public Health* 96, no. 2 (2006), 233–243. doi:10.2105/ajph.2005.065409.

While Prohibition in the United States may be long gone, alcohol continues to be regulated, but inconsistently. In Puerto Rico and the U.S. Virgin Islands, the legal drinking age is 18, but in the rest of the United States, the legal drinking age is 21, higher than in most of the world. People under the age of 21 may not purchase alcohol or drink it in public. In many states, however, people younger than 21 are allowed to drink alcohol at home with parental presence and consent, in religious ceremonies, or in private premises. Laws regarding the sale of alcohol vary by state. Many states prohibit the sale of alcohol on Sundays. In some states, any type of liquor can be bought in grocery stores, while in others only beer can be sold in grocery stores; in still other states, only state-run stores sell alcohol.

One area where alcohol use is highly regulated is when it comes to driving a motor vehicle. There is a consensus that alcohol leads to dangerous driving, which imperils the driver and others. In most countries, people who drive with a blood alcohol level of 0.08% or over are judged to be driving while intoxicated. Blood alcohol level, sometimes known as blood alcohol concentration or content, is the percentage of blood containing alcohol, or grams of alcohol per 100 milliliters of blood. Breathalyzers analyze the amount of exhaled alcohol in the breath and provide a rough estimate of the blood alcohol concentration. Breathalyzers are convenient, noninvasive, fairly reliable, and easy to use. (In contrast, it is not so easy to assess if one is driving under the influence of marijuana.)

Development and Causes

The development of an AUD is complex. Only some alcohol drinkers become dependent on it. Is the brain of an alcohol-dependent person different from a "normal" brain even before one begins to drink? If so, how might that difference make one more vulnerable to becoming dependent?

A genetic loading for alcoholism will put a person at greater risk than a person without that burden. In twin studies, researchers have compared the incidence of alcoholism in fraternal and identical twins. Most twins share a common upbringing, but only identical twins have the same genes. Identical twins are more alike in their rates of alcoholism than are fraternal twins, suggesting a genetic component to alcoholism. Studies of biological children of people with alcoholism who are adopted by people without alcoholism also show higher-than-expected rates of AUDs. These and other studies taken together suggest that about half of a person's vulnerability to an AUD is hereditary (Verhulst, Neale, and Kendler 2014).

The earlier in life that a person begins to drink, the more likely it is that he or she may develop an AUD. People with anxiety, depression, bipolar disorder, or schizophrenia are at greater risk for developing AUDS than those without these disorders. A history of childhood and adolescent stressors and trauma also increases the risk.

Environment or cultural factors also play a role. In cultures where drinking is associated with families and meals, alcohol is thought to be less problematic than when drinking is done alone or in bars. For example, the consumption of alcohol in the European Mediterranean region is reported to be associated with less harm, since alcohol (often wine) is usually drunk with families and at meals. In countries such as Ireland or Finland where alcohol tends to be drunk in bars or other places without food, alcohol may be more harmful.

Alcohol consumption can be particularly harmful for indigenous peoples worldwide, perhaps due to differences in metabolism and the consequences of economic and social marginalization.

We now view AUDs as resulting from a combination of genetic, cultural, economic, and environmental factors. But there are, or have been, other ways of understanding how one can "fall victim" to an AUD, that are larger hearted. In an address to a temperance movement, Abraham Lincoln said:

> In my judgment, such of us as have never fallen victims have been spared more by the absence of appetite, than from any mental or moral superiority over those who have. Indeed, I believe, if we take habitual drunkards as a class, their heads and their hearts will bear an advantageous comparison with those of any other class. There seems ever to have been a proneness in the brilliant and warm-blooded to fall into this vice. The demon of intemperance ever seems to have delighted in sucking the blood of genius and of generosity. (www.abrahamlincolnonline.org/lincoln/speeches /temperance)

Up Close—In Society
Alcohol is a valued part of meals and entertainment. But when more than a moderate amount of alcohol is drunk quickly, the result is intoxication, inebriation, or drunkenness. An intoxicated person can be impulsive and have poor judgment and volatile emotions, being overly friendly one moment and sobbing or angry the next.

In his novel Saturday, *Ian McEwan perfectly describes this behavior. He writes of a family gathering, attended by the protagonist's father-in-law, a poet. This man was a connoisseur of fine wine, but as he grew older, he began to drink more, often drinking gin and tonic before dinner, wine through dinner, and then beer and scotch later in the evening.*

> *Becoming drunk is a journey that generally elates him in the early stages—he's good company, expansive, mischievous and fun, the famous old poet, almost as happy listening as talking. But once the destination is met, once established up there on that unsunny plateau, a fully qualified drunk, the nastier muses, the goblins of aggression, paranoia, self-pity take control.*
>
> *(McEwan 2006, 141)*

An intoxicated person is often physically uncoordinated, slurs his or her speech, and can either be sedated or overexcited. Alcohol intoxication leads to falls, injuries, and many accidents, particularly car and pedestrian fatalities. Intoxicated drivers can be unreasonably confident in their driving prowess, even though their coordination and reaction times are impaired. Accidents caused by inebriated pedestrians are less well publicized, but the causes are similar: intoxicated people making bad judgments with poor control over their physical movements.

Alcohol intoxication is also associated with violence, including homicide, intimate partner violence, and sexual assault. Intoxicated people fight more often with strangers and family members than do sober people. Alcohol is associated with an increased incidence of sexual assaults in colleges and universities (Abbey 2002).

Intoxicated people are at a greater risk of suicide because alcohol can diminish inhibitions and increase impulsivity and emotional volatility. The Centers for Disease Control and Prevention analyzed data from the National Violent Death Reporting System for 2005 and 2006 and found that, in suicide deaths, among people tested for alcohol, the blood alcohol concentration was at or above 0.08% in almost a quarter of all cases (Centers for Disease Control and Prevention 2009).

Binge drinking is when a person drinks enough alcohol to have a blood alcohol level of 0.08% or more or has more than five drinks at one time if male or more than four drinks at one time if female. Binge drinking can be associated with alcohol addiction. Many young people binge-drink during their high school and college years; some people do this at public athletic events. Binge drinking is a troubling issue on college campuses where almost half of all students drink to excess (Wechsler et al. 1994). Some people experience "blackouts" when they drink heavily. During the blackout, the person may act in violent or self-destructive ways and have no memory of these events afterward. Alcohol drunk quickly and in large amounts can lead to alcohol poisoning, which can be lethal. Large amounts of alcohol rapidly consumed can interfere with the control of heart rate and breathing. It can also inhibit the gag reflex, so the person may aspirate or choke after vomiting. The combination of large amounts of alcohol and other drugs is particularly dangerous. Many fatal polysubstance overdoses involve alcohol as one of the substances.

The problems of heavy and/or excessive drinking are magnified when the person develops an AUD. An AUD diminishes a person's quality of life even when the person is not intoxicated because of the symptoms described earlier: craving, inability to see or act on the bad consequences of their drinking, and the dominance of drinking alcohol in the person's life. A person with a severe AUD will have difficulty maintaining employment or relationships.

Case Study

John is a 65-year-old man who has just come into an urban hospital's emergency room (ER)—and not for the first time. He is disheveled and malodorous. He is coughing and walking unsteadily. He is thin and has a bleeding gash on his forehead. He does not know how he was injured. The ER team is worried about a possible brain injury and orders a head CT scan, which shows no acute changes. His chest x-ray is normal. Laboratory testing shows some indications of liver damage and a blood alcohol level of 0.275%. (This level is more than three times higher than the level indicating inability to drive safely. A person who rarely drinks alcohol would be unconscious with a blood alcohol level this high.) John tells a social worker that he has no family, friends, or fixed address. The social worker tries to find a detoxification facility for him, but there are no available beds in the city. The nursing staff—who know him well— help him shower. They give him a meal and find him some clean clothes, and he spends the night in the ER. In the morning, he sees the next day's team. He is less intoxicated, with his blood alcohol level having fallen to 0.07%. His gait is steadier and he looks better. The team urges him to consider an alcohol treatment program. John thanks the ER staff for their help but insists on leaving. He is anxious to resume smoking and to have a drink. He refuses to wait to see if any beds have become available. The ER team wonders when they will see him next.

Up Close—At Work

About 9% of full-time workers drink alcohol heavily. The highest rates of drinking are found in the mining (18%) and construction (17%)

industries (Bush and Lipari 2015). Some people drink alcohol while at work. Such use is generally accepted to be harmful when engaged in to excess or when the person has become addicted. Workplace drinking can be found everywhere, but particularly where the workers are predominantly male and the work is perceived as tedious, there is little supervision, and alcohol is available (National Institute on Alcohol Abuse and Alcoholism 1999). Drinking alcohol while at work is associated with absenteeism, leaving early or arriving late, doing less work, doing work of a poorer quality, and arguing with coworkers.

Sometimes alcohol is used as a compensation for or celebration of work. There is a venerable history of alcohol being used to reward workers. Perhaps this began in Egypt, where the people who built the pyramids were paid with beer. Some companies now supply their employees with beer and wine. In some cultures, it is expected that people will drink heavily with their colleagues after the work day.

Case Study

Susan is a 35-year-old woman who has drunk heavily since her teens and always enjoyed it. She worked as a nurse for six years in an ER and then five years in a nursing home. However, she was not getting along well with some of her coworkers and began to dread going to work. Two or three glasses of wine helped her go to sleep, and then another glass helped her go back to sleep if she woke up in the middle of the night. She sometimes had a glass of wine before she went to work to help her feel less anxious about the day. She wondered if she had a drinking problem but thought that she was too young. Besides, she was holding down a full-time job and saw no similarity between herself and some of the alcoholic patients whom she saw when working in the ER. On one occasion, though, she had a disagreement with another staff member that degenerated into a physical fight. When the supervisor of the nursing home intervened, he smelled alcohol on Susan's breath and immediately fired her. She entered an alcohol rehabilitation program and became sober. She now attends Alcoholics Anonymous (AA) meetings regularly, has a sponsor, and is maintaining her sobriety. She left nursing, feeling that it was too stressful, and retrained in graphics design.

She now works for a small company that recently has begun to stock the kitchen with fruit, cheese, and wine. Some employees have a glass of wine at the end of the day, especially if they work late. The company directors say: "Our employees work long hours. We profit from their hard work and their creativity; we want to treat them like adults and make this a nice place to work." For the most part, the employees are delighted, but Susan, who has not told anyone at work about her past struggles with addiction, is nervous about the availability of alcohol.

Up Close—In Relationships

The effects of an AUD are often apparent at home. The person who is addicted to alcohol puts the need for alcohol above other needs, including those of the family. Such a person may be distracted or irritable much of the time. If the alcohol addiction interferes with the person's performance at work, worries about this or financial stresses will aggravate tensions at home.

The choices that family members have in such situations are difficult. They may choose to intervene, or they may be reluctant to intervene and do the opposite, which is to enable the person. Some examples of enablement are making excuses for their behavior, blaming others, paying their debts, or bailing them out of trouble. Children living with alcoholic parents may blame themselves or suffer from the parent's anger or difficulty in behaving in an appropriately parental role.

Experts often suggest support groups such as Al-Anon or Alateen for people who have family members who misuse alcohol.

Case Study

Jake is a 43-year-old real-estate lawyer who is married with three children. His mother was a heavy drinker and smoker who died of lung cancer five years ago. His father drinks moderately, and his two brothers do not drink at all. Jake began to drink when he was 12. He has had several periods of sobriety but always resumes drinking, and he has been drinking heavily for the last year. While he says that he drinks because he has been having trouble at work, his wife says that it his drinking that is causing the trouble. When he takes his clients or colleagues out to lunch or dinner, he will usually have several drinks. His wife is upset because at times he comes home from work intoxicated. He has become increasingly preoccupied and spends little time with the family. Once she found a bottle of vodka hidden in his car. She has been going to Al-Anon and wants Jake to go to AA; he has gone a few times but dislikes the emphasis on a higher power. The two argue about his drinking, and Jake tells her that if she stopped nagging him so much, he would drink less. One evening they found their 13-year-old son in his bedroom intoxicated. Jake's wife said to him, "This is your fault. He sees you drinking and of course he is going to drink too. You're just like your mother. If you don't stop drinking, I am leaving and taking the children with me."

Effects and Costs

Adverse Medical Effects

Alcohol exacerbates or increases the risk of many medical illnesses. It irritates the esophagus and stomach, sometimes to the point of bleeding. It is associated with acute pancreatitis and liver damage. Chronic exposure to alcohol is also associated with fatty liver, liver failure, and cirrhosis of the liver, which is irreversible. In those with chronic hepatitis, even moderate alcohol intake may increase the risk of cirrhosis and liver cancer. Hepatitis of any type is worsened by alcohol intake. Drinking more than a moderate amount of alcohol is associated with cardiovascular morbidity, such as high blood pressure, cardiomyopathy, and atrial fibrillation. Alcohol harms both the bones and bone marrow. It can cause neuropathies, in which the feet or hands become both numb and painful, and it complicates the course of diabetes. Alcohol is associated with an increase in the rate of many malignancies, including oral, esophageal, breast, and rectal cancers. Many of these medical risks are further increased in drinkers who are malnourished and/or smoke cigarettes or misuse other substances.

Because more men drink than do women, more men suffer from the consequences of alcohol than do women. But women are more sensitive than men to the toxic effects of alcohol because of differences in body makeup and metabolism. Therefore, women are more susceptible to all the medical problems caused by alcohol. Women who drink alcohol increase their risk of sexual assault. Pregnant women who drink heavily risk giving birth to babies with alcohol-related birth defects or developmental problems, at their most extreme known as Fetal Alcohol Syndrome (FAS). A baby with FAS is small, with a small head with small eyes and jaw, flat nose, no furrow between the upper lip and nose, and extra skin at the inside edge of the eyes. The baby may also have malformations of the heart, brain, kidneys, and skeletal system. Children with FAS may have learning and attentional difficulties and varying degrees of mental retardation. Described in all parts of the world, FAS is one of the leading causes of mental retardation in the United States. As these children grow up, their learning disabilities and impulsivity might increase their own risk for drinking alcohol. Many physicians and American medical authorities, such as the American College of Obstetricians and Gynecologists and the Centers for Disease Control and Prevention, recommend that pregnant women drink no alcohol.

Other Adverse Effects

Alcohol is harmful to the brain, and some heavy drinkers develop brain damage, particularly if they are malnourished. This situation is sometimes found in people with AUDs who have worn out the patience of their families and employers and end up living alone or in shelters. Wernicke-Korsakoff syndrome, caused by thiamine deficiency, is sometimes seen in malnourished heavy drinkers. Wernicke's encephalopathy is the acute part of this syndrome and is marked by confusion, oculomotor signs (weakness of the muscles moving the eyes), and ataxia (poor motor coordination). In people with this syndrome, the ataxia usually affects the legs and may be so severe that the patient cannot walk. It is often worsened by other medical problems that the person may have.

Wernicke's encephalopathy may develop into a memory disorder, known as Korsakoff's psychosis, in which a person cannot remember the past or form new memories. Korsakoff's psychosis is often accompanied by apathy and lack of insight, and occasionally by confabulation, or the fabrication of stories. Without the ability to form new memories, the person will have great difficulty living independently (Reuler, Girard, and Cooney 1985).

Wernicke's encephalopathy is difficult to diagnose—and usually missed clinically—because the person may be intoxicated when seen by doctors, thus making a good clinical exam difficult. The confusion of the patient may be attributed to intoxication, withdrawal, or perhaps concurrent other illnesses or head injuries. For example, in a study of 131 cases, it was diagnosed before death in only 20% of cases (Harper 1983). Repeated episodes of Wernicke's encephalopathy may play a role in the development of alcoholic dementia or cerebellar degeneration.

AUDs are associated with anxiety and mood disorders. It is often difficult to determine if an anxious and depressed person who is drinking heavily has a mood disorder caused by alcohol or has the mood disorder independent of alcohol and is in part drinking to treat that mood disorder. Drinking to treat an anxiety disorder or depression is common, even though it usually exacerbates the symptoms of those disorders. Whether or not the depressed person should be treated with antidepressants while still drinking is a difficult decision for several reasons. All medications have side effects and can be expensive. Furthermore, the prescription of a medication may dilute the message to the depressed person about the importance of stopping alcohol consumption. But for some people, an antidepressant can be sufficiently mood lifting so that the person feels able to stop drinking alcohol.

One of the most serious sequelae of an AUD is suicidality. AUDs are associated with suicide for many reasons. Alcohol can exacerbate feelings of hopelessness, depression, or shame. Having an AUD increases the risk of depression, although having either problem increases the risk of having the other (Boden and Fergusson 2011). As noted, intoxication can increase impulsivity, decrease inhibitions, and interfere with judgment. A person with an AUD may commit suicide in either an intoxicated or a sober state. Among people with AUD, the risk of completed suicide is about 10 times the risk seen in people without an AUD (Kõlves et al. 2017).

When it comes to the risk of suicide, the type of alcohol may be important. When national rates of drinking alcohol are compared, per capita alcohol consumption is related to suicide rate, but not when wine alone is examined. In contrast, higher per capita consumption of spirits is associated with higher rates of suicide. Perhaps this is due to the ways in which these types of alcohol are consumed. The World Health Organization defines *risky drinking* as including drinking done in large amounts, on festive occasions, often leading to intoxication, and in public places. Less risky drinking includes daily or nearly daily drinking and with meals, if consumption is moderate. Spirits are more often drunk in a risky fashion and wine more often in a less risky fashion (Roche, Rogers, and Pridemore 2018, 17).

Beneficial Effects of Alcohol

There are beneficial effects of alcohol consumption. Moderate use of alcohol increases conviviality, improves the flavor of food, enhances conversation, and lessens stress. Many people drink alcohol to help them relax in the evening, and some feel it might also improve their sleep—hence the term "nightcap"—despite evidence to the contrary.

Alcohol may also expand our ways of thinking. William James, the great philosopher of pragmatism, had a family history of alcohol misuse and wrote compassionately about this aspect of alcohol, even when it involved intoxication:

> The sway of alcohol over mankind is unquestionably due to its power to stimulate the mystical faculties of human nature, usually crushed to earth by the cold facts and dry criticisms of the sober hour. Sobriety diminishes, discriminates, and says no; drunkenness expands, unites, and says yes. It is in fact the great exciter of the *Yes* function in man. It brings its votary from the chill periphery of things to the radiant core. It makes him for the moment one with truth. Not through mere perversity do men run after it. To the poor and the unlettered it stands in the place of symphony concerts and of literature; and it is part of the deeper mystery and tragedy of life that whiffs and gleams of something that we immediately recognize

as excellent should be vouchsafed to so many of us only in the fleeting earlier phases of what in its totality is so degrading a poisoning. (James 1958, 297)

Despite the medical problems caused by alcohol there is a long-held belief that alcohol, at least in small or moderate amounts, has health-promoting effects. Many studies have shown that, when compared to nondrinkers, moderate drinkers are healthier and live longer (Ferrari et al. 2014). People who have up to one a drink a day have less cardiovascular morbidity and mortality compared to nondrinkers, possibly due to a change in clotting mechanisms or an increase in the proteins that remove cholesterol from the blood vessel walls (Brien et al. 2011; Ronksley et al. 2011). However, these benefits of alcohol have not yet been firmly established. A large study proposed by the National Institute on Alcohol Abuse and Alcoholism (NIAAA) to explore the possible beneficial amounts of alcohol might have provided more information, but it was cancelled in 2018 because of revelations of funding and influence from alcohol corporations.

Costs

Alcohol is so widely used and its effects are so numerous that it is difficult to calculate the costs of addiction with precision. Nevertheless, the Centers for Disease Control and Prevention estimated in 2015 that excessive drinking cost the United States over $249 billion in 2010, mostly because of binge drinking. These costs are due to a combination of medical illnesses, property damage from fires and car accidents, alcohol-related crime, and lost productivity (Sacks et al. 2015). With respect to the economic costs of alcohol worldwide, the indirect costs due to productivity loss were the main drivers of financial burden (Rehm et al. 2009).

Theory and Research

Alcohol interacts with many neurotransmitter systems and has multiple dose-dependent effects on the brain. Research suggests alcohol works at least in part because of its effects on the neurotransmitters gamma-aminobutyric acid (GABA), glutamate, and dopamine, but why alcohol is so addictive is not fully understood. GABA, a common amino acid, is the chief inhibitory neurotransmitter in the brain. Alcohol binds to the GABA receptor in such a way that the effect of GABA is increased, resulting in a temporary relief of anxiety. If a person who is taking large quantities of alcohol suddenly stops this use, GABA activity will decrease, and this, along with changes in the N-methyl-D-aspartate (NMDA) receptor, can lead to an increase in anxiety. (This is similar to what happens to a person withdrawing from sedatives and hypnotics.)

Another effect of alcohol on some GABA receptors might lead to an increase in the activity in the dopamine pathways running from the ventral tegmental area to the nucleus accumbens (Davies 2003). As is discussed elsewhere, dopamine activity in the reward system is thought to be a key component of addiction. Alcohol also activates pathways in the brain used by the brain's endorphins and endocannabinoids (opiate and cannabis-like substances), increasing its pleasurable and addicting effects.

Glutamate, another amino acid, is the main excitatory neurotransmitter in the brain. There are several types of glutamate receptors. The NMDA glutamate receptor is the most complicated of all the neurotransmitter receptors, is affected by many drugs, and is involved in memory. (NMDA is a *synthetic* substance that binds to and activates this receptor, and it gave its name to the receptor.) A memory can be understood as a strong connection between two neurons, or a stronger synapse, meaning that the presynaptic neuron is more likely to activate a postsynaptic neuron. NMDA receptors are found throughout the brain but are most densely concentrated in the cerebral cortex, particularly the hippocampus, as well as the amygdala and basal ganglia.

Alcohol has the opposite effect on glutamate receptors than it does on GABA receptors; it antagonizes them. Glutamate pathways run from the prefrontal cortex to the ventral tegmental area and nucleus accumbens and regulate the sensitivity of the dopaminergic reward pathway. They are also involved with the memory of experiences with alcohol and thus may be part of craving for alcohol.

If a person stops drinking alcohol, a subsequent increase in glutamate activity at the NMDA receptor is associated with withdrawal seizures.

Treatments

Prevention is preferable to treatment of alcohol addiction. Without alcohol there would be no AUDs, so the simplest approach to prevention would be to ban alcohol. As reviewed earlier, however, Prohibition was not a success, but there are several other approaches to AUD prevention. One successful approach is to limit the availability of alcohol by keeping the price high and regulating how it can be sold (Österberg 2004).

Another approach to prevention is education, but it is not as success-ful as limiting availability (Edwards 2003; Österberg 2004). The alco-hol companies sponsor education in schools and programs to encourage people to drink sensibly. The best approach to education is not clear though. Some suggest that students in elementary and high schools simply be instructed not to drink. Others suggest that the students be provided with examples of the harm alcohol can cause or alternative activities they can engage in. The prevention of alcohol misuse is perhaps even more important in colleges, since the rate of binge drinking in col-leges are so high. Binge drinking does not necessarily lead to addiction but is itself harmful.

Despite regulations concerning availability and attempts at prevention, AUDs, of course, do exist. Most people with an AUD get no treatment. In the study of the prevalence of AUDs (as defined by *DSM-5*) between 2012 and 2013, only 20% of those with a lifetime AUD had ever been treated for it (Grant et al. 2015). Some people with an AUD who want to become sober either cannot afford or do not want treatment. If a person with an addiction wants to stop drinking without treatment, the person is more likely to succeed if he or she can find another focus of activity and another way of filling time. Avoidance of triggers, cues that lead to a person feeling that he or she "must" drink again, is likely to help. Environmental triggers can be the presence of others who drink, such as "drinking buddies" or places associated with alcohol. Other triggers can include certain stresses or events, loneliness, or even positive events— leading the person to think that he or she deserves a reward.

Other people may stop drinking as they make attachments to others, acquire responsibilities or obligations, or just develop different interests. Using NESARC interview data, researchers found that, considering the year before the interview, of people with a history of alcohol dependence in the time *prior* to the year before the interview (as defined by *DSM-IV*), only 25% continued to be dependent on alcohol, and nearly half were in remission at the time of the interview, and of these, most had been in remission for at least five years. Only one quarter of people with alcohol dependence had ever received treatment. Nearly a quarter of people with a history of alcohol dependence had stopped problematic drinking with-out treatment. Treatment increased the chances of staying sober but was not a prerequisite. Other factors that increased the chances of becoming sober were increasing age, having at least a high school education, and being married (Dawson et al. 2005; Dawson et al. 2006).

Treatment for an AUD sometimes is prompted by an "intervention" in which the friends and/or family of the person with the addiction talk with that individual about the problems that alcohol is causing, break through the person's denial, and suggest options. When treatment for AUD does take place, it can be divided into three phases: detoxification to allow safe withdrawal; stabilization; and finally, maintenance of sobriety. Not all people will go through all phases.

Alcohol detoxification, sometimes just referred to as "detox," refers to the supportive and/or medical treatment of the person who stops drinking alcohol. Someone who has been drinking heavily for years will have a difficult time lessening his or her alcohol intake for multiple reasons—habit, psychological dependence, pressure from friends who drink, reluctance to lose the pleasure obtained from alcohol, the fear of withdrawal, and/or the discomfort experienced with a reduced alcohol intake.

Withdrawal from alcohol is often managed in detoxification facilities that may be inpatient hospital units. The treatment is guided by the need to treat the distressing symptoms while making sure that the patient stays medically stable. Symptoms include tremulousness, irritability, nausea, vomiting, and insomnia, and they are usually at their worst two to three days after the person stops drinking. The person may have seizures or develop delirium tremens, which is characterized by agitation, confusion, tremors, fever, sweating, and rapid heartbeat. Anxiety and visual hallucinations are common. A person who has had previous episodes of delirium tremens is at risk for undergoing the disorder again. The mortality rate of delirium tremens is high. Withdrawal from alcohol, and not from any of the other substances discussed in this book, can be fatal.

Treatments for withdrawal vary but usually consist of immediate cessation of drinking and the use of medications, most often benzodiazepines, to treat insomnia and agitation and lessen the chance of the development of delirium tremens or seizures. Benzodiazepines are often used at high doses and then tapered down. They may be given on a prearranged schedule or as triggered by symptoms. If the person is experiencing confusion and hallucinations, dopamine antagonists such as haloperidol are sometimes used. In extreme cases, the person may need admission to an intensive care unit where general anesthetics (phenobarbital or propofol), intubation, and mechanical ventilation may be used. Thiamine is given to prevent Wernicke's encephalopathy. Withdrawal can last for several days and may become more difficult with age. Cravings for alcohol and sleep disturbance can persist for months.

Alcohol detoxification programs have high success rates—at least in the short term. Once the person is sober and has withdrawn, he or she can begin to work on maintaining sobriety. Knowing what treatment works best to help a person stay sober is difficult because there are so many ways to define success and differences in follow up and selection of subjects.

Possibly the best-known treatment for alcohol addiction is AA. In 1934, businessman Bill Wilson, known in AA as Bill W., was, for the fourth time, hospitalized because of his alcoholism at the Towns Hospital in New York, a hospital that treated well-to-do alcoholics. He was sedated with chloral hydrate and given an anticholinergic drug, belladonna, a drug that can lead to hallucinations. He saw a flash of light and experienced serenity. This experience had a profound effect on him and he stopped drinking. He later cofounded AA with an alcoholic surgeon from Ohio, Bob Smith, known in AA as Dr. Bob. AA is based on or borrowed features from the Oxford Group, an active Christian evangelical movement of the time. In both movements, there is little institutional hierarchy or organization and no physical buildings. Both emphasize fellowship and honesty about one's failings with oneself and others. While his work with AA helped Bill W. stay sober, he remained addicted to cigarettes for the rest of his life.

AA has paradoxical beliefs: that alcoholism is an illness, but that "treatment" for this disease is a set of 12 spiritual steps. The first step is to admit powerlessness over the addiction. This acknowledgment of powerlessness empowers some people. Other steps include accepting a higher power, taking a "fearless moral inventory," admitting "the exact nature of our wrongs," and asking God to remove all character defects (Alcoholics Anonymous 2001, 59). Much of the work of AA takes place in meetings, where people introduce themselves by their first name and say, "I'm an alcoholic." People will often recount their stories of alcoholism, and there may be readings from the AA literature. AA encourages anonymity and working with a sponsor. It has given rise to many other self-help or mutual-aid societies.

Whether or not AA works is controversial. Acceptance of the disorder and lessening of shame and isolation are probably helpful; however, any rigorous studies are impossible because of AA's emphasis on anonymity and confidentiality, its nonmedical nature, and the difficulty of doing randomized controlled trials (the usual way of assessing the effectiveness of treatments). Nonetheless, AA is often included in treatment programs, and courts may mandate attendance at AA for alcohol-related convictions.

Psychological or supportive therapies are often recommended to help the person learn other ways of coping with stress besides drinking alcohol and to come to terms with the damage that alcohol might have done to the person's life. Two techniques often used are cognitive behavioral therapy or motivational interviewing/motivational enhancement therapy.

Cognitive behavioral therapy teaches people how to recognize and avoid triggers for their drinking and how to cope with other behaviors associated with alcohol misuse. People learn strategies to manage craving.

Motivational interviewing (MI) addresses the inevitable ambivalence that people have about change. MI is useful for people who have not yet made the decision to give up alcohol. Motivational enhancement therapy (MET) is based on MI and includes specific personalized assessment. MET begins with a session to assess the problem, followed by four sessions of structured feedback and discussions about the person's goals and how the addiction affects those goals. MI/MET differs from other techniques that might include giving advice, persuading, or challenging the person who does not admit to the severity of his or her addiction. MI/MET therapists do not confront denial or minimization of the problem but rather are supportive, avoid arguing, and encourage patients to realize that they can make changes. They help the person see how becoming sober could improve their life.

The NIAAA organized an eight-year multimillion-dollar study to try to determine which types of alcoholics responded best to which type of treatment, called the Matching Alcoholism Treatments to Client Heterogeneity, or the MATCH study. Three types of treatment were evaluated: cognitive behavioral skills training, MET, and 12-step facilitation therapy (similar to AA).

All three techniques were found to be equally effective, and the study did not find any benefit in "matching" patients to treatment. There was no control group in this study, but people usually assume (from other studies) that MI/MET is more effective than no treatment at all (Project Match Group 1997).

A similar study was carried out in England, where a study compared MET with a different form of therapy that involved people in the patient's social network. No differences between the two treatments were found (United Kingdom Alcohol Treatment Trial [UKATT] Research Team 2005).

Treatment programs may be outpatient or residential. Many can be resort-like and expensive. Some famous treatment programs include Silver Springs, Hazelden, and Betty Ford. Addiction programs that are associated with some professions work well. For example, programs for pilots and doctors with alcohol misuse have excellent response rates. These successful programs may owe their good results to the high motivation of these professionals. The programs use random drug screens and close follow-up, which might be important.

Griffith Edwards, an English expert on alcohol misuse, wrote, "The message is thus not that all treatments are equally good, but that many good treatments are equally good . . . Treatments which are useful have in common the capacity to catalyse and support natural processes of recovery" (Edwards 2003, 141–142).

Medication

The idea of treating AUDs with medication may seem antithetical to the goal of sobriety. Why treat a substance use disorder with another substance? This caution is strengthened by anecdotes from the 1950s and 1960s when physicians sometimes treated heavy drinkers, insomniacs, or anxious people with high doses of sedatives and hypnotics, and addiction resulted. However, because intensive inpatient and residential treatment programs have high relapse rates, there has been much interest in psychopharmacologic agents that may be more helpful, in conjunction with psychosocial treatment.

AA cofounder Bill W. became interested in the use of drugs to treat addiction. Twenty years after he became sober, he used lysergic acid diethylamide (LSD) at a Veterans Administration Hospital in Los Angeles. People thought that LSD could mimic the horrors of delirium tremens and deter people from drinking alcohol. But Bill W. and others thought that it brought great insights and was helpful for people struggling with alcoholism. As is discussed in the hallucinogen chapter, Humphry Osmond used LSD to treat alcohol addiction for 13 years in Saskatchewan with good results. Despite Bill W.'s enthusiasm, AA never did support the use of hallucinogens.

Medication-assisted treatment (MAT) is now recommended by many medical and addiction agencies. Three medications—disulfiram, naltrexone, and acamprosate—are approved by the Food and Drug Administration for the treatment of AUDs.

Disulfiram (Antabuse), one of the oldest medications used to treat alcohol addiction, works by interfering with the metabolism of alcohol. Alcohol is broken down in the liver into a toxic molecule, acetaldehyde. Disulfiram inhibits aldehyde dehydrogenase, the enzyme that metabolizes acetaldehyde. If a person drinks alcohol while taking disulfiram, the accumulation of acetaldehyde leads to flushing, nausea, vomiting, and headaches. However, it does not treat withdrawal or craving. Disulfiram is not used often now, since most studies have not found it to be effective.

Naltrexone, an opioid receptor antagonist, was synthesized in 1963 and originally used as a treatment for opiate addiction. Clinical trials using naltrexone as a treatment for heroin addiction began in 1973.

In 1985, Joseph Volpicelli and Charles O'Brien began to study naltrexone in alcoholics at the Veterans Administration Hospital in Philadelphia. They found that it tempers the amount of pleasure that alcohol causes and decreases craving and the anticipatory excitement that sometimes occurs in response to a trigger. Naltrexone was discovered to be particularly helpful in decreasing relapses when combined with supportive treatment (Volpicelli et al. 1992).

An extended-release injectable version of the drug naltrexone can be administered once a month and may be easier for people recovering from alcohol use disorder to use consistently since one does not have to remember to take a daily pill. Some reports suggest that it is more effective and safer than the oral drug.

The third drug, acamprosate, may work by stabilizing the brain's glutamate receptors and decreasing the craving for alcohol.

Other medications sometimes tried include baclofen, topiramate, gabapentin, and namlefene.

As previously noted, most people with alcoholism receive no treatment at all, let alone some of the specialized psychotherapeutic treatments or new medications mentioned in this chapter. There has long been interest in making treatment more accessible. One method has been to use brief interventions that involve one to four sessions focusing on moderating alcohol consumption. Bien, Miller, and Tonigan (1993) found that brief interventions were more effective than no treatment and just as effective as some more extended treatments.

To address the practical questions about how better to approach the problem of the large number of people with untreated AUDS, the NIAAA sponsored another large study of alcohol treatment, Combined Pharmacotherapies and Behavioral Interventions (COMBINE) (Anton et al. 2006). In this study of 1,300 patients with an AUD, nine combinations of treatment, using medication, combinations of medications, medical management, and combined behavioral intervention—a form of specialized therapy combining elements of MET, CBT, and 12-step programs—were employed. Some of the questions to be answered included: Is routine medical counseling as effective as specialized therapy? Do medications work? Is the combination of naltrexone and acamprosate, which work in different ways, synergistic? Medical management involved one 45-minute initial meeting, followed by nine 20-minute meetings between patient and medical professional that stressed medication adherence, support, and encouragement. Specialized therapy involved hour-long meetings with highly trained specialists.

The authors found acamprosate to be ineffective. The best results were obtained with the combination of naltrexone and medical management, or specialized therapy and placebo and medical management, or naltrexone and medical management and specialized therapy. The worst results were in the group receiving specialized therapy with no pills and no medical management. The findings supported the usefulness of medical management. The group treated with combined behavioral intervention, delivered without active drug, placebo, or medical management did poorly. As well, it seemed that giving a placebo pill was more helpful than giving no pill at all. Although conclusions are difficult to make in this complex study, placebo and structured medical advice seem to be as or more effective than the highly developed specialized therapies. The importance of the study is that people with AUDs do not necessarily need specialized treatments.

Bibliography

Abbey, Antonia. "Alcohol-Related Sexual Assault: A Common Problem among College Students." *J Stud Alcohol Suppl* no. s14 (2002), 118–128. doi:10.15288/jsas.2002.s14.118.

Abraham Lincoln Online—Your Source for Lincoln News and Information. Accessed October 6, 2018. www.abrahamlincolnonline.org /lincoln/speeches/temperance.

Alcoholics Anonymous. *Alcoholics Anonymous: The Story of How Many Thousands of Men and Women Have Recovered from Alcoholism,* 4th ed. New York: Alcoholics Anonymous World Services, 2001.

American Psychiatric Association. *Diagnostic and Statistical Manual of Mental Disorders (DSM-5),* 5th ed. Arlington, VA: American Psychiatric Association, 2013.

Anton, Raymond F., Stephanie S. O'Malley, Domenic A. Ciraulo, Ron A. Cisler, David Couper, Dennis M. Donovan, David R. Gastfriend, et al. "Combined Pharmacotherapies and Behavioral Interventions for Alcohol Dependence." *JAMA* 295, no. 17 (2006), 2003–2017. doi:10.1001/jama.295.17.2003.

Bien, Thomas H., William R. Miller, and J. S. Tonigan. "Brief Interventions for Alcohol Problems: A Review." *Addiction* 88, no. 3 (1993), 315–336. doi:10.1111/j.1360-0443.1993.tb00820.x.

Boden, Joseph M., and David M. Fergusson. "Alcohol and Depression." *Addiction* 106, no. 5 (2011), 906–914. doi:10.1111/j.1360 -0443.2010.03351.x.

Brien, Susan E., Paul E. Ronksley, Barbara J. Turner, Ken J. Mukamal, and William A. Ghali. "Effect of Alcohol Consumption on Biological Markers Associated with Risk of Coronary Heart Disease: Systematic

Review and Meta-Analysis of Interventional Studies." *BMJ* 342 (2011), d636. doi:10.1136/bmj.d636.

Bush, Donna M., and Rachel N. Lipari. *Substance Use and Substance Use Disorder, by Industry*. The CBHSQ Report. Rockville, MD: Substance Abuse and Mental Health Services Administration, 2015.

Centers for Disease Control and Prevention. "Alcohol and Suicide Among Racial/Ethnic Populations—17 States, 2005–2006." *MMWR* 58 (2009), 637–641.

Davies, Martin. "The Role of GABAA Receptors in Mediating the Effects of Alcohol in the Central Nervous System." *J Psychiatry Neurosci* 28, no. 4 (July 2003), 263–274.

Dawson, Deborah A., Bridget F. Grant, Frederick S. Stinson, and Patricia S. Chou. "Estimating the Effect of Help-Seeking on Achieving Recovery from Alcohol Dependence." *Addiction* 101, no. 6 (2006), 824–834. doi:10.1111/j.1360-0443.2006.01433.x.

Dawson, Deborah A., Bridget F. Grant, Frederick S. Stinson, Patricia S. Chou, Boji Huang, and W. J. Ruan. "Recovery from DSM-IV Alcohol Dependence: United States, 2001–2002." *Addiction* 100, no. 3 (2005), 281–292. doi:10.1111/j.1360-0443.2004.00964.x.

Edwards, Griffith. *Alcohol: The World's Favorite Drug*. New York: St. Martin's Press, 2003.

Ewing, John A. "Detecting Alcoholism." *JAMA* 252, no. 14 (1984), 1905–1907. doi:10.1001/jama.1984.03350140051025.

Ferrari, Pietro, Idlir Licaj, David C. Muller, Per K. Andersen, Mattias Johansson, Heiner Boeing, Elisabete Weiderpass, et al. "Lifetime Alcohol Use and Overall and Cause-Specific Mortality in the European Prospective Investigation into Cancer and Nutrition (EPIC) Study." *BMJ Open* 4, no. 7 (2014), e005245. doi:10.1136/bmjopen-2014-005245.

Grant, Bridget F., Risë B. Goldstein, Tulshi D. Saha, S. P. Chou, Jeesun Jung, Haitao Zhang, Roger P. Pickering, et al. "Epidemiology of DSM-5 Alcohol Use Disorder." *JAMA Psychiatry* 72, no. 8 (2015), 757–766. doi:10.1001/jamapsychiatry.2015.0584.

Harper, Clive. "The Incidence of Wernicke's Encephalopathy in Australia—A Neuropathological Study of 131 Cases." *J Neurol Neurosurg Psychiatry* 46, no. 7 (1983), 593–598. doi:10.1136/jnnp.46.7.593.

James, William. *The Varieties of Religious Experience*. New York: Mentor Books, 1958.

Kõlves, Kairi, Brian M. Draper, John Snowdon, and Diego De Leo. "Alcohol-Use Disorders and Suicide: Results from a Psychological Autopsy Study in Australia." *Alcohol* 64 (2017), 29–35. doi:10.1016/j.alcohol.2017.05.005.

McEwan, Ian. *Saturday*. New York: Anchor, 2006.

National Institutes on Alcohol Abuse and Alcoholism. Number 44. *Alcohol and the Workplace*. National Institutes of Health, 1999. Accessed July 29, 2019. https://pubs.niaaa.nih.gov/publications/aa44.htm.

Österberg, E. *What are the Most Effective and Cost-Effective Interventions in Alcohol Control?* Copenhagen, WHO Regional Office for Europe: Health Evidence Network report, 2004. Accessed March 15, 2004. http://www.euro.who.int/document/E82969.pdf.

Project Match Group. "Matching Alcoholism Treatments to Client Heterogeneity: Project MATCH Posttreatment Drinking Outcomes." *J Stud Alcohol* 58, no. 1 (1997), 7–29. doi:10.15288/jsa.1997.58.7.

Rehm, Jürgen, Colin Mathers, Svetlana Popova, Montarat Thavorncharoensap, Yot Teerawattananon, and Jayadeep Patra. "Global Burden of Disease and Injury and Economic Cost Attributable to Alcohol Use and Alcohol-Use Disorders." *Lancet* 373, no. 9682 (2009), 2223–2233. doi:10.1016/s0140-6736(09)60746-7.

Reuler, James B., Donald E. Girard, and Thomas G. Cooney. "Wernicke's Encephalopathy." *New Engl J Med* 312, no. 16 (1985), 1035–1039. doi:10.1056/nejm198504183121606.

Roche, Sean P., Meghan L. Rogers, and William A. Pridemore. "A Cross-National Study of the Population-Level Association between Alcohol Consumption and Suicide Rates." *Drug Alcohol Depend* 188 (2018), 16–23. doi:10.1016/j.drugalcdep.2018.02.036.

Ronksley, Paul E., Susan E. Brien, Barbara J. Turner, Ken J. Mukamal, and William A. Ghali. "Association of Alcohol Consumption with Selected Cardiovascular Disease Outcomes: A Systematic Review and Meta-Analysis." *BMJ* 342 (2011), d671. doi:10.1136/bmj.d671.

Sacks, Jeffrey J., Katherine R. Gonzales, Ellen E. Bouchery, Laura E. Tomedi, and Robert D. Brewer. "2010 National and State Costs of Excessive Alcohol Consumption." *Am J Prev Med* 49, no. 5 (2015), e73–e79. doi:10.1016/j.amepre.2015.05.031. Epub 2015 Oct 1.

Saunders, John B., Olaf G. Aasland, Thomas F. Babor, Juan R. De La Fuente, and Marcus Grant. "Development of the Alcohol Use Disorders Identification Test (AUDIT): WHO Collaborative Project on Early Detection of Persons with Harmful Alcohol Consumption-II." *Addiction* 88, no. 6 (1993), 791–804. doi:10.1111/j.1360-0443.1993.tb02093.x.

Substance Abuse and Mental Health Services Administration. *Key Substance Use and Mental Health Indicators in the United States: Results from the 2017 National Survey on Drug Use and Health (HHS Publication No. SMA 18-5068, NSDUH Series H-53)*. Rockville, MD: Center for Behavioral Health Statistics and Quality, Substance

Abuse and Mental Health Services Administration, 2018. Accessed July 29, 2019. http://www.samhsa.gov/data/.

United Kingdom Alcohol Treatment Trial (UKATT) Research Team. "Effectiveness of Treatment for Alcohol Problems: Findings of the Randomised UK Alcohol Treatment trial (UKATT)." *BMJ* 331, no. 7516 (2005), 541–544. doi:10.1136/bmj.331.7516.541.

Verhulst, Brad, Michael C. Neale, and Kenneth S. Kendler. "The Heritability of Alcohol Use Disorders: A Meta-Analysis of Twin and Adoption Studies." *Psychol Med* 45, no. 5 (2014), 1061–1072. doi:10.1017/s0033291714002165.

Volpicelli, Joseph R., A. I. Alterman, M. Hayashida, and C. P. O'Brien. "Naltrexone in the Treatment of Alcohol Dependence." *Arch Gen Psychiatry* 49, no. 11 (1992), 876–880. doi:10.1001/archpsyc.1992.01820110040006.

Wechsler, Henry, Andrea Davenport, George Dowdall, Barbara Moeykens, and Sonia Castillo. "Health and Behavioral Consequences of Binge Drinking in College." *JAMA* 272, no. 21 (December 1994), 1672–1677. doi:10.1001/jama.1994.03520210056032.

CHAPTER 2

Cannabis

Frances R. Frankenburg

Some experts see cannabis as a powerful and potentially dangerous addictive drug associated with the misuse of other substances, driving accidents, violence, psychotic episodes, and perhaps even the development of schizophrenia. Others perceive it to be safe, particularly in comparison with other substances of abuse, because cannabis overdoses have never been associated with deaths, and cannabis has long been used as a safe medicine. The latter point of view is gaining favor, and the trend in the United States in 2019 is to decriminalize cannabis or, in some states, to legalize its recreational or medical use.

The words *cannabis* and *marijuana* are often used interchangeably and refer either to the cannabis plant or to its products, which alter the consciousness of the person consuming them. However, *cannabis* is becoming the preferred word because of the perceived pejorative implications of the word *marijuana*. The word *marijuana* is generally used only in three circumstances: when referring to its medical uses, because of the widely used term "medical marijuana"; when discussing cannabis with respect to Mexico because the word may come from Mexican Spanish (its etymology is uncertain); and when referring to legislation or commissions using the word *marihuana* (for some years a variant spelling of *marijuana*).

Although there is debate about the taxonomy, most experts agree that there are two main species of the *Cannabis* genus. *Cannabis indica* is a short, bushy, and frost-tolerant plant with wide leaves, native to Asian mountainous regions. *Cannabis sativa* is a tall plant with narrow leaves, native to warm or equatorial climates. *Cannabis* is sometimes known as

Indian hemp, although that name applies to other plants as well. The word *hemp* can refer to the fiber itself or to a variety of *C. sativa* that produces fiber used for the manufacture of many products, including paper, rope, building materials, and textiles. Hemp seeds are popular birdfeed. Hemp seed oil is used for a variety of industrial purposes, such as the manufacture of paint or as a moisturizing agent, and for medical purposes, discussed in this chapter.

Tiny glandular hairs on the leaves and flowering tops of female cannabis plants (sometimes known as buds) produce a resin containing many compounds, including terpenes and cannabinoids. Found in many plants, terpenes are hydrocarbon compounds with a characteristic pungent smell. Cannabinoids are 21 carbon compounds and are agonists (chemicals that bind to a receptor and activate the receptor to produce a biological response) at the cannabinoid receptors in the brain. Receptors are proteins on cell membranes that recognize some compounds as signals or messages. Cannabinoids can be divided into three types:

1. Phytocannabinoids, meaning cannabinoids produced by cannabis plants. The best known is delta-9-tetrahydrocannabinol (Δ-9-THC), or THC, the psychoactive component in cannabis plants. Psychoactive chemicals change how people think or perceive. The other important phytocannabinoid, cannabidiol (CBD), has no psychoactive effects. The hemp variety of cannabis produces CBD and negligible amounts of THC.
2. Endogenous cannabinoids, also known as endocannabinoids, such as anandamide and 2-arachidonyl glycerol. They are produced by all animals, including humans.
3. Synthetic cannabinoids such as dronabinol, or laboratory-made THC.

Another group of compounds, such as spice and K2, are chemically dissimilar from cannabinoids but are active at the cannabinoid receptors. They are made in laboratories and sprayed on to dry plant material that can be smoked or vaporized. They are illegal, potent, and harmful and *also* known as synthetic cannabinoids. In this book they will be referred to as illegal synthetic cannabinoids.

This chapter will mostly be concerned with recreational uses of cannabis that can lead to addiction. Medical marijuana will be briefly reviewed. As cannabis is legalized in more states, becomes increasingly potent due to horticultural advances, and is promoted for its therapeutic uses, harm associated with its use may become more evident.

Symptoms, Diagnosis, and Incidence

Symptoms

The person who is using cannabis for recreational purposes usually feels relaxed and mildly euphoric. Time seems to slow down and sensations are more vivid. However, some people may feel anxious, suspicious, or even have panic attacks. An individual using cannabis may have a shortened attention span, impaired concentration, poor memory, red eyes, poor muscle coordination, increased appetite, and slow reaction times. Colloquially, this state is known as being *high* or *stoned*.

Cannabis can be consumed in various ways, but it is usually smoked, vaped, or added to foods and then eaten. When smoked in the form of the well-known "joint," there is a quick onset of symptoms that usually dissipate within an hour or so. To vape cannabis, dried cannabis is heated to a temperature below its combustion point and then the vapor is inhaled. The vapors have higher concentrations of THC than burning cannabis and are (currently) thought to be safer than the smoke from burning cannabis, which contains multiple other chemicals, including carcinogenic toxins also common in tobacco smoke (Eisenberg, Ogintz, and Almog 2014). The safety of the additives, such as polyethylene glycol or propylene glycol used in preparing cannabis for vaporization, has not been established. Finally, one can eat foods containing cannabis products. Symptoms take longer to appear but last for several hours.

Regular cannabis users will develop tolerance, meaning that over time, they will require greater amounts of cannabis to experience the desired effects. If these users stop or significantly reduce their use, they may experience withdrawal symptoms. The withdrawal, presumably caused by hypoactive CB-1 receptors (see later in this chapter), leads to irritability, anxiety, depression, insomnia, disturbed sleep, weight loss, tremors, sweats, fever or chills, and headache. The person also craves cannabis. The symptoms are milder than those associated with withdrawal from other substances, such as alcohol, cocaine, or opioids. Withdrawal from illegal synthetic cannabinoids, in comparison, is associated with more severe symptoms, including fast heart rate, high blood pressure, and sweating.

Diagnosis

In the American Psychiatric Association's 2013 *Diagnostic and Statistical Manual of Mental Disorders* (*DSM-5*), cannabis use disorder (CUD) is diagnosed when the person using cannabis is not doing well due to at least two of the following criteria during a 12-month period: using more cannabis than was originally planned; inability to reduce cannabis use; being occupied much of the time with cannabis-related activities; craving cannabis; using cannabis even though being "high" or "stoned" interferes with other activities; experiencing social problems due to cannabis, such as the disapproval of others; preferring the use of cannabis over other activities that have become less meaningful; using cannabis despite it being dangerous in certain situations (such as driving); using cannabis despite being aware of medical or other problems (such as dizziness or paranoia) due to the cannabis; becoming tolerant of the drug, meaning that higher doses are needed for the desired effects; and developing withdrawal symptoms when cannabis use is stopped.

Cannabis withdrawal was added to the *DSM-5* criteria for CUD. Depending on the number of criteria met, the person is diagnosed with mild (2–3 criteria), moderate (4–5 criteria), or severe (6 or more criteria) CUD. Meeting six or more of the previously listed criteria is equivalent to what in the past would have been called (and still is by many) an addiction to cannabis.

Incidence

The 2017 National Survey on Drug Use and Health (NSDUH) found that in the United States, about 9.6% of the population aged 12 or older used cannabis in the past month with about 1.5% of people aged 12 or over, or 4.1 million people, meeting *DSM-IV* (an earlier version of *DSM-5*) criteria for cannabis use disorder in the past year (Substance Abuse and Mental Health Services Administration 2018). Similarly, Weiss, Howlett, and Baler (2017) report that about 9% of people who use cannabis may become addicted to it. Although there may seem to be two groups of people who use cannabis—either for recreation or for medical reasons—the groups overlap.

It is difficult to know if the incidence of cannabis misuse has increased along with its changing legal status. According to the 2017 NSDUH survey, there has been little change in the rates of CUD. The National Epidemiologic Survey on Alcohol and Related Conditions (NESARC), comparing waves of data collection between 2001–2002 and 2012–2013, found that the rates of cannabis use and CUD substantially increased in little over a decade (Hasin et al. 2015). As noted in the introduction, differences in methodology may explain these discrepant findings. People who are using cannabis may not be forthcoming when it comes to answering questions to an interviewer in person, as happens in the NSDUH surveys but not the NESARC surveys. NESARC also changed some of their interview methods between the different waves. The interviewers in the 2001–2002 survey were United States Census Bureau employees and did not offer participants incentives for participation. The 2012–2013 wave, however, was conducted by a private contractor. Participants provided saliva and were paid for participation (Grucza, Agrawal, and Bierut 2016; Grucza et al. 2016). Currently, then, it is difficult to determine the effects of legal changes on the incidence of CUD.

History

Cannabis has been used for almost 5,000 years. It was first used by the Chinese in about 2700 BCE for medicinal reasons. In his possibly apocryphal stories from the Orient, Marco Polo popularized the idea of the Old Man of the Mountains who, in the 11th century, controlled a group of men who murdered promiscuously, fueled by *hashish*, another name for cannabis. Hashish gave rise to the word *assassin*.

An Irish physician with skills in telegraphy, chemistry, botany, and pharmacology helped introduce cannabis to the Western world. William O'Shaughnessy, born in 1809, received his medical degree from the University of Edinburgh. He began his career in England investigating the safety of the coloring agents used in candies. In 1833, he took a job with the British East India Company in Calcutta as an assistant surgeon. While there he tested the medicinal properties of indigenous plants. He investigated *Cannabis indica* methodically, experimenting at first on animals and then on children. He wrote "On the Preparations of the Indian Hemp, or Gunjah" in which he explained how he successfully used it to treat pain, convulsions, and the spasms experienced in tetanus and rabies (O'Shaughnessy 1843). (*Gunjah*, also spelled *ganja*, is the Hindi word for *Cannabis indica*.)

O'Shaughnessy returned to England in 1841 and brought back *C. indica* for the Royal Botanical Gardens at Kew. On O'Shaughnessy's advice, Queen Victoria's personal physician advocated the use of cannabis to ease menstrual cramps. In 1844, O'Shaughnessy compiled the *Bengal Pharmacopeia* and included a 25-page section on cannabis. (A pharmacopeia is a book that identifies and describes drugs, chemicals, and plants used as medicines.) In 1848, he was elected a fellow of the Royal Society. His work was influential, and by the mid-1800s, cannabis was used for multiple medical purposes, including as an analgesic, in England and the United States. It would continue to be used for these purposes for most of the next century.

In 1851, the *United States Dispensatory* (like a pharmacopeia but less selective) described "extract of hemp" as:

> Causing exhilaration, intoxication, delirious hallucinations, and, in its subsequent action, drowsiness and stupor, with little effect upon the circulation. It is asserted also to act as a decided aphrodisiac, to increase the appetite, and occasionally to induce the cataleptic state. In morbid states of the system, it has been found to cause sleep, to allay spasm, to compose nervous disquietude, and to relieve pain. In these respects, it resembles opium; but it differs from that narcotic in not diminishing the appetite, checking the secretions, or constipating the bowels. It is much less certain in its effects. (Brecher 1972, 405)

In 1844, French intellectuals, such as Charles Baudelaire, Theophile Gautier, and Alexandre Dumas père, formed a club where they and other members of the Parisian elite would meet to sample drugs and discuss their effects. A favorite was cannabis, known to them as *hashish*. In 1846, Gautier wrote an essay, "Le Club des Hashischins," and in 1860, Baudelaire wrote a book, *Les Paradis Artificiels*; both were about the psychoactive effects of cannabis.

Dr. Jacques-Joseph Moreau, a French psychiatrist who was a member of the club, described its uses as an experimental psychotomimetic, a drug that causes psychosis, and noted that it changes how the user experiences time.

In 1892, William Osler, professor of medicine first at Johns Hopkins and then at Oxford, a respected and serious medical authority, recommended the use of C. *indica* as the best of several options for the prevention and treatment of migraine.

Cannabis was not as popular a medicine as opium because it was not as potent or as quick acting. It was difficult to prepare, and it could not be used intravenously because it is not soluble in water. Its popularity as an analgesic further waned when aspirin and acetaminophen were developed because these medications were more reliable, easier to produce, and more consistent. Botanical or herbal medicines cannot easily be standardized as growing conditions can affect their potency, and quality control is often poor.

In the 1920s, cannabis began to be used for its psychoactive properties in New Orleans where it was associated with jazz. When Prohibition came into force, it may have been used more widely. Cannabis moved into northern cities in the United States where it continued to be associated with musicians and minorities.

In the 1920s and 1930s, public opinion, largely in the Southwest, shifted against marijuana because of its connection with Mexican workers who smoked it. Organized labor wanted to protect its American members from wage competition from Mexicans who were willing to work for lower wages. Some of the anti-Mexican feelings of the time were displaced onto marijuana. Newspaper publisher William Randolph Hearst also stoked the antimarijuana sentiment, popularizing theories that marijuana turned its users into madmen, rapists, and murderers.

In 1937, President Franklin Delano Roosevelt signed the Marihuana Tax Act. People buying or selling marijuana, even for medical use, now had to acquire a "tax stamp" by registering and paying fees and taxes. The law did not criminalize the sale, possession, or use of marijuana but did impose heavy penalties if the required tax stamps were not obtained. The use of marijuana as a medicine virtually disappeared since the process of getting these stamps was tedious, expensive, and as will be seen later in this chapter, legally confusing. By this time, possession of marijuana had also been made illegal in many states, further confusing the matter.

The Marihuana Tax Act was unpopular in some parts of the country, particularly New York. New York City mayor Fiorello LaGuardia was opposed to the act because when he had been a member of the House of Representatives, he had heard about the use of marijuana by soldiers stationed in Panama. An Army Board of Inquiry found that the drug was sold by Panamanian farmers to the American soldiers who either smoked it or drank it as a form of tea. The army had not been concerned, finding that these practices were relatively harmless (Lee 2012, 43).

In 1938, LaGuardia asked the New York Academy of Medicine to study the question of the alleged harmfulness of marijuana. A group of 31 distinguished scientists, including physicians, psychiatrists, and sociologists, surveyed its use in the city and examined its effects on 72 prisoners, many of whom had previous experience with marijuana, and 5 non-prisoners who had never used marijuana. (The use of prisoners would not be allowed today because they would be seen as a vulnerable population who could be exploited.) In 1944, their report, *The Marihuana Problem in the City of New York*, concluded that marijuana was a mild drug that caused no harm, was not addicting, and did not lead to the use of more dangerous drugs. This report was ignored and the Marihuana Tax Act remained in effect.

In the 1960s, the use of marijuana became associated with the counterculture movement, the anti–Vietnam War movement, and hippies. In December 1965, psychologist Timothy Leary crossed the border from Mexico to Texas, where customs officers found marijuana seeds and five ounces of marijuana in his car. (See hallucinogen chapter for more discussion of Leary.) He was arrested for illegal possession under the Marihuana Tax Act of 1937 because he did not have the mandatory tax stamp. But to obtain it, he would have had to produce marijuana, and then he would have been in violation of Texas state law, which prohibited the possession of marijuana. Thus, the Marihuana Tax Act required him to violate state law and incriminate himself to government officials to comply with federal law. This proved to be a great opportunity for Leary. His lawyers argued successfully that the federal law violated the Fifth Amendment to the Constitution, barring mandatory self-incrimination. In 1969, in a unanimous decision, the U.S. Supreme Court ruled that the Marihuana Tax Act was in violation of Leary's Fifth Amendment right and was thus unconstitutional. This decision ended federal marijuana prohibition, but only temporarily.

In the Controlled Substances Act of the 1970s, cannabis was placed in Schedule I along with other drugs that are thought to have no medical use and to be highly addictive. This placement was temporary, pending the results of more inquiry. President Nixon appointed Raymond Shafer, a former Republican governor of Pennsylvania, to chair a commission reviewing marijuana. In 1972, the Shafer Commission, officially known as the National Commission on Marihuana and Drug Abuse, concluded that marijuana was relatively benign, that there was no need for harsh laws, and that the distribution or possession of small amounts should not be penalized in the criminal system. (The Canadian LeDain Commission of 1969–1973 arrived at similar conclusions.) Once again, a report was ignored, and as of February 2019, cannabis remains a Schedule I drug.

The history of cannabis has taken another turn with horticultural and technological advances. Botanists are creating hybrids of C. *sativa* and

---

Sidebar 2.1 The Changing Legal Status of Cannabis

Cannabis is widely grown and used, and it is perceived to be less addictive and harmful than other psychoactive drugs (such as alcohol, cocaine, and opioids) and to have medical benefits. Yet it is also disapproved of by many. Because of these factors, its legal status has always been complicated and has become more so in the last 25 years.

In 1996, California was the first state to approve the use of medical marijuana. In 2012, Colorado became the first state to vote for legal recreational marijuana for those over the age of 21. Recreational cannabis went on sale in that state in 2014, and in 2016, Colorado reported over a billion dollars' worth of cannabis sales. Other states have legalized recreational cannabis, and legal cannabis is now a multibillion-dollar industry in the United States.

Because cannabis (the whole plant) is still classified as a Schedule I drug, it is illegal federally. As of February 2019, medical marijuana is legal in 33 states, the District of Columbia, and the territories of Guam, Puerto Rico, the Northern Mariana Islands, and the U.S. Virgin Islands. At federal medical facilities, such as Veterans Administration hospitals, medical marijuana is illegal, even if the host state has legalized it. Fourteen other states have legalized CBD. Recreational cannabis is legal in 10 states, the District of Columbia, and the Northern Mariana Islands.

The advantages of legalization are many. Police and legal forces can be diverted to dealing with more harmful activities. Legalization lessens the power and profitability of drug dealers and increases tax revenue. In addition, the government can regulate the production and sale of cannabis (much as it does for tobacco and alcohol). Opponents worry, however, that legalization will lead to increased use by youth and others because of availability and promotion by companies selling cannabis.

Another approach, short of legalization, is to keep cannabis illegal but to reduce or eliminate criminal penalties involved with its sale or use. As of February 2019, cannabis has been decriminalized in 13 states and the U.S. Virgin Islands. Production and sale are unregulated. Instead, people who use or possess small amounts of cannabis in these states face civil penalties such as fines. The definition of "small" varies between the states, as do other aspects of the decriminalization laws.

Some of the complications of the contradiction between federal and state law are financial. Cannabis businesses may have difficulty using banks (which are federally regulated), deducting business expenses on federal income tax forms, and using water from federally managed resources.

The use of cannabis might seem to be a liberal issue because of its historical association with youth and the anti–Vietnam War movement. But many people who subscribe to right-wing, conservative, or libertarian politics also support the legalization of cannabis because of their objections to government intrusion into people's personal lives. Indeed, one of the first attorneys to work for its legalization was James R. White who described himself as "to the right of Barry Goldwater" (Lee 2012, 97–98).

In December 2018, industrial hemp became legal federally in an effort to support farmers and to encourage the development of industries associated with the use of hemp. Hemp plants yield oil high in CBD and very low in THC. In order to be legal, no part of the hemp plant can contain more than 0.3 % THC. Whether this oil is regulated by the Drug Enforcement Administration (DEA) and/or the Food and Drug Administration (FDA) is not clear; and therefore, its federal status is not clear. Despite this, hemp CBD oil is aggressively advertised in the United States as a safe and effective treatment for pain and inflammation.

Bibliography

Lee, Martin A. *Smoke Signals: A Social History of Marijuana: Medical, Recreational & Scientific*. New York: Scribner, 2012.

C. indica that are genetically programmed to produce high concentrations of THC. To further boost THC content, growers raise cannabis in greenhouses with carefully controlled environments.

Some recent research findings document the changing nature of cannabis. In the 1960s, cannabis contained about 4% THC; in 2014, it contained about 12% (D'Souza et al. 2017); the ratio of THC to CBD has also increased, which may change the psychoactive properties of cannabis (ElSohly et al. 2016).

Different hybrids are promoted as having different psychoactive properties. Cannabis growers promise consumers that they can pick the strain to give them whichever desired effects they want, such as energy, relaxation, sedation, vivid perceptions, diminished anxiety, or enhanced concentration. Some strains may be more likely to cause fearfulness, dizziness, or paranoia.

At the same time, interest in medical marijuana is growing. Many want to use marijuana for its medical effects (discussed later in this chapter) without becoming "stoned." High-CBD strains of marijuana or hemp-derived CBD are becoming increasingly popular because of their limited psychoactive effects.

Beginning in the 2000s, chemists in foreign (and illegal domestic) laboratories have synthesized over a hundred drugs that are distinct from THC but are active at cannabinoid receptors. These illegal synthetic cannabinoids are stronger than the phytocannabinoids or our own gentle, short-lived endocannabinoids (see later in this chapter), and are not diluted or modified by the myriad of other cannabinoids, terpenes, and substances in the cannabis plant. They are more likely to lead to aggression, hallucinations, vomiting, and rapid heart rate than are phytocannabinoids.

The history of hemp is slightly different from that of cannabis. Hemp has been grown for several thousand years for its fiber. Presidents George Washington and Thomas Jefferson grew hemp to be used as rope, fabric, and paper, and it was a major crop in Kentucky from pioneer times until the early 20th century. The use of American-grown hemp diminished with the increasing popularity of cotton, wool, synthetic fibers, and imported cheaper hemp. It further decreased after the passage of the 1937 Marihuana Tax Act but is now experiencing a resurgence (see Sidebar 2.1). The confusion about nomenclature and legality may continue.

Development and Causes

People in the United States who are most likely to report using cannabis are males between the ages of 18 and 25 who do poorly at school or who have little education, are unemployed, unmarried, and who also use tobacco. Some people begin to use cannabis at an early age and use it persistently, while others begin at a later age and use it only occasionally. Those who become dependent on cannabis are usually those who use it heavily. Genetic susceptibility may play a role.

Up Close—In Society
Societal attitudes and responses to cannabis use are complicated by its changing legal status and the variety of opinions about it. Many worry about its effect on motivation and possible precipitation of psychosis (discussed later in this chapter). But intoxication with cannabis is often seen as humorous.

Case Study
Morris is a 15-year-old Caucasian male who is getting poor grades at school. He says he just doesn't like school or understand why it is so important, and he finds it difficult to sit in class and pay attention. In his free time, Morris smokes as much cannabis as he can. He has begun to vape it because he knows that this is safer for his lungs than is smoking. He lives in a state where medical and recreational cannabis are legal, and when his parents confront him about his usage, he argues, "It's legal! Why shouldn't I use it? Everyone knows it's better for you than alcohol or cigarettes." Morris's parents say that recreational cannabis is for adults, not for children. They wonder if cannabis is causing his problems at school. They tell him that they will not let him get a driver's license while he is smoking so much cannabis. Morris scoffs at their concerns, saying, "Who cares about school? Steve Jobs and Bill Gates smoked and were dropouts and they did just fine. And I've seen you drive after a couple of drinks." Morris's parents read more about cannabis and discover that cannabis may increase the risk of developing schizophrenia. A couple of times while vaping Morris has become agitated. His mother has a brother with schizophrenia, and she is afraid that the agitation Morris sometimes experiences after smoking may indicate an increased susceptibility to cannabis-related schizophrenia. When she talks to Morris about her brother and her worry about Morris becoming ill, he just laughs.

Up Close—At Work
Cannabis misuse may interfere with work. A person who consumes large amounts of cannabis is known colloquially as a "stoner" or "pothead" and supposedly lacks ambition or the ability to work hard. If the reports

that cannabis use in adolescents interferes with memory and ability to learn are borne out, this too will have implications for the cannabis user's productivity. On the other hand, some believe that cannabis is helpful for creativity. If there is such an association, it could be that cannabis aids creativity or that creativity is linked with the open-mindedness that might go along with using cannabis.

As more people use medicinal and recreational cannabis, cannabis use in the workplace may become common, along with increasing concerns about idleness, possible cognitive impairment, and accidents. It is difficult, however, to know how to proceed with such concerns as there is no easy or accepted laboratory way of assessing cannabis intoxication. Blood testing is not routinely performed because there are no quick or well-accepted tests, the current tests do not indicate the level of impairment, and the tests are positive only briefly after ingestion. Urine and hair tests are also not very useful because they may test positive for cannabinoid metabolites for several days or weeks after use, and there is no link between positive urines and impairment. Nonetheless, in most cases, states and federal laws allow employers to test employees if there is reason to be concerned. Illegal synthetic cannabinoids are not detected by conventional urine testing.

Case Study

Harry is a 27-year-old male who smokes cannabis every day and has lost two jobs because of his poor motivation, possibly due to his cannabis use. Harry has had one driving accident after having smoked cannabis but does not believe that cannabis was to blame. He is currently working as a salesman for a friend who is aware of his cannabis use. His friend tells him that he will not tolerate cannabis use and that he will request urine drug testing if he has reasonable suspicion that Harry was impaired because of drug use. Harry has been working for his friend now for two months, and the friend is becoming annoyed by Harry's frequent tardiness and poor job performance. He thinks that he smells cannabis on Harry's clothes. He talks to Harry about his concerns, but Harry doesn't really care. His main interest is music. He thinks that once he finds a job involving music, his cannabis use will not be problematic because of what he believes is the more tolerant attitude of musicians toward cannabis. He lives in a state where cannabis is not yet legal, but he says that he has never been in trouble. He says to his friend, "The real problem is that I smoke cigarettes. Now that's bad for you. The only thing I want to do is listen to music and maybe write some. And everyone knows that music sounds better when you're stoned. And you compose better music when you're stoned. Look at Bob Marley. Have you ever listened to Willie Nelson?" His friend requests that Harry submit to drug testing and provide a urine sample, saying, "I gave you fair warning about this. I told you to stop using cannabis as soon as you started working here. If your urine tests positive, you are fired."

Up Close—In Relationships
Cannabis is not associated with the type of family conflicts that are seen in the families of those who gamble or drink too much alcohol. Nonetheless, family members are often unhappy about a loved one's cannabis use.

Case Study
Karen is a 24-year-old woman who uses medical marijuana to control her migraines. Her parents think that she uses it excessively, and they want her to quit. She has tried to cut down and once quit for a couple of months but says that her headaches get worse when she is not smoking marijuana regularly. She is willing to try to reduce her use to please her parents but says that she will not quit altogether. Her boyfriend sides with Karen's parents. He would like the two of them to have a baby but does not want Karen to be smoking marijuana while pregnant. He says, "Why take any risks when you are pregnant? I don't want our baby exposed to something that the federal government has not said is safe." She says, "You don't know how bad my headaches are, and anything else I take could be bad for the baby. My body, my baby, my decision."

Effects and Costs

Effects

Unlike many of the other substances dealt with in this book, cannabis does not seem to be associated with acute, serious, or chronic medical problems. Overdoses do not lead to morbidity or mortality. However, there are several areas of concern regarding its effects, including cognitive defects, the development of schizophrenia or depression, violence, driving accidents, toxicity, and introduction to other drugs of misuse. Cannabinoids and medical marijuana may have some beneficial effects.

Early work suggested that young people who smoked cannabis had decrements in executive functioning. A recent review of the literature found that cognitive problems associated with cannabis might have been due to acute use or withdrawal, and that within 72 hours of stopping cannabis use, there are virtually no cognitive deficits (Scott et al. 2018). Authorities are still concerned that younger people who use large quantities of high-THC cannabis may be sustaining some damage to their brains.

By comparison, older people who use medical marijuana with higher quantities of CBD to treat pain or anxiety may see improved brain functioning. Recent research done at Harvard Medical School, using functional magnetic resonance imaging (fMRI)—a technique for measuring and mapping brain activity by measuring changes in blood oxygenation—and a test of executive functioning, showed an improvement in both imaging and actual test performance in subjects who used CBD (Gruber et al. 2017).

Long-term or heavy use of cannabis in adolescence may be a risk factor for schizophrenia, particularly if the person has ever had an episode of cannabis-induced psychosis or is vulnerable because of a family history of schizophrenia (D'Souza et al. 2017; Radhakrishnan et al. 2014). A concern about the increasing legalization of cannabis is that it might lead to more cases of psychosis, although there is no clear evidence that legalization of cannabis leads to increased use by adolescents (Gruczka, Agrawal, and Bierut 2016). Studies about the rates of depression and violence in cannabis users have found conflicting results. Driving while under the influence of cannabis may be problematic particularly when combined with alcohol. Smoked cannabis may be toxic to the lungs; the safety of vaporized cannabis has not been established.

Some experts worry that cannabis is a gateway drug, meaning that someone will begin using cannabis and then move on to more harmful drugs, such as opioids or cocaine. Others suggest that although cannabis users are more likely to use these drugs than cannabis nonusers, it is only because those people who go on to misuse other drugs have a susceptibility to drug misuse and would have misused the other drugs in any event.

Many believe that there are medical benefits to be obtained from the use of cannabinoids. Dronabinol (synthetic THC) is approved by the Food and Drug Administration (FDA) for the treatment of anorexia in AIDS and nausea and vomiting associated with chemotherapy. It is a Schedule III drug, meaning that it has some potential for abuse and may lead to dependence. Psychoactive effects are rare. In June 2018, the FDA approved the use of plant-based CBD (Epidiolex) for the treatment of two rare diseases that cause epilepsy in children. Epidiolex is a Schedule V drug, meaning that there is low potential for misuse. Apart from these two medications, the FDA has not approved cannabinoids for medical use.

Legal in 47 states, medical marijuana is marijuana that has been prescribed by a physician and is available in a dispensary. It can be the whole plant or certain extracts. It has benefits in some conditions, decreasing pain and spasticity in multiple sclerosis, increasing appetite in those with HIV and AIDS, and decreasing nausea and vomiting in people taking chemotherapy. An extract of marijuana with equal amounts of THC and CBD (nabiximols) is available in 27 countries (but not the United States) for the treatment of complications of multiple sclerosis, such as spasticity and pain.

There is some overlap between the medical effects of THC and CBD; each may be helpful for pain. CBD is thought to be anti-inflammatory. Many believe that with respect to medical uses, marijuana is more effective than dronabinol because there are ingredients in marijuana that are synergistic with the THC itself. In other words, substances in marijuana such as CBD and terpenes, among others, might work together to increase their beneficial effects; this is called the *entourage effect* (Russo, 2019).

Medical marijuana may decrease intraocular pressure and thus be helpful for glaucoma, but research shows that the effect only lasts for three to four hours so that it must be used throughout the day. Currently, ophthalmologists do not recommend medical marijuana for patients with glaucoma.

Those opposed to medical marijuana note that, with the exception of Epidiolex, the FDA has not approved medical uses of the cannabis plant or extracts. The dosing and delivery methods have not yet been rigorously studied in large samples, and quality control cannot be ensured. The American College of Obstetricians and Gynecologists recommends against its use in pregnant or breastfeeding women for the same reasons (ACOG 2017). The long-term effects of cannabis on the developing brain, both in the fetus and the adolescent, have not been studied, but there is some indication that it may interfere with the brain's own endocannabinoid system, as described in this chapter. Those supporting the use of medical marijuana note that it has been used for centuries with no clear evidence of harm.

Costs

Most of the literature about the costs of cannabis misuse concerns the legalization debate and the possible increase in tax revenue. Little is known about the actual costs of cannabis use disorder or addiction.

Theory and Research

In the mid-1960s, organic chemist Raphael Mechoulam and his team at the Hebrew University in Jerusalem identified and synthesized THC, thus making research on cannabis easier. The next landmark discovery took place in the American Midwest. In 1988, neuroscientist Allyn Howlett and her graduate student William Devane at the St. Louis University School of Medicine discovered that the mammalian brain has receptors that respond to cannabis compounds. These G-protein-coupled receptors (GPCRs) are found in the hippocampus, cerebral cortex, cerebellum, basal ganglia, hypothalamus, and amygdala and are the most common type of GPCRs. They are not found in the brain stem, the region that controls breathing and heartbeat, perhaps explaining in part the safety of high doses of cannabis compared to opioids.

By 1990, molecular biologist Lisa Matsuda and colleagues at the National Institute of Mental Health had described the exact DNA sequence that encodes a THC-sensitive receptor in the rat's brain and had cloned the cannabinoid receptor, thus allowing yet more research.

Researchers also identified a second type of cannabinoid receptor found throughout the peripheral nervous system, gut, spleen, liver, heart, kidneys, bones, blood vessels, lymph cells, endocrine glands, and reproductive organs. The first receptor, known as CB-1, mediates psychoactive effects and the second receptor, CB-2, regulates immune response.

In 1992, almost 30 years after his original discovery, Raphael Mechoulam, in collaboration with William Devane, now at NIMH, and Dr. Lumír Hanuš, a Czech chemist working in Israel, found a novel neurotransmitter, an "endocannabinoid," that attaches to the same mammalian brain cell receptors as THC. Devane named it "anandamide," deriving from the Sanskrit word for "bliss." In 1995, this group discovered a second major endocannabinoid molecule, 2-AG (2-arachidonoylglycerol), which binds to both CB-1 and CB-2 receptors. Endocannabinoids and their receptors are present in fish, reptiles, earthworms, leeches, amphibians, birds, and mammals—every type of animal except insects.

Endocannabinoids (and nitric oxide) are "retrograde signaling molecules." Usually, a signal goes from a presynaptic neuron across a synapse to the postsynaptic neuron. But retrograde transmitters diffuse *backward* from postsynaptic neurons (where they are synthesized "on demand") across the synapse to terminals on presynaptic neurons where they bind to specific GPCRs and inhibit neurotransmitter release for a few seconds, thus modulating neurotransmission. The retrograde signaling inhibits immune response, reduces inflammation, relaxes musculature, lowers blood pressure, dilates bronchial passages, and increases cerebral blood flow.

The endocannabinoids are metabolized rapidly. THC, in contrast, is broken down slowly so its effects on the brain persist (Pertwee 2009).

Prolonged exposure to THC may change the body's own endocannabinoid system. This fact is concerning for adolescents whose brains are still developing because the endocannabinoid system may become less sensitive to endogenous cannabinoids. Illegal synthetic cannabinoids are potent agonists and have higher affinity for receptors than THC and thus may be more dangerous.

Much drug research is done by federal agencies, such as the National Institutes for Drug Abuse, but this work is hampered by cannabis's illegal status. For example, federal agencies are not allowed to work with cannabis that is sold in the states that have legalized it; they can only work with cannabis that is grown in a University of Mississippi facility. In 1968, this facility was established as the first (and still only) legal cannabis farm in the United States. Additionally, numerous layers of bureaucracy still exist when agencies work with cannabis. Rigorous research supporting the medical uses of marijuana is sparse.

Treatments

The treatment of CUD is still evolving. Currently there are no medications that have proven useful for treating CUD, and none have been approved by the FDA. A few groups are using oral THC as a way of lessening the symptoms of withdrawal, which is analogous to using methadone or suboxone to ameliorate the symptoms of opioid withdrawal. However, in most treatment facilities, medications are not used.

The treatment for CUD is usually an outpatient process involving the use of psychosocial interventions such as cognitive behavioral therapy (CBT) or motivational enhancement therapy (MET) or a combination of the two. (These treatments are described in more detail in the alcohol chapter.) Contingency management—providing vouchers or rewards of some sort for "negative" urine screens (or "clean urines") or attending therapy—can be used also (Budney et al. 2007).

Treatment of CUD is challenging. Because cannabis is commonly used and perceived to be safer than other drugs, such as tobacco and alcohol, some users prefer to lessen their use rather than give it up entirely. Another challenge is the person who is in treatment for opioid and cocaine misuse but who wants to continue using cannabis. Experts are concerned that the individual who continues to misuse cannabis is at greater risk for relapsing to misuse of the other substances, including opioids (Olfson et al. 2018); other research suggests that medical marijuana may decrease opioid analgesic overdose mortality (Bachhuber et al. 2014). Some treatment programs compromise by discouraging recreational cannabis use without imposing harsh consequences.

Bibliography

ACOG (American College of Obstetricians and Gynecologists). "ACOG Committee Opinion: Marijuana Use During Pregnancy and Lactation, Bulletin no. 722." *Obstet Gynecol* 130 (October 2017), e205–209.

American Psychiatric Association. *Diagnostic and Statistical Manual of Mental Disorders (DSM-5)*, 5th ed. Arlington, VA: American Psychiatric Association, 2013.

Bachhuber, Marcus A., Brendan Saloner, Chinazo O. Cunningham, and Colleen L. Barry. "Medical Cannabis Laws and Opioid Analgesic Overdose Mortality in the United States, 1999–2010." *JAMA Int Med* 174, no. 10 (2014), 1668–1673. doi:10.1001/jamainternmed.2014.4005.

Brecher, Edward M. *Licit and Illicit Drugs: The Consumers Union Report on Narcotics, Stimulants, Depressants, Inhalants, Hallucinogens, and Marijuana—Including Caffeine, Nicotine, and Alcohol.* Boston: Little, Brown, 1972.

Budney, Alan, Roger Roffman, Robert Stephens, and Denise Walker. "Marijuana Dependence and Its Treatment." *Addict Sci Clin Pract* 4, no. 1 (2007), 4–16. doi:10.1151/ascp07414.

D'Souza, Deepak C., Rajiv Radhakrishnan, Mohamed Sherif, Jose Cortes-Briones, John Cahill, Swapnil Gupta, Patrick D. Skosnik, and Mohini Ranganathan. "Cannabinoids and Psychosis." *Curr Pharm Des* 22, no. 42 (2017), 6380–6391.

Eisenberg, Elon, Miri Ogintz, and Shlomo Almog. "The Pharmacokinetics, Efficacy, Safety, and Ease of Use of a Novel Portable Metered-Dose Cannabis Inhaler in Patients With Chronic Neuropathic Pain: A Phase 1a Study." *J Pain Palliat Care Pharmacother* 28, no. 3 (2014), 216–225. doi:10.3109/15360288.2014.941130.

ElSohly, Mahmoud A., Zlatko Mehmedic, Susan Foster, Chandrani Gon, Suman Chandra, and James C. Church. "Changes in Cannabis Potency Over the Last 2 Decades (1995–2014): Analysis of Current Data in the United States." *Biol Psychiatry* 79, no. 7 (2016), 613–619. doi:10.1016/j.biopsych.2016.01.004.

Gruber, Staci A., Kelly A. Sagar, Mary K. Dahlgren, Atilla Gonenc, Rosemary T. Smith, Ashley M. Lambros, Korine B. Cabrera, and Scott E. Lukas. "The Grass Might Be Greener: Medical Marijuana Patients Exhibit Altered Brain Activity and Improved Executive Function after

3 Months of Treatment." *Front Pharmacol* 8 (January 2018), 983. doi:10.3389/fphar.2017.00983. eCollection 2017.

Grucza, Richard A., Arpana Agrawal, and Laura J. Bierut. "NESARC Findings on Increased Prevalence of Marijuana Use Disorders— Reply." *JAMA Psychiatry* 73, no. 5 (2016), 532–533. doi:10.1001/jamapsychiatry.2016.0244.

Grucza, Richard A., Arpana Agrawal, Melissa J. Krauss, Patricia A. Cavazos-Rehg, and Laura J. Bierut. "Recent Trends in the Prevalence of Marijuana Use and Associated Disorders in the United States." *JAMA Psychiatry* 73, no. 3 (2016), 300–301. doi:10.1001/jamapsychiatry.2015.3111.

Hasin, Deborah S., Tulshi D. Saha, Bradley T. Kerridge, Risë B. Goldstein, S. P. Chou, Haitao Zhang, Jeesun Jung, et al. "Prevalence of Marijuana Use Disorders in the United States Between 2001–2002 and 2012–2013." *JAMA Psychiatry* 72, no. 12 (2015), 1235–1242. doi:10.1001/jamapsychiatry.2015.1858.

Lee, Martin A. *Smoke Signals: A Social History of Marijuana: Medical, Recreational & Scientific.* New York: Scribner, 2012.

Olfson, Mark, Melanie M. Wall, Shang-Min Liu, and Carlos Blanco. "Cannabis Use and Risk of Prescription Opioid Use Disorder in the United States." *Am J Psychiatry* 175, no. 1 (2018), 47–53. doi:10.1176/appi.ajp.2017.17040413.

O'Shaughnessy, William B. "On the Preparations of the Indian Hemp, or Gunjah: Cannabis Indica Their Effects on the Animal System in Health, and their Utility in the Treatment of Tetanus and other Convulsive Diseases." *BMJ* s1-5, no. 123 (1843), 363–369. doi:10.1136/bmj.s1-5.123.363.

Pertwee, Roger G. "Cannabinoid Pharmacology: The First 66 Years." *Br J Pharmacol* 147, no. S1 (2009), S163–S171. doi:10.1038/sj.bjp.0706406.

Radhakrishnan, Rajiv, Peter H. Addy, R. A. Sewell, Patrick D. Skosnik, Mohini Ranganathan, and Deepak C. D'Souza. "Cannabis, Cannabinoids, and the Association with Psychosis." *The Effects of Drug Abuse on the Human Nervous System*, 2014, 423–474. doi:10.1016/b978-0-12-418679-8.00014-9.

Russo, Ethan B. "The Case for the Entourage Effect and Conventional Breeding of Clinical Cannabis: No 'Strain,' No Gain." *Front Plant Sci* 9 (2019). doi:10.3389/fpls.2018.01969. eCollection 2018.

Scott, J. C., Samantha T. Slomiak, Jason D. Jones, Adon F. Rosen, Tyler M. Moore, and Ruben C. Gur. "Association of Cannabis With Cognitive

Functioning in Adolescents and Young Adults." *JAMA Psychiatry* 75, no. 6 (2018), 585–595. doi:10.1001/jamapsychiatry.2018.0335.

Substance Abuse and Mental Health Services Administration. *Key substance use and mental health indicators in the United States: Results from the 2017 National Survey on Drug Use and Health (HHS Publication No. SMA 18-5068, NSDUH Series H-53).* Rockville, MD: Center for Behavioral Health Statistics and Quality, Substance Abuse and Mental Health Services Administration, 2018. Accessed July 29, 2019. http://www.samhsa.gov/data/.

Weiss, Susan R., Katia D. Howlett, and Ruben D. Baler. "Building Smart Cannabis Policy from the Science Up." *Int J Drug Policy* 42 (2017), 39–49. doi:10.1016/j.drugpo.2017.01.007.

CHAPTER 3

Gambling

Jennifer Grant, Joshua B. Grubbs, and Shane W. Kraus

Addiction has typically been associated with substance misuse, but some behaviors can also be understood as addictive. Gambling is one such behavior, which, when indulged in to excess, harms an individual's health, community, and finances. *Gambling* is defined as "risking something of value in the hopes of attaining something of greater value" (American Psychiatric Association 2013, 586), and therefore encompasses many activities. Sometimes skill and knowledge play a part in the outcome of the activity, and chance—or its close neighbor, luck—is always involved. Chance has to do with events that seem to be random; luck is how people perceive these events. For example, poker involves skill and chance, sports betting involves knowledge and chance, while playing the lottery or slot machines involves only chance. The person who wins at these games is said to be "lucky." Lotteries, raffles, office pools, and casino gambling are the most common forms of gambling in the United States (Welte et al. 2015). The term *gambling* can also refer to taking risks of any sort when the outcome is uncertain; but that is not the sense in which gambling is used in this book.

Despite being included in the American Psychiatric Association's *Diagnostic and Statistical Manual of Mental Disorders (DSM)* (2013) since 1980, gambling disorder has only been officially considered an addiction since the fifth edition of the manual, *DSM-5*, was published in 2013. It is the only behavioral addiction with enough empirical support to be included in the *DSM-5*. Gambling has high rates of comorbidity with other psychiatric disorders.

Symptoms, Diagnosis, and Incidence

Symptoms

Most people realize that gambling will cost, not earn, them money. As a form of entertainment, it may be worth the mild thrill of betting even if one does lose some money on lottery or scratch tickets or a bet on a horse. For some people, however, gambling stops being a diversion and becomes the central activity of their lives, despite the harm it causes. These individuals believe that they will eventually profit from their gambling, and their gambling becomes impulsive or compulsive. Consider people who go to a casino and lose several thousand dollars playing blackjack. Most people realize that continuing to play will almost certainly lead to more losses and therefore will decide to "cut" their losses and stop playing. By contrast, a person with a gambling disorder thinks: "If I keep playing for just a little longer, I'm certain to win back what I've lost. I've almost won a few times, so I have to keep playing." This individual will realize at some level that such behavior is not sensible, feel some shame and or guilt, and so may choose to hide such activities from his or her family. In severe cases of gambling addiction, individuals may even resort to theft or fraud to be able to continue to play.

Diagnosis

The *DSM* first included gambling as a disorder in 1980 under the name "Pathological Gambling." The diagnosis was included under the umbrella of "impulse-control disorders" and was based on subjective evaluations of clinicians and researchers. However, as more data have been collected and analyzed, the criteria for gambling disorder have changed, and in the *DSM-5*, it is now considered an addictive disorder. This change in classification took place after years of debate and is due to the increasing recognition of the overlap between problem gambling and substance misuse in their symptoms, natural history, epidemiology, comorbidity, and neurobiology.

Although gambling disorder is placed in its own section in the *DSM-5*, "Non-Substance-Related Disorders," its general features are like those of substance use disorders, with emphasis on the financial aspects of the behavior (American Psychiatric Association 2013). The *DSM* outlines nine criteria for the disorder: spending increasing amounts of money on gambling; feeling irritable when not gambling; trying time and again to stop or reduce gambling; thinking about gambling for much of the time; gambling when upset; "chasing" losses, meaning that the person continues to gamble to win back the money lost in prior gambles; lying to others about the frequency of gambling or how much money has been lost; losing or risking losing a job or relationship because of the time or money spent gambling; and losing so much money gambling that must depend on others for money to continue gambling. As with most disorders, gambling disorder can cause significant problems in an individual's relationships, job, career, or education. It can also cause major financial problems, such as debts, which may persist long after recovery.

People are said to have "problem gambling" if they have some symptoms or some adverse consequences from gambling. Those with four to seven symptoms in a 12-month period have a mild gambling disorder; those with eight or nine have a severe gambling disorder.

Incidence

Almost 80% of Americans gamble at some point in their lifetime, but only a few become addicted (Kessler et al. 2008, 1351). A small number of adults meet some criteria for gambling disorder: the numbers vary depending on the way that problem gambling is defined or ascertained (Petry 2005; Welte et al. 2015). Adolescents have higher rates of gambling disorder (4%–6%) or problem gambling (8%–10%) compared to adults (Shaffer and Hall 2001). Rates of problem gambling are higher for men than women, and the gap is growing: gambling rates are increasing for men and decreasing for women (Welte et al. 2015, 695). Those struggling with gambling problems are more likely to be single or divorced, to be from a lower socioeconomic background, and to have less education (Welte et al. 2017). A larger proportion of individuals with gambling disorder belong to ethnic and racial minorities compared to the general population. African Americans are overrepresented in the rates of gambling disorder compared to the general population (Welte et al. 2015, 695). Those who are in the military, in prison, or in treatment due to other disorders have a higher likelihood of being diagnosed with gambling disorder (Shaffer and Hall 2001; Stefanovics, Potenza, and Pietrzak 2017).

Prevalence rates of disordered gambling seem to be similar throughout the world (Petry 2005, 16–20) and may be rising as individuals have more leisure time and different types of gambling are being developed (Petry 2005, 32).

Gambling has high rates of comorbidity with substance use disorders, post–traumatic stress disorder (PTSD), antisocial personality disorder, and generalized anxiety disorder (Grubbs et al. 2018; Kessler et al. 2008; Shaw et al. 2007). Gambling is associated with high rates of suicide ideation and suicide attempts (Battersby et al. 2006; Cunningham-Williams et al. 2005); this risk is even higher among individuals with gambling disorder and PTSD (Najavits 2010).

History

People have been gambling for millennia. For example, some Chinese and Japanese games are said to have been invented by Emperor Yao in about 2100 BCE (France 1902, 364). Ancient Romans gambled enthusiastically, betting, for example, on the outcomes of chariot races.

Throughout history, authorities have repeatedly tried to regulate gambling because of the problems often associated with it. Because ancient Roman officials noticed the negative consequences of gambling, they outlawed it except during certain holidays. Roman law allowed a debtor, including one whose debts were from gambling, to be enslaved to his creditor (Petry 2005, 6). Native American tribes did not allow individuals to gamble with items that they had borrowed, helping members avoid debt (Petry 2005, 6). In England, Henry VIII made gambling illegal for the common people—except at Christmas (France 1902, 368).

Europeans did not understand the mathematics of gambling and chance until Hindu-Arabic numerals were introduced, making computation easier and facilitating the work of individuals such as physician and polymath Gerolamo Cardano and mathematician Blaise Pascal. People in India and China had probably begun to understand chance much earlier.

Around the start of the 17th century, the casino, a large public space equipped with entertainment and gambling devices, appeared in Italy. Before the advent of the casino, gambling was most often conducted in private bets with zero-sum outcomes, meaning that what one person loses the other wins. However, casinos use formulas to ensure that the odds favor "the house," while still providing patrons with enough wins to give the impression that the odds are fair. Between the 17th and 19th centuries, games of chance, such as baccarat, blackjack, craps, and roulette, became popular. A feature of these "table games" is the presence of a croupier or dealer who directs or organizes them.

Settlers in the United States brought many of the European games with them. Gambling grew popular throughout the colonies—and even more so in the West. (The image of cowboys playing poker in a saloon is iconic.) Perhaps those willing to risk the uncertainties of migration to improve their fortune were also willing to gamble in other ways. But by the 18th and 19th centuries, there was a backlash. Hymns and sermons from that time refer to gambling as a disease similar to leprosy and drunkenness (Flavin 2003, 222–223). Conservative religious movements in the United States denounced gambling and it fell out of favor. During the Great Depression, gambling was only permitted in churches and other charitable organizations as a form of fundraising, and only specific forms of gambling, such as bingo, were allowed. (The relationship between religion and gambling is discussed in Sidebar 3.1.) Other forms of gambling moved underground and became associated with organized crime.

Governments have long used lotteries to raise revenue, and the history of lotteries in the United States is complex. In the early 1600s, English lottery revenue was involved in the establishment of Virginia, the first permanent British colony in North America (Schwartz 2006, 124–125). Before the American Revolution, the British Crown passed a restriction on lotteries, which partly fueled rising tensions and revealed the colonies' financial dependence on lotteries. After the Revolution, lotteries were revived and continued for some years. Each of the 13 colonies used them to raise revenue. Because of the 18th- and 19th-century disapproval of

---

Sidebar 3.1 The Relationship between Gambling and Religion

Five of the world's major religions—Buddhism, Christianity, Hinduism, Islam, and Judaism—warn about the negative consequences of excessive gambling. In most cases, religious texts discuss the problems it can create not only for the individual but also for others. A passage from the Hindu *Rig Veda Mandala 10: Sukta 34* describes how gambling can cause people to lose everything and how it leads to sadness for those around them. The Buddhist *Sigalovada Sutta* details major negative consequences associated with gambling. If individuals did begin to gamble problematically, it was thought that they were choosing to harm themselves and society and going against the teachings of their religion.

The extent of prohibition recommended by each religion is different. For example, the Catholic Church allows gambling if it is not harmful or excessive, and many parishes use bingo or raffles to raise funds for their church. More recently, with the advent of the belief that excessive gambling is a disorder, the view of this activity as a moral failing is lessening.

gambling, lotteries disappeared. Lotteries resurged briefly after the Civil War, especially in some of the Southern states, which used the revenue to help recover from the war. But by 1895, all state lotteries had once again disappeared.

Gambling made a comeback in the early 20th century. In 1931, Nevada legalized most types of gambling as a way of providing revenue for the state, and Las Vegas became a hub for gambling. Between the 1950s and 1980s, Southern Maryland and Atlantic City, New Jersey, also legalized gambling, revitalizing these areas. In 1979, the Seminole tribe attempted to secure their economy by opening the first reservation casino. Other tribes did the same. Reservation casinos are protected by the Indian Gaming Regulatory Act of 1988.

In 1964, New Hampshire became the first state to reintroduce a state lottery to increase revenue. Since then, 44 other states have followed, using the revenue to help fund public services such as education. In many cases, retailers that sell these tickets are paid a commission and bonuses for selling a winning ticket, which means that the lottery also supports businesses (Gerstein et al. 1999).

At about the same time that New Hampshire revived the state lottery, sports and horse-race betting were being gradually legalized throughout the United States. However, because of perceived harms, in 1992, the U.S. Congress passed the Professional and Amateur Sports Protection Act to curb sports betting. This act was overturned in 2018 because of claims that it was unconstitutional and conflicted with the Tenth Amendment. Now states can regulate their own sports betting.

The first machine game was invented in 1891 as an automatic poker game, with winners receiving cigars as prizes. In 1898, Charles Fey invented the first slot machine with cash prizes (Schwartz 2006, 325–346). In 1909, California banned these machines and other states followed. However, noncash slot machines were permitted, where prizes included gum and trinkets. By the 1980s, these machines had been replaced first by electromechanical machines and then by fully digital machines, which determine outcomes by a computerized pseudo-random number generator. This type of "random" number generator still allowed the house to have the odds in its favor. By the beginning of the 21st century, these machines accounted for much of casino revenue. Electronic gaming (or gambling) machines (EGMs) are the preferred method of gambling for many who gamble problematically and for women.

Internet gambling has grown in popularity worldwide since the beginning of the 21st century. However, even though it is legal in some states, international and interstate transactions are illegal because of the 1961

Federal Wire Act and the 2006 Unlawful Internet Gambling Enforcement Act. As of 2019, only Utah and Hawaii have made all types of gambling illegal in the United States.

It is likely that the development of EGMs and online gambling has changed gambling as much as did the development of casinos. The speed of the activity, lack of distraction by other people or activities, cleverly designed audio-visual input, and carefully manipulated response rates exacerbate gambling disorder in some gamblers.

Development and Causes

Gambling disorder can develop in adolescence or adulthood, although earlier onset is more typical in men and those who gamble with family and friends. The disorder most commonly occurs in young and middle-aged individuals (Welte et al. 2015). High school and college students who have it often grow out of it. Early onset is associated with comorbid substance use and impulsivity. Gambling disorder tends to develop over the course of a couple of years and may develop faster in women than in men. As the disorder progresses, individuals gamble more frequently and with larger amounts of money. Gambling waxes and wanes, and people may cycle in and out of having gambling problems. Individuals may resume gambling after having stopped, only to have it become problematic again. People usually have one or two favorite types of gambling. The type differs by age and gender; for example, women and older individuals prefer slot machines and bingo (Welte et al. 2002).

Biological Etiology

The cause of problem gambling is not known with certainty, though there is some evidence that it runs in families. Twin studies suggest that genetics may play a role (Walters 2001). Gambling disorder also has a high comorbidity with substance use disorders (Eisen et al. 1998; Slutske et al. 2000). Gamblers experience more excitement and anticipation of pleasure than do nongamblers when gambling, possibly due to their biological responses to the activity, increasing the likelihood of developing gambling problems (Blanchard et al. 2000). Other studies have suggested that the frontal lobe and prefrontal cortex of gamblers may be impaired, thus explaining the problems they have with making sensible decisions (Gehring and Willoughby 2002; Potenza et al. 2003). Environmental factors and exposure to stressors such as trauma and poverty also play a role in the development of a gambling disorder.

Cognitive Behavioral Theory

According to behavioral theory, all behavior, including gambling and associated behaviors, is learned via one (or more) of three mechanisms: *classical conditioning, operant conditioning,* and *modeling.* In classical conditioning, learning occurs when two stimuli are paired, so that the response to the first stimulus will eventually occur also to the second (conditioned) stimulus. For example, if a bell rings when a dog is presented with food, eventually the dog will salivate at the sound of the bell, the conditioned stimulus. Classical conditioning explains some of the superstitions of gamblers. If a gambler wins when playing at a certain slot machine, she will associate that machine with winning. Operant conditioning is to do with "rewards" for behaviors. If a gambler wins, he will keep gambling. The gambler may also be rewarded by feelings of excitement and euphoria when playing, regardless of whether he wins. The best way to encourage a behavior is to reward it immediately, randomly, or intermittently, explaining why gambling disorder develops quickly (Petry 2005, 199–203). In modeling, individuals learn disordered gambling through watching others and copying their behavior. Studies show, for example, that children of those with gambling problems have higher rates of gambling problems themselves (Jacobs et al. 1989).

Cognitive fallacies, such as expecting a "big win" after several losses, are important in the development of gambling disorder, as is the failure to account for realistic probabilities of winning. These biases may interact with behavioral mechanisms, leading to increased gambling (Sharpe and Tarrier 1993).

Up Close—In Society
Gambling disorder is a problem in members and veterans of the armed forces (Westermeyer et al. 2013). Among veterans, gambling disorder has been associated with mental health problems, including higher rates of suicidality/suicide attempts, PTSD, depression, substance use, and poor quality of life (Shirk et al. 2018). In a study of more than 3,000 veterans, 35.1% gambled recreationally and 2.2% met criteria for at-risk or problem gambling (Stefanovics, Potenza, and Pietrzak 2017). Approximately 4.2% of veterans who returned recently from Iraq or Afghanistan deployments met diagnostic criteria for gambling disorder (Whiting et al. 2016). This rate is higher than gambling disorder prevalence rates in the general population (Welte et al. 2015). In 2018, a bill was signed into law requiring members of the U.S. armed forces to be screened for problem gambling.

Case Study

Joseph is a 32-year-old veteran who has served two tours in Afghanistan. During his second tour of duty, Joseph's unit was hit by an improvised explosive device (IED). Joseph sustained serious injuries, but several members of his unit, including a close friend, were killed by the blast. After recuperating in a military hospital, Joseph was reassigned to a base in Germany. Joseph began to experience flashbacks and intrusive thoughts about the IED event and the loss of his friends. He became depressed and anxious. Joseph began to drink heavily and gamble at the base's slot machines.(Slot machines are only allowed on overseas military bases.) Sometimes he tried to stop both activities, but he then felt irritable and more anxious. Within a few months, Joseph had used all his savings, reached his credit limit on several credit cards, and had borrowed money from friends. His friends suggested that he attend Gamblers Anonymous (GA), but Joseph dismissed this suggestion, explaining that he had had some "near misses" recently so he was sure that he would make all his money back soon. Over the past month, Joseph sold government-owned property to support his habit. Because of the pervasiveness of his gambling, he wasn't getting enough sleep and fell asleep while on duty. These behaviors were discovered, and Joseph is now facing a potential court-martial. He begins to think about suicide.

Up Close—At Work

One of the symptoms of gambling disorder is borrowing or stealing money. In the previous version of the DSM, the DSM-IV, legal consequences were listed as one of the criteria that could be used to diagnose gambling disorder; however, this criterion was eliminated in the DSM-5. Nevertheless, people with gambling problems commonly borrow and steal. If an individual is discovered to be stealing from work, he or she will likely be fired. The person may face legal consequences and have difficulties finding future work.

Absenteeism may increase as problem gamblers prioritize gambling over working. As online gambling grows, people will increasingly gamble on devices at work, further decreasing productivity.

Case Study

Robert is a 50-year-old businessman who has had legal problems in the past. He is an adventurous man who skis, rides a motorcycle, and bets on sports games. He enjoys playing poker with his friends and is proud of his skills. However, over recent years, he has become bored with these games, and he has begun to play poker "online." Unconcerned about its murky legal status, he has spent all his money and incurred several thousands of dollars of debt. He no longer has sufficient credit to borrow money. Now desperate, Robert begins to skim profits from his own company to pay off his debts. As a result, he shortchanges investors and fails to meet productivity goals for clients. Although he had previously been able to make excuses for missed deadlines and hide his withdrawals from company accounts, his business partner has recently noticed the discrepancies; he is now threatening to press charges in criminal court and sue in civil court for damages unless Robert can pay back the stolen funds. To try to replace the missing funds, Robert decides to increase his gambling because he knows that he is "due" for a win.

Up Close—In Relationships

Each person with gambling disorder harms between 10 and 17 other people (Politzer, Yesalis, and Hudak 1992). Indeed, a key feature of this disorder is its damage to relationships with loved ones, friends, and professional acquaintances. Family members suffer the most, perhaps even losing their home or struggling to pay for necessities. When someone with a gambling disorder lies to conceal losses or winnings—another feature of the disorder—the deception can damage the person's relationships with others, especially with those who trust the person. People with gambling disorder may steal from family members or friends, and some relationships may be damaged or lost as a result. Additionally, as previously reviewed, gamblers may lose their jobs and get into legal trouble if they steal money from work; this will affect both their professional and personal relationships. Gambling problems can also be associated with divorce, child abuse, and domestic violence, the latter probably because of the association with antisocial personality disorder (Grinols 2004; Shaw et al. 2007).

Resources are available to help affected spouses and family members, for example, helplines and Gam-Anon, the counterpart to GA. Spouses are the ones who most often seek help, either for themselves or for their gambling spouse. However, spouses can also be enabling, helping their spouses continue gambling by taking their "side" when criticized by others, making excuses for their behavior, or bailing them out of debt. The child of someone with gambling disorder is more likely to develop a gambling problem, abuse drugs, or be depressed than those without a parent with the disorder (Jacobs et al. 1989).

Case Study

Gabby, a 57-year-old woman, and Tom, her husband of 34 years, have been quarreling because of her gambling. She always enjoyed traveling to Las Vegas with her girlfriends for special occasions or weekend getaways. They played the slot machines, watched some shows, and enjoyed eating at the restaurants. She usually lost more money than she thought she would, but her losses were minimal, and her gambling was limited to those weekend trips. Two years ago, her state legalized casino gambling, and a neighboring town quickly built a casino. She stopped going to Las Vegas and drove to the casino to gamble by herself. A pastime that had previously cost a few hundred dollars a year quickly escalated to a monthly, then weekly, then daily habit at the local casino. She began to gamble for several hours at a time at the EGMs. She carried lucky charms with her and tapped the machines in certain ways. Gabby lost over $60,000, accumulated credit card debt, and withdrew money from her husband's retirement account without his knowledge. When Tom found out about Gabby's financial indiscretions, he was hurt and surprised that she was able to keep this secret from him for so long. He told her that he would leave her if she does not stop gambling immediately. She promised that she would, but Tom asks her how he can ever trust her again.

Effects and Costs

The American Gaming Association (Kilsby et al. 2018) reports that in 2017 people spent $89.4 billion at casinos, including those operated by Native American tribes. Eight-two percent of this money was spent on gambling itself. According to the *2016 Survey of Problem Gambling Services in the United States* (Marotta et al. 2017), $80.5 billion was spent on lotteries, roughly equivalent to the amount spent at casinos.

The majority of lottery tickets are bought by lower-educated and poorer individuals and they spend a higher proportion of their income on the lotteries than do the rich (Gerstein et al. 1999). Even though lottery proceeds go to public service, some have argued that lotteries are a regressive or unfair tax on the poor (Perez and Humphreys 2013).

Individuals who gamble heavily—many of whom have a gambling disorder—typically lose considerable sums of money, even if they experience a couple of "big wins," and this is harmful for them and for society at large. Stealing to pay for gambling can lead to prosecution for theft and embezzlement, which can be associated with legal expenses, loss of income, and jail time. Violent and criminal behavior is related to gambling problems and may lead to severe social and legal consequences (Laursen et al. 2016). Grinols and Mustard (2006) estimated that the social crime cost associated with casinos amounted to $75 per adult in the United States in 1996.

Gambling problems are related to many other issues that have costs to them, such as an increased risk of PTSD, generalized anxiety disorder, and most often, substance use disorders (Grubbs et al. 2018; Kessler et al. 2008). A higher likelihood of suicide ideation and behavior is also associated with more gambling problems (Battersby et al. 2006; Cunningham-Williams et al. 2005). Gambling is also associated with poor physical health and quality of life (Black et al. 2013). Increased debt and mental and physical concerns will put individuals at risk of homelessness and raise their chances of being below the poverty line (Nower et al. 2013).

On the other hand, the gambling industry often argues that gambling has benefits for the economy, providing many jobs and contributing taxes to the government. In a detailed study of the economic impact of gambling, Grinols (2004) demonstrated that after considering jobs and taxes, the social impact of gambling costs the U.S. economy more than $50 billion a year. Using 2003 data, he estimated that each pathological gambler (similar to a person with a gambling disorder) costs society over $10,000 a year. Even though the gambling industry brings in taxes for governments and profits for the gambling industry, gambling costs outweigh those benefits. Most of the costs to society are caused by problem or pathological gamblers.

Despite these costs, the government spends little money on treatment for gambling disorder. The United States allocated $73 million for gambling problem services in 2016; however, this funding varied by state, and no money was allocated on the federal level (Marotta et al. 2017, 2). Perhaps this lack of funding has something to do with the gambling industry's effective lobbying efforts (Grinols, 2004) and the fact that all gambling winnings are taxed. The immediate appeal of taxes seems to blind governments to the costs of gambling.

Theory and Research

Problem gamblers can be divided into three groups: *action or impulsive gamblers, escape or emotional gamblers*, and *"normal" or behavioral gamblers* (Milosevic and Ledgerwood 2010). Action gamblers are impulsive and gamble to increase their arousal or reduce boredom. They are more egotistical, neurotic, and antisocial, and more likely to be male and to play skill-based games—poker, horse- or dog-race betting, and sports betting—than other types of gamblers. Individuals who play these games think they can pick the winners or find a "strategy" to win or to "beat the odds."

Escape gamblers tend to be more anxious and depressed than action gamblers and to gamble to try to avoid these emotions. They are more likely to be female and play luck-based games, such as Keno, lotteries, or slot machines. They are also the ones most likely to seek treatment, probably because of the negative emotions driving their gambling.

Finally, "normal" or behaviorally conditioned gamblers do not have any characteristic mental health problems. Instead, they gamble primarily due to social pressure and have dysfunctional cognitive processes, such as believing in gambling fallacies. One common fallacy, referred to earlier, is the belief in the usefulness of "chasing one's losses." Often, this behavior is associated with the belief that you are "owed" a win after so many losses. This group develops problematic gambling due to behavioral conditioning and faulty cognitive mechanisms.

The prevailing model for understanding gambling disorder is the pathways model of Blaszczynski and Nower (2002). Cognitive biases and operant conditioning, through arousal during gambling like that of a drug "high," are present in all pathways.

The first pathway pertains to gamblers who are behaviorally conditioned. These individuals do not have any preexisting psychopathologies. In this pathway, the gamblers begin to gamble for socialization or entertainment, but if they begin to "chase their losses," they may develop problem gambling. For these individuals, the symptoms are consequences, not causes, of problem gambling behavior. According to Blaszczynski and Nower (2002), these gamblers have the least severe problems. Individuals fluctuate between problematic gambling and non-problematic but frequent gambling. They respond well to treatment.

The second pathway pertains to gamblers who are emotionally vulnerable. This pathway is the same as the first but includes preexisting psychopathology, such as premorbid depression and/or anxiety, childhood difficulties, and substance use. As gambling relieves the immediate feelings of distress by distracting the person, conditioning mechanisms begin to work, and then the pathway is the same as the pathway for behaviorally conditioned gamblers. In other words, this pathway is likely to result in the escape type of gambler described by Milosevic and Ledgerwood (2010). According to Blaszczynski and Nower (2002), gamblers who developed through this pathway are more resistant to change than those from the first pathway. Treatment should also address the underlying psychological distress.

The third pathway is characteristic for antisocial and impulsive gamblers. In this pathway, the gambler has an emotional and/or biological vulnerability, as in the second pathway, but also has antisocial personality disorder and difficulty with attention and impulse control, resulting in overall poor psychosocial functioning. Gamblers from this pathway tend to begin gambling at an early age. Problematic behaviors, such as gambling-related crimes, develop quickly. These gamblers are the least motivated to get and complete treatment.

Valleur et al. (2016) conducted a study using 372 problem gamblers in France to attempt to validate this model. They found that their sample split into three groups, which matched the descriptions given by Blaszczynski and Nower (2002). The "emotionally vulnerable" group preferred games of chance, and the "impulsive" group preferred semi-skillful games. However, the "behaviorally conditioned" gamblers did not seem to have unique characteristics, but instead fit between the other two groups on most dimensions, such as income, game choice, and so on. Their results support the pathways model and suggest that the pathways may be seen on a continuum, whereby "emotionally vulnerable" and "impulsive" gamblers are on the extreme ends and "behaviorally conditioned" gamblers are in the middle.

Mader (2017) also conducted a study to evaluate the pathways model using 125 problem gamblers. His three groups corresponded with those suggested by Blaszczynski and Nower (2002). However, the group similar to the "emotionally vulnerable" gamblers was less consistent with the pathway model description than the other two groups. Depression and anxiety were not found to significantly predict group membership, suggesting some variability with the "emotionally vulnerable" gambler group. Moreover, the "emotionally vulnerable" and "behaviorally conditioned" gambler groups were not as different as the pathways model suggests.

Treatments

Psychodynamic

In the past, psychotherapy for individuals with gambling disorder was conducted using a psychodynamic approach, which focuses on how childhood experiences may affect an individual's functioning later in life. Rosenthal and Rugle (1994) suggested that therapists should encourage gambling abstinence and point out inconsistencies in the gambler's narrative, while also being nonjudgmental and supportive. Transference, or redirecting childhood emotions toward the therapist, is likely to occur, especially in those who grew up in abusive households or have more narcissistic tendencies.

Cognitive Behavioral Therapy

Cognitive behavioral therapy (CBT) aims to explore and change maladaptive beliefs and behaviors. For example, a common gambling belief is that a succession of losses will be followed by a win. In other words, "chasing losses" is understood as a reasonable activity. This is also known as "the gambler's fallacy" or the Monte Carlo fallacy. If a roulette wheel spins five times and comes up "red" five times, it might seem more likely that the next spin will come up "black." But each spin is independent of the one before. Another common cognitive distortion is the "illusion of control." Some gamblers believe that they are more likely to win if they choose a number in a lottery (rather than be assigned a number) or throw the dice themselves rather than having someone else throw them. Related to this is the "attributional bias," which is the belief that an individual can control the outcome due to his or her special skills and knowledge. Many gamblers also acquire superstitions, such as wearing certain clothes, picking numbers that have a personal significance, or throwing dice in a special way. The person may develop a "talismanic superstition," such as carrying a lucky rabbit's foot. The CBT therapist discusses these and other fallacies and attempts to point out how irrational they are. The CBT therapist also encourages more adaptive activities. For example, a therapist may encourage an individual to go to dinner with friends or family as a reward for not gambling for a certain period. Some researchers find that CBT is the most effective treatment for gambling (Toneatto and Ladouceur 2003).

Motivational Interviewing

Motivational interviewing (MI) is a useful tool in the treatment of substance use disorders. This therapy helps people change by encouraging them to talk about problems and possible solutions without being judged (Prochaska and Velicer 1997). Carlbring, Jonsson, Josephson, and Forsberg (2010) compared MI to a group version of CBT for 150 individuals with problem gambling. Their results suggested that four sessions of MI may be as effective as eight sessions of group CBT in reducing gambling problems.

Pharmacotherapies

Several drugs have been tested for their efficacy in reducing problem and disordered gambling. Selective serotonin reuptake inhibitors (SSRIs) and mood stabilizers have been studied, but effects are small, and placebo response rates are high (Hollander et al. 2000; Pallanti et al. 2002). There is some interest in the use of N-acetyl cysteine, a glutamate-modulating agent, in the treatment of problem gambling (Grant, Kim and Odlaug 2007). Finally, opioid antagonists have been studied. Grant et al. (2010) found that nalmefene hydrochloride, an opioid antagonist, did not reduce problematic gambling. There was a suggestion from the data that patients who tolerated a higher dose of the nalmefene might have received some benefit. Naltrexone, another opioid antagonist, has been shown to be effective in several clinical trials (Grant, Kim, and Hartman 2008; Kim et al. 2001). More research is needed to understand and find effective pharmacological treatments for gambling disorder.

Natural Recovery and Gamblers Anonymous

Rates of natural recovery from gambling disorder are relatively high. For example, Slutske (2006) found that one-third of 206 individuals who met criteria for gambling disorder recovered without professional help. Only about 8% of people with gambling disorder seek treatment, with the rates being even lower for men and younger individuals (Gerstein et al. 1999). Resources are available for those who try to stop gambling by themselves. One of the best known and utilized programs is GA, based on the Alcoholics Anonymous 12-step program. Those who attend GA tend to be older and more likely to be married than others. Only about 10% of people who attend GA actually become active participants (Petry 2005, 161–173).

Bibliography

American Psychiatric Association. *Diagnostic and Statistical Manual of Mental Disorders: Fifth Edition.* Arlington, VA: American Psychiatric Association, 2013. doi:10.1176/appi.books.9780890425596.744053.

Battersby, Malcolm, Barry Tolchard, Mark Scurrah, and Lyndall Thomas. "Suicide Ideation and Behaviour in People with Pathological Gambling Attending a Treatment Service." *Int J Mental Health Addict* 4, no. 3 (2006), 233–246. doi:10.1007/s11469-006-9022-z.

Black, Donald W., Martha Shaw, Brett McCormick, and Jeff Allen. "Pathological Gambling: Relationship to Obesity, Self-Reported Chronic Medical Conditions, Poor Lifestyle Choices, and Impaired Quality of Life." *Compr Psychiatry* 54, no. 2 (2013), 97–104. doi:10.1016/j.comppsych.2012.07.001.

Blanchard, Edward B., Edelgard Wulfert, Brian M. Freidenberg, and Loretta S. Malta. "Psychophysiological Assessment of Compulsive Gamblers' Arousal to Gambling Cues: A Pilot Study." *Appl Psychophysiol Biofeedback* 25, no. 3 (2000), 155–165. doi:10.1023/A:100 9550724836.

Blaszczynski, Alex, and Lia Nower. "A Pathways Model of Problem and Pathological Gambling." *Addiction* 97, no. 5 (2002), 487–499. doi:10.1046/j.1360-0443.2002.00015.x.

Carlbring, Per, Jakob Jonsson, Henrik Josephson, and Lars Forsberg. "Motivational Interviewing versus Cognitive Behavioral Group Therapy in the Treatment of Problem and Pathological Gambling: A Randomized Controlled Trial." *Cogn Behav Ther* 39, no. 2 (2010), 92–103. doi:10.1080/16506070903190245.

Cunningham-Williams, Renee M., Richard A. Grucza, Linda B. Cottler, Sharon B. Womack, Samantha J. Books, Thomas R. Przybeck, Edward L. Spitznagel, and C. Robert Cloninger. "Prevalence and Predictors of Pathological Gambling: Results from the St. Louis Personality, Health and Lifestyle (SLPHL) Study." *J Psychiatric Res* 39, no. 4 (2005), 377–390. doi:10.1016/j.jpsychires.2004.09.002.

Eisen, Seth A., Nong Lin, Michael J. Lyons, Jeffrey Frank Scherrer, Kristin Griffith, William R. True, Jack Goldberg, and Ming T. Tsuang. "Familial Influences on Gambling Behavior: An Analysis of 3359 Twin Pairs." *Addiction* 93, no. 9 (1998), 1375–1384. doi:10.1046/j.1360-0443.1998.93913758.x.

Flavin, Michael. *Gambling in the Nineteenth-Century English Novel: A Leprosy Is o'er the Land*. Brighton: Sussex Academic Press, 2003.

France, Clemens J. "The Gambling Impulse." *Am J Psychol* 13, no. 3 (1902), 364–407.

Gehring, William J., and Adrian R. Willoughby. "The Medial Frontal Cortex and the Rapid Processing of Monetary Gains and Losses." *Science* 295 (2002), 2279–2282. doi:10.1126/science.1066893.

Gerstein, Dean, John Hoffmann, Cindy Larison, Laszlo Engelman, Sally Murphy, and Amanda Palmer. "Gambling Impact and Behavior Study." Report to the National Gambling Impact Study Commission. NORC, University of Chicago, IL, 1999.

Grant, Jon E., Brian L. Odlaug, Marc N. Potenza, Eric Hollander, and Suck Won Kim. "Nalmefene in the Treatment of Pathological Gambling: Multicentre, Double-Blind, Placebo-Controlled Study." *Br J Psychiatry* 197, no. 4 (2010), 330–331. doi:10.1192/bjp.bp.110.078105.

Grant, Jon E., Suck Won Kim, and Boyd K. Hartman. "A Double-Blind, Placebo-Controlled Study of the Opiate Antagonist Naltrexone in the

Treatment of Pathological Gambling Urges." *J Clin Psychiatry* 69, no. 5 (2008), 783–789.

Grant, Jon E., Suck Won Kim, and Brian L. Odlaug. "N-acetyl Cysteine, a Glutamate-modulating Agent, in the Treatment of Pathological Gambling: A Pilot Study." *Biol Psychiatry* 62, no. 6 (2007), 652–657.

Grinols, Earl L. *Gambling in America: Costs and Benefits.* Cambridge: Cambridge University Press, 2004.

Grinols, Earl L., and David B. Mustard. "Casinos, Crime, and Community Costs." *Rev Econ Stat* 88, no. 1 (February 2006), 28–45. doi. org/10.1162/rest.2006.88.1.28.

Grubbs, Joshua B., Heather Chapman, Lauren Milner, Ian A. Gutierrez, and David F. Bradley. "Examining Links between Post-Traumatic Stress and Gambling Motives : The Role of Positive Gambling Expectancies." *Psychol Addict Behav* 32, no. 7 (2018), 821–831. doi:10.17605/ OSF.IO/ZXW6D.

Hollander, Eric, Concetta M. Decaria, Jared N. Finkell, Tomer Begaz, Cheryl M. Wong, and Charles Cartwright. "A Randomized Double-Blind Fluvoxamine / Placebo Crossover Trial in Pathologic Gambling." *Biol Psychiatry* 47, no. 9 (2000), 813–817.

Jacobs, Durand F., Albert R. Marston, Robert D. Singer, Keith Widaman, Todd Little, and Jeannette Veizades. "Children of Problem Gamblers." *J Gambl Behav* 5, no. 4 (1989), 261–268.

Kessler, Ronald. C., Irving Hwang, Richard LaBrie, Maria Petukhova, Nancy A. Sampson, Ken C. Winters, and Howard J. Shaffer. "DSM-IV Pathological Gambling in the National Comorbidity Survey Replication." *Psychol Med* 38, no. 9 (2008), 1351–1360. doi:10.1017/ S0033291708002900.

Kilsby, James, Chris Krafcik, Daniel Stone, Tony Batt, and Kristal Rovira. *State of the States 2018. The AGA Survey of the Commercial Casino Industry.* American Gaming Association. Accessed July 29, 2019. https://www.americangaming.org/.

Kim, Suck Won, Jon E. Grant, David E. Adson, and Young Chul Shin. "Double-Blind Naltrexone and Placebo Comparison Study in the Treatment of Pathological Gambling." *Biol Psychiatry* 49, no. 11 (2001), 914–21. doi:10.1016/S0006-3223(01)01079-4.

Laursen, Bjarne, Rikke Plauborg, Ola Ekholm, Christina Viskum Lytken Larsen, and Knud Juel. "Problem Gambling Associated with Violent and Criminal Behaviour: A Danish Population-Based Survey and Register Study." *J Gambl Stud* 32, no. 1 (2016), 25–34. doi:10.1007/ s10899-015-9536-z.

Mader, Joel. "An Evaluation of the Pathways Model of Problem Gambling." MEd dissertation, University of Lethbridge, 2017.

Marotta, Jeffrey, Julie Hynes, Loreen Rugle, Keith S. Whyte, Kathleen M. Scanlan, Jimmy Sheldrup, and Janina Dukart. *2016 Survey of Problem Gambling Services in the United State*s. Boston MA: Association of Problem Gambling Service Administrators, 2017.

Milosevic, Aleks and David M. Ledgerwood. "The Subtyping of Pathological Gambling: A Comprehensive Review." *Clin Psychol Rev* 30, no. 8 (2010), 988–998. doi:10.1016/j.cpr.2010.06.013.

Najavits, Lisa M. "Treatment Utilization of Pathological Gamblers with and without PTSD." *J Gambl Stud* 26, no. 4 (2010), 583–592. doi:10.1007/s10899-010-9179-z.

Nower, Lia, Karin M. Eyrich-Garg, David E. Pollio, and Carol S. North. "Problem Gambling and Homelessness: Results from an Epidemiologic Study." *J Gambl Stud* 31, no. 2 (2013), 533–545. doi:10.1007/s10899-013-9435-0.

Pallanti, Stefano, Leonardo Quercioli, Erica Sood, and Eric Hollander. "Lithium and Valproate Treatment of Pathological Gambling: A Randomized Single-Blind Study." *J Clin Psychiatry* 63, no. 7 (2002), 559–564.

Perez, Levi, and Brad Humphreys. "The 'Who and Why' of Lottery: Empirical Highlights from the Seminal Economic Literature." *J Econ Surveys* 27, no. 5 (2013), 915–940. doi:10.1111/j.1467-6419.2012.00732.x.

Petry, Nancy M. *Pathological Gambling: Etiology, Comorbidity, and Treatment.* Washington, DC: American Psychological Association, 2005. doi:10.1037/0022-006X.74.3.555.

Politzer, Robert C., Charles E. Yesalis, and Clark J. Hudak. "The Epidemiologic Model and the Risk of Legalized Gambling: Where Are We Headed?" *Health Values* 16 (1992), 20–27.

Potenza, Marc N., Marvin A. Steinberg, Pawel Skudlarski, Robert K. Fulbright, Cheryl M. Lacadie, Mary K. Wilber, Bruce J. Rounsaville, John C. Gore, and Bruce E. Wexler. "Gambling Urges in Pathological Gambling." *Arch Gen Psychiatry* 60 no. 8 (2003), 828–836. doi:10.1001/archpsyc.60.8.828.

Prochaska, James O., and Wayne F. Velicer. "The Transtheoretical Change Model of Health Behavior." *Am J Health Promot* 12, no. 1 (1997), 38–48. doi:10.4278/0890-1171-12.1.38.

Rosenthal, Richard J., and Loreen J. Rugle. "A Psychodynamic Approach to the Treatment of Pathological Gambling: Part I. Achieving Abstinence." *J Gam Stud* 10, no. 1 (1994), 21–42. doi:10.1007/BF02109777.

Schwartz, David G. *Roll the Bones*. New York: Gotham Books, 2006.

Shaffer, Howard J., and Matthew N. Hall. "Updating and Refining Prevalence Estimates of Disordered Gambling Behavior in the United States and Canada." *Can J Public Health* 92, no. 3 (2001), 168–172.

Sharpe, Louise, and Nicholas Tarrier. "Towards a Cognitive-Behavioural Theory of Problem Gambling." *Br J Psychiatry* 162, no. 3 March (1993), 407–412. doi:10.1192/bjp.162.3.407.

Shaw, Martha C., Kelsie T. Forbush, Jessica Schlinder, Eugene Rosenman, and Donald W. Black. "The Effect of Pathological Gambling on Families, Marriages, and Children." *CNS Spectrums* 12, no. 8 (2007), 615–622. doi:10.1017/S1092852900021416.

Shirk, Steven D., Megan M. Kelly, Shane W. Kraus, Marc N. Potenza, Kendra Pugh, Christopher Waltrous, Edward Federman, Christopher Krebs, and Charles E. Drebing. "Gambling-Related Cognitive Distortions Predict Level of Function among US Veterans Seeking Treatment for Gambling Disorders." *Am J Addict* 27, no. 2 (2018), 108–115. doi:10.1111/ajad.12685.

Slutske, Wendy S. "Natural Recovery and Treatment-Seeking in Pathological Gambling: Results of Two U.S. National Surveys." *Am J Psychiatry* 163, no. 2 (2006), 297–302. doi:10.1176/appi.ajp.163.2.297.

Slutske, Wendy S., Seth Eisen, William R. True, Michael J. Lyons, Jack Goldberg, and Ming Tsuang. "Common Genetic Vulnerability for Pathological Gambling and Alcohol Dependence in Men." *Arch Gen Psychiatry* 57, no. 7 (2000), 666–673. doi:10.1001/archpsyc.57.7.666.

Stefanovics, Elina A., Marc N. Potenza, and Robert H. Pietrzak. "Gambling in a National U.S. Veteran Population: Prevalence, Socio-Demographics, and Psychiatric Comorbidities." *J Gambl Stud* 33, no. 4 (2017), 1099–1120. doi:10.1007/s10899-017-9678-2.

Toneatto, Tony, and Robert Ladouceur. "Treatment of Pathological Gambling: A Critical Review of the Literature." *Psychol Addict Behav* 17, no. 4 (2003), 284–292. doi:10.1037/0893-164X.17.4.284.

Valleur, Marc, Irène Codina, Jean Luc Vénisse, Lucia Romo, David Magalon, Mélina Fatséas, Isabelle Chéreau-Boudet, et al. "Towards a Validation of the Three Pathways Model of Pathological Gambling." *J Gambl Stud* 32, no. 2 (2016), 757–771. doi:10.1007/s10899-015-9545-y.

Walters, Glenn D. "Behavior Genetic Research on Gambling and Problem Gambling: A Preliminary Meta-Analysis of Available Data." *J Gambl Stud* 17, no. 4 (2001), 255–271. doi:10.1023/A:1013652328999.

Welte, John W., Grace M. Barnes, Marie Cecile O. Tidwell, Joseph H. Hoffman, and William F. Wieczorek. "Gambling and Problem Gambling in the United States: Changes between 1999 and 2013." *J Gambl Stud* 31, no. 3 (2015), 695–715. doi:10.1007/s10899-014-9471-4.

Welte, John W., Grace M. Barnes, Marie Cecile O. Tidwell, and William F. Wieczorek. "Predictors of Problem Gambling in the U.S." *J Gambl Stud* 33, no. 2 (2017), 327–342. doi:10.1007/s10899-016-9639-1.

Welte, John W., Grace M. Barnes, William F. Wieczorek, Marie-Cecile Tidwell, and John Parker. "Gambling Participation in the U.S.: Results from a National Survey." *J Gambl Stud* 18, no. 4 (2002), 313–337. doi:10.1023/A.

Westermeyer, Joe, Jose Canive, Paul Thuras, Michael Oakes, and Marline Spring. "Pathological and Problem Gambling among Veterans in Clinical Care: Prevalence, Demography, and Clinical Correlates." *Am J Addict* 22, no. 3 (2013), 218–225. doi:10.1111/j.1521-0391.2012.12011.x.

Whiting, Seth W., Marc N. Potenza, Crystal L. Park, Sherry A. McKee, Carolyn M. Mazure, and Rani A. Hoff. "Investigating Veterans' Pre-, Peri-, and Post-Deployment Experiences as Potential Risk Factors for Problem Gambling." *J Behav Addict* 5, no. 2 (2016), 213–220. doi:10.1556/2006.5.2016.027.

CHAPTER 4

Hallucinogens

Frances R. Frankenburg

Hallucinogens change our perceptions and cognitions in stranger ways than the other drugs described in this book. People who use hallucinogens often feel as though these substances let them have a deeper, more meaningful and more spiritual connection with the world. As with most of the other substances, there are therapeutic uses of hallucinogens. Unlike other substances, though, the hallucinogens are increasingly being used to treat addiction and other psychiatric disorders. Despite their relative safety and possible utility, they are still classified as Schedule I controlled drugs, the category of drugs considered to be most dangerous and without medical value.

The term *hallucinogen* refers to a substance that can cause hallucinations—that is, seeing, hearing, smelling, or feeling things that are not there. Sometimes these substances distort perceptions but can also convey sensations of understanding the cosmos. Although we see ourselves as the most developed species in existence, lower organisms synthesize these molecules that change our brain functioning in ways that many experience as an enhancement. For millennia, people have deliberately used fungi, cacti, and other flowering plants for their hallucinogenic effects. The cultural significance of hallucinogenic plants and mushrooms is probably strongest in Mexico and Central America, where they are highly valued, and weakest in Africa (Schultes, Hofmann, and Rätsch 2001, 26).

The geography of hallucinogen use changed in the 1960s. As European and North American baby boomers had the time, health, freedom, and financial security to travel and to participate in the civil rights and anti–Vietnam War movements as well as the sexual revolution (helped by the availability of oral contraception), they began to experiment with mind- and mood-altering substances more exotic than the nicotine, alcohol, and sedatives used by their parents. Their embrace of hallucinogens is reflected in the art, fashion, and music of the times. Some hallucinogens began to come not from the world of fungi and plants but from the laboratory.

Symptoms, Diagnosis, and Incidence

Symptoms

Each hallucinogen produces somewhat different symptoms, which also vary by individual, the setting in which the substance is taken, and the individual's own expectations of the drug's effects.

The main symptoms are: hallucinations, which are often visual; alterations in sense of time; and increased vividness of sensations. The person may experience dissociation or feeling separate from his or her thoughts and sensations. Many people report spiritual feelings, a clarity of vision, and a sense of comprehending the universe. Often people say that when under the influence of hallucinogens, they realize the importance of love.

Diagnosis

The fifth version of the *Diagnostic and Statistical Manual of Mental Disorders (DSM-5)* (American Psychiatric Association 2013), a manual prepared by the American Psychiatric Association containing descriptions, symptoms, and other criteria for diagnosing mental disorders, describes hallucinogen use disorder along a continuum. Phencyclidine (along with related substances such as ketamine) is classified separately because it is associated with more severe symptoms of intoxication. The *DSM* refers to the use of all other hallucinogens as "Other Hallucinogen Use Disorder." However, most hallucinogens, including the classic hallucinogens (d-Lysergic acid diethylamide [LSD], mescaline, and psilocybin) are included in this category. Throughout this book, the term *hallucinogens* will refer to all hallucinogens.

The criteria for a hallucinogen use disorder are: using hallucinogens in larger amounts or over a longer period than the person originally meant to; inability to stop or limit hallucinogen use; spending much time involved with the use of hallucinogens; craving hallucinogens; inability to carry out tasks because of hallucinogen use (although some people now say that low doses might actually help improve performance on some tasks, perhaps by leading to new ways of understanding problems); continuing to use hallucinogens even though the use causes problems, such as disagreements with others; choosing to use hallucinogens rather than engaging in other activities in part because the hallucinogen use seems more important or interesting; using hallucinogens even when there are physical hazards (such as exhaustion or metabolic problems from phencyclidine [PCP] or 3,4-methylenedioxymethamphetamine [MDMA]); continuing to use hallucinogens even though they cause medical or psychological problems (occurring with phencyclidine and MDMA in particular); or building up tolerance, so that one might want to use higher doses (for example, of mescaline) to experience the same mind-altering effects.

Anyone meeting any two of the criteria during the same 12-month period receives a diagnosis of hallucinogen use disorder. The severity—mild, moderate, or severe—is based on the number of criteria met. The person who has two or three symptoms has a mild disorder. The person with four or five symptoms is said to have a moderate disorder. The person with a severe disorder meets six or more symptoms of the disorder within one year and would be said to have an addiction. Addiction is a word falling out of favor, but in any event, addiction to hallucinogens is unusual.

A difference between these criteria and the criteria discussed in most other chapters of this book (except inhalants and gambling) is that withdrawal is not a criterion. However, some experts do describe a withdrawal syndrome associated with the use of phencyclidine and MDMA. People who use those drugs repeatedly may experience cravings, headaches, depression, and sweating if they stop using the drug.

Incidence

The National Survey on Drug Use and Health (NSDUH), sponsored by the Substance Abuse and Mental Health Services Administration (SAMHSA), is an annual survey of people over the age of 12. The 2017 NSDUH asked about the use of the hallucinogens lysergic acid diethylamide (LSD), ecstasy, psilocybin, peyote, ketamine, dimethyltryptamine (DMT), salvia, and phencyclidine. In 2017, 0.5% of the population aged

12 or over used hallucinogens in the month before the survey (Substance Abuse and Mental Health Services Administration 2018).

With respect to hallucinogen use disorder, the National Epidemiologic Survey on Alcohol and Related Conditions (NESARC) is a study conducted by the United States Census Bureau on behalf of the National Institute on Alcohol Abuse and Alcoholism. It conducts in-depth diagnostic interviews of people over the age of 18 and asks about a variety of disorders. It surveys civilians but not people in the military or living in institutions. The third NESARC survey collected data between April 2012 and June 2013. They reported a 12-month prevalence of hallucinogen use disorder of 0.05% and of lifetime hallucinogen use disorder of 0.6%. Most of the cases of hallucinogen use disorder were mild (Shalit, Rehm, and Lev-Ran 2019).

History

There are several types of hallucinogens, or psychedelic substances, each with a distinct history. The mechanisms of action and possible therapeutic uses of these substances are reviewed separately.

Amanita Muscaria Mushrooms

Amanita muscaria (fly agaric) is a large mushroom that has a red cap, sometimes flecked with white, and white gills and stem. It grows in forests, under birch, fir, and larch trees. It may be the oldest hallucinogen and was once the most widely used (Spinella 2001, 387). Fly agaric is not much used now, but descriptions of its use can be found in the accounts of past travelers to Eurasia.

Writer Lewis Carroll may have read and been influenced by some of these tales. In his 1865 novel, *Alice's Adventures in Wonderland*, Alice follows a white rabbit, eats bits of a mushroom, and then feels herself changing size and shape. While it's also possible that Carroll's description may have been based on his migraines, a connection between Alice, mushrooms, and altered perceptions became a theme of the psychedelic-fueled 1960s. This connection might have been clearest in the song "White Rabbit," written by Grace Slick, in which the listener, who has just eaten "some kind of mushroom," is told to "go ask Alice," now "ten feet tall," about pills. However, the connection is misleading because Slick conflated *Amanita muscaria*—the mushrooms that might have inspired the wonderful creation of Lewis Carroll—with *Psilocybe* mushrooms (discussed in the following section), which are the famous "magic mushrooms" of the 1960s.

Psilocybe Mushrooms

Many mushrooms in the *Psilocybe* genus have hallucinogenic properties and were well known to the Native American civilizations in Central America. The Aztec, the indigenous people of the central region of
present-day Mexico, used them in religious ceremonies, where they were
known as teonanacatl (from the Aztec for "sacred mushroom" or "God's
flesh"). In the 16th century, Spanish conquistadors, while looting silver
and gold from Native Americans, tried to eradicate their customs, seeing
them as antithetical to their own Roman Catholic beliefs. (The conquistadors also tried to stop Andean Native Americans from using coca leaf
for similar reasons.)

The conquistadors did not eliminate the use of *Psilocybe*, but instead
drove it underground. Mazatecs, the indigenous people of Oaxaca in
present-day Mexico, continued to use mushrooms in their ceremonies,
but did so in secret, reluctant to let outsiders know any details. The
first Caucasian person to use teonanacatl might have been R. Gordon
Wasson, vice president of J.P. Morgan and Company. He and his wife
traveled to Mexico in 1953 and, by 1955, had sufficiently befriended the
Mazatecs that they were allowed to participate in a ceremony involving
their sacred mushrooms. Wasson describes consuming the mushroom
and seeing geometric, colored patterns and then visions of colonnades
and palaces.

The Swiss pharmaceutical company Sandoz became interested in these
mushrooms, and in 1958, one of their chemists, Albert Hofmann, isolated and synthesized psilocybin and psilocin, the two hallucinogenic
substances in *Psilocybe mexicana*. In 1962, Hofmann and Wasson traveled together to Mexico where Mazatecs confirmed that the psychoactive effects of synthetic psilocybin were equivalent to the effects of the
Psilocybe mushroom itself. These mushrooms intrigued many people,
including Timothy Leary, a charismatic psychologist then working at
Harvard University's Center for Research in Personality. In August 1960,
during a vacation in Cuernavaca, Mexico, he experimented with *Psilocybe* mushrooms and became convinced that their use would revolution-
ize psychology (Stevens 1987, 134). At around the same time, Sandoz
marketed synthetic psilocybin for physicians to use as an experimental
agent in psychotherapy.

Later that year, Leary started the Harvard Psilocybin Project. He
and his colleague, Dr. Richard Alpert, obtained psilocybin from Sandoz. Interested in its effects on creativity, they gave it to several writers, including Aldous Huxley, Allen Ginsberg, and William Burroughs.

In 1961, Leary conducted an experiment at Concord State Prison in Massachusetts and reported that the prisoners who took psilocybin were less likely to be rearrested and returned for parole violation than those who had not taken the drug (Brecher 1972, 368; Stevens 1987, 156). Later research, however, has shed doubt on these findings (Doblin 1998).

In the 1960s, *Psilocybe* mushrooms became known as "magic mushrooms," or, as they are sometimes called, "shrooms."

Peyote Cactuses and Mescaline

Mescaline is a naturally occurring psychedelic substance found in several cactus species, most notably peyote (*Lophophora williamsii*) and San Pedro (*Trichocereus pachanoi*). (The words "peyote" and "mescaline" are often used interchangeably.) The peyote cactus is a small, round, and spineless plant. The only part of the cactus that is above ground, the crown, consists of disc-shaped protrusions called buttons. Peyote was used in ceremonies of the Aztecs and other indigenous peoples of Mexico for centuries. In the late 1800s, its use spread northward to the Native Americans in the United States who also used it in their ceremonies.

Parke-Davis, an American pharmaceutical company (mentioned also in the cocaine chapter), was interested in peyote, and in 1888, sent "cactus buttons" to a well-respected Berlin toxicologist, Louis Lewin, who then traveled to the American Southwest to study peyote. He identified the psychoactive alkaloid present in the cactus and named it "mescal." Peyote buttons became quite popular in the late 19th century and were used by well-known physicians such as neurologist Weir Mitchell and Philadelphia sexologist Havelock Ellis and by poets such as W. B. Yeats.

Humphry Osmond, an English psychiatrist, became interested in mescaline in the 1940s because it sometimes led to symptoms that were like those seen in schizophrenia. John Smythies, a neuropsychiatrist, and Osmond noted that the chemical formula for mescaline was similar to that of adrenaline. They wondered if the body, when stressed, changed adrenaline into something like mescaline, which caused psychotic symptoms. Osmond took some mescaline, experienced a change in how he perceived reality, and thought that it helped him understand the perceptions of the person with schizophrenia (Kaplan 2014, 118).

Osmond coined the word *psychedelic*, an adjective often applied to hallucinogenic substances, from two Greek words, *psyche* (meaning "mind," "soul," or "spirit") and *delos* (meaning "to manifest" or "make visible"). *Psychedelic* has been defined as "mind manifesting" or "soul revealing." Osmond thought that a person under the influence of a psychedelic drug could perceive more vividly and deeply.

Aldous Huxley—the author of *Brave New World*, a novel that offers a terrifying vision of a totalitarian society in which the population is controlled by a drug known as "soma"—also wanted to take mescaline. While Huxley recognized that human freedom could be compromised by drugs, he was intrigued by their ability to alter perceptions. Huxley read about Osmond's work and asked the psychiatrist to administer mescaline to him. Under Osmond's supervision, Huxley took mescaline in May 1953. Huxley described this and subsequent mescaline experiences in the book *Doors of Perception*. The title comes from a line in William Blake's poem "The Marriage of Heaven and Hell": "If the doors of perception were cleansed everything would appear to man as it is, Infinite." (The 1960s American rock band The Doors named itself after this book.)

As previously noted, peyote had an important role in religious ceremonies in Mexico and was then incorporated into the rituals and ceremonies of Native Americans. The 1994 American Indian Religious Freedom Act Amendments allow members of the Native American Church to use peyote in their ceremonies. (Peyote is a Schedule I drug; therefore, it is illegal for anyone not associated with this church to buy, distribute, or possess the drug.)

The effects of mescaline are complex and variable. Perhaps its best-known effects are the production of rich visual hallucinations, often accompanied by synesthesia, the experience of receiving information in one sensory modality but experiencing it in another. For example, a person with synesthesia "sees" music or "hears" a painting. These experiences are sometimes accompanied by a sense of spiritual or mystical insight.

Ergot and Lysergic Alkaloids, Including LSD

Ergot (*Claviceps purpurea*) is a parasitic fungus that grows on rye and other grasses during wet seasons. The fungus produces a variety of alkaloids, some of them lysergic acid alkaloids, which have a complex array of effects on humans. The word *ergot* can refer to the fungus itself or its alkaloids.

One ergot alkaloid, ergotamine, constricts or tightens blood vessels and is used to treat migraine. Another alkaloid, ergometrine, leads to uterine contractions and has been used in the past to induce labor; it is still used to control postpartum bleeding. Perhaps the most striking properties of ergot, however, are its hallucinogenic effects.

If bread is made from rye contaminated with ergot, a serious illness, ergotism, can result. One type of ergotism is marked by neurological symptoms consisting of seizures and hallucinations. The other form of the illness is marked by constriction of blood vessels in the extremities. If severe, this vasoconstriction leads to gangrene and possible loss of limbs.

Some historians suggest that there was a link between accusations of witchcraft and ergotism. Many European witchcraft trials took place in areas where rye was a staple, and where there were frequent prolonged periods of cool wet weather (Hudler 2000, 76). In 1692 in Salem, Massachusetts, villagers claimed that they had been "bewitched." Some historians suggest that they might have instead been suffering from hallucinations caused by ergotism (Caporeal 1976).

In the 1930s, Sandoz Pharmaceuticals became interested in synthesizing ergot-like drugs because of their vasoconstrictive properties. Albert Hofmann, the Sandoz chemist who later synthesized psilocybin and psilocin, produced a series of derivatives of the core molecule of ergotamine, lysergic acid. In 1938, he synthesized the 25th derivative, lysergic acid diethylamide, or the famous LSD-25. He set it aside for years only to discover its psychoactive properties by accident in 1943, after licking his fingers while working in the lab. He felt unwell and rode his bicycle home. Hofmann had no reason to expect anything from his accidental exposure to LSD. His description of these experiences is valuable because future work was to show that one's experience of LSD depended in part on individual expectations.

> Last Friday, April 16, 1943, I was forced to interrupt my work in the laboratory in the middle of the afternoon and proceed home, being affected by a remarkable restlessness, combined with a slight dizziness. At home I lay down and sank into a not unpleasant intoxicated-like condition, characterized by an extremely stimulated imagination. In a dreamlike state, with eyes closed (I found the daylight to be unpleasantly glaring), I perceived an uninterrupted stream of fantastic pictures, extraordinary shapes with intense, kaleidoscopic play of colors. After some two hours this condition faded away. (Hofmann 1980)

Sandoz saw a marketing opportunity and distributed LSD to physicians and researchers to determine if it had clinical applications.

Timothy Leary, mentioned earlier in connection with psilocybin, described LSD as the more powerful of the two drugs. He lost interest in his psilocybin project and became more interested in LSD, mysticism, and Eastern religions. He became famous as a kind of guru, and for coining phrases such as "turn on, tune in, drop out." Leary left Harvard in the spring of 1963 to proselytize for the use of LSD and other drugs. He was arrested and imprisoned for violation of drug offenses (see description in the cannabis chapter). In 1971, Richard Nixon described him as the most dangerous man in America, seeing him as a leading figure in the counterculture.

LSD became associated with the "hippies" and "flower children" of the 1960s and was used by music groups of the time, many of whom produced music known as psychedelic rock or acid rock. Aldous Huxley continued to be interested in psychedelic drugs, including LSD. Perhaps in honor of Huxley's devotion to mind-altering substances, the Beatles included a picture of him on the famous cover of their album *Sgt. Pepper's Lonely Hearts Club Band*. The cover is a colorful collage of objects, garish uniforms, and celebrities. One of the songs, "Lucy in the Sky with Diamonds," was thought to be a reference to LSD. However, John Lennon always attributed the title and idea of the song to a drawing by his son and his reading of *Alice's Adventures in Wonderland*. (Lewis Carroll also has a place on the album cover.) A strange bond formed between some "hippies" and another group of people interested in LSD—the intelligence community (see Sidebar 4.1).

LSD became feared in the late 1960s possibly because of an outpouring in the popular press about it leading to prolonged psychotic reactions, suicides, or chromosomal damage. Much of this reporting turned out to be false or misleading (Pollan 2018, 209; Stevens 1987, 273–282). LSD is now a Schedule I controlled substance.

Sidebar 4.1 Ken Kesey and MK ULTRA

Ken Kesey was born in Colorado and brought up on a farm in Oregon. He was an outstanding high school student and wrestler. In 1958, he began to study writing at Stanford University in California. Kesey worked as a night orderly in the psychiatric wing of the Veterans Administration (VA) Hospital at Menlo Park and used that experience in his first novel, *One Flew over the Cuckoo's Nest*, published in 1962. To make more money, he volunteered to take part in an experimental program at the hospital that involved taking LSD, psilocybin, and other hallucinogenic drugs. He shared some of the LSD from the program with friends. Although it was not known at the time, the program at the VA in California was funded by the CIA and was part of the secret program known as MK ULTRA. The CIA and the Army Chemical Corps had begun to carry out research using LSD and other hallucinogens in the 1950s because of concerns that enemies of the United States might use or have used hallucinogens to brainwash or to confuse American prisoners of war or American allies. The CIA and army also investigated the idea of weaponizing hallucinogens for their own use by the United States, using them, for example, as knockout pills or as an aid in interrogations (Lee and Shlain 1985, xxi–xxv, 282–283).

Kesey became enchanted with LSD, and in 1964, he bought an old Harvester school bus. With some friends, he traveled in the flamboyantly painted bus from California to New York. Throughout the trip, the group, who called themselves the Merry Pranksters, took LSD and distributed it to others. Described in raucous prose in Tom Wolfe's *Electric Kool-Aid Acid Test*, the trip became one of the signature events of the 1960s.

Bibliography

Lee, Martin A., and Bruce Shlain. *Acid Dreams: The Complete Social History of LSD: The CIA, the Sixties, and Beyond*. New York: Grove Press, 1985.

Solanaceous Plants

Solanaceae (nightshade) is a large family of herbs, shrubs, and trees, which are often scented and sometimes poisonous. The Latin name comes from the name for the potato, *Solanum tuberosum*. Other common solanaceous plants are *Capsicum* (sweet and chili peppers), *Solanum lycopersicum* (tomato), and *Nicotiana tabacum* (tobacco). Less common solanaceous plants include *Datura stramonium* (Jimson, Jamestown, locoweed, or thorn apple), *Hyoscyamus niger* (henbane), *Mandragora officinarum* (mandrake), and *Brugmansia* (golden angel's trumpet). This entire latter group of plants contains potent hallucinogenic anticholinergic alkaloids. Of the anticholinergic alkaloids, scopolamine, also known as hyoscine, is used as a treatment for motion sickness and is reputedly most likely to lead to hallucinations.

Atropa belladonna, commonly known as belladonna or deadly nightshade, gives its name to atropine, an anticholinergic medication that can cause hallucinations. When applied to the eye, it dilates the pupil, which is supposed to make women more attractive, hence the name, which means "beautiful woman" in Italian. Belladonna, in the form of an extract of the plant, was used in a New York hospital where addiction to alcohol was treated. In 1934, a patient named Bill Wilson received it (along with other drugs) and had a sort of mystical experience, following which he never drank alcohol again. Wilson went on to found Alcoholics Anonymous.

Ayahuasca

Another hallucinogenic substance is ayahuasca, also known as yage. Ayahuasca is a beverage made from ingredients from the perennial shrub chacruna (*Psychotria viridis*) and the ayahuasca vine (*Banisteriopsis caapi*). Chacruna contains the hallucinogenic indole alkaloid dimethyltryptamine (DMT), and the ayahuasca vine contains a monoamine oxidase inhibitor that prevents the body's breakdown of DMT. The word *ayahuasca* refers to both the beverage and the vine and comes from a Quechua term meaning "vine of the souls" (McKenna 2004). The brew is an important part of shamanism among the indigenous and mestizo peoples in Peru, Columbia, and Ecuador. It causes hallucinogenic experiences—and violent vomiting.

The legal status of DMT-containing plants in the United States is not clear. Ayahuasca plants themselves are legal, but any preparation containing DMT is not because DMT is a Schedule I drug. However, a small religious sect originating in Brazil won permission from the Supreme Court in 2006 to use ayahuasca in their rituals, basing their argument on the Religious Freedom Restoration Act.

Salvia Divinorum

Known as the diviner's sage or seer's sage, *Salvia divinorum* grows in the cloud forests in Mexico (especially Oaxaca), Central America, and South America. The plant is used by the Mazatecs and associated with the Virgin Mary. Its leaves can be chewed or smoked, and its effects are intense but short-lived. In the United States, it is legal at the federal level but outlawed in many states.

3,4-Methylenedioxymethamphetamine (MDMA)

The pharmaceutical company Merck synthesized MDMA in 1912 while it was looking for a new blood-clotting agent. It was set aside for decades (Freudenmann, Oxler, and Bernschneider-Reif 2006). In 1974, the biochemist Alexander Shulgin, searching for new psychedelic drugs, resynthesized it and discovered that it was a hallucinogen with stimulant properties, which Shulgin thought could be used as an aid in psychotherapy. It became a "party drug" with street names of "ecstasy" or "Molly" (short for "molecule"). In 1985, the U.S. Drug Enforcement Administration labeled MDMA as a Schedule I drug. It fell out of favor after the 1980s because so much of what was sold as MDMA was highly adulterated; however, there is now a resurgence of MDMA availability.

Sometimes it is sold as a powder or in capsules, and it is reported to be more potent than the MDMA of the 1980s but is still often contaminated by other drugs.

People who use MDMA report increased energy, pleasure, empathy for others, and distorted sensations. Of the substances discussed in this chapter, MDMA is the most harmful. It causes amphetamine-like symptoms and may be addictive. It can also cause hyperactivity, increase in body temperature, jaw clenching, and, rarely, heart or kidney damage. Some users report symptoms of depression for a day or so after using it (National Institute on Drug Abuse, 2018).

Phenyl-cyclohexyl-piperidine (Phencyclidine)

In the 1950s, pharmaceutical company Parke-Davis synthesized phenyl-cyclohexyl-piperidine, or phencyclidine, while searching for new anesthetic agents, naming it Semyl. Semyl was an improvement over other agents because it did not affect the heart rate or breathing, but patients became excited after its use and hallucinated, so its use in humans was discontinued. It is still, however, used in veterinary anesthesia (Mion 2017). People now use phencyclidine illegally for the same effects that made it unsuitable for anesthesia: excitement and hallucinations. It can cause seizures and has been associated with possible addiction, violence, flashbacks, and suicide. Interactions with other drugs consumed at the same time can lead to coma or death. It has many street names, including "PCP" and "angel dust," and can be swallowed, smoked, snorted, or injected. Phencyclidine is a Schedule II drug, meaning that it is legal but has high potential for abuse and dependence. Possession of phencyclidine is illegal. Phencyclidine has its own category in *DSM-5*. If used in high doses, it is associated with seizures, muscle breakdown, psychosis, violence, and flashbacks. When used with other drugs it can lead to coma. Phencyclidine intoxication has been associated with accidents leading to death or suicide (National Institute on Drug Abuse; Hallucinogens 2016).

Ketamine

In 1962, Parke-Davis synthesized a derivative of phencyclidine that was both a ketone and an amine and thus named *ketamine*. Ketamine turned out to be a better anesthetic drug than phencyclidine and was widely used as such during the Vietnam War. It continues to be used as an anesthetic drug both for humans and animals. It is now misused as a recreational drug, often by snorting, and known by a variety of names, including "special K." It leads to dissociation. It is shorter-acting than phencyclidine and is not associated with the violence linked to that drug. It is used illegally for its psychedelic and dissociative effects and is a Schedule III drug, meaning that there is some potential for abuse, and it may lead to dependence. There is now great interest in ketamine's possible use as a rapidly acting antidepressant agent.

Development and Causes

Little is known about the natural history of hallucinogen misuse. What is known is that both the reasons people use hallucinogens and the profile of the people using them have changed. There has been little or no research into the development and causes of the misuse of hallucinogens, nor has there been a sense of urgency to this research because, apart from PCP and MDMA, it is uncertain how much harm is done by these substances.

Up Close—In Society

In the 1960s, those who used hallucinogens tended to be young people who dissented from the mores of the time. Many wanted to protest what they saw as the confining and hypocritical expectations of a corrupt social system. Today, people who use hallucinogens seem less politically and socially motivated and often use them with other drugs or alcohol (Shalit, Rehm, and Lev-Ran 2019). There is less interest in transcendence and more of a craving for excitement.

Case Study

Ms. A is a 20-year-old woman who goes to a techno concert with loud, pulsing music and flashing lights. She is drinking alcohol and smoking marijuana. A young man gives her a capsule containing a white powder that he says is ecstasy, and he promises her that it will allow her to connect with others and to experience the music in a deeper way. She takes the tablet and dances energetically for several hours. Then she becomes agitated and complains that she is "burning up." Her friends encourage her to drink large quantities of water. She says that she feels worse, and her friends take her to a hospital where her pulse, blood pressure, and temperature are all found to be dangerously high; she also has low serum sodium. She is treated and told that the capsule she was given might have been ecstasy (MDMA) but that it might also have been adulterated with other drugs such as phencyclidine.

Up Close—At Work

Some people take hallucinogens such as LSD or psilocybin to alter their perceptions, and they say that it improves their productivity. Successful people have used LSD and claimed that it helped their work. It could also be that some individuals are creative despite, not because of, psychedelic drugs. Or perhaps the creative process is so demanding and strenuous that psychedelic drugs help people relax.

Case Studies

Biochemist Kary Mullis invented a simple technique with far-reaching scientific ramifications. He refined the polymerase chain reaction (PCR) technique, which makes identical copies of a single segment of deoxyribonucleic acid (DNA); in 1993, he won the Nobel Prize in Chemistry for this work. PCR allows DNA to be quickly amplified and thus revolutionized molecular biology. Four times married, he is known for his love of surfing and his beliefs, not shared by most scientists, that HIV does not cause AIDS and that astrology has value. He said, "Would I have invented PCR if I hadn't taken LSD? I seriously doubt it . . . I could sit on a DNA molecule and watch the polymers go by. I learnt that partly on psychedelic drugs" (Nichols 2016, 332).

Steve Jobs, founder of Apple, was a billionaire entrepreneur. A brilliant student, he dropped out of Reed College. He traveled to Japan. As a youngster he was interested in electronics and then developed an interest in literature. He visited ashrams in India for seven months. He connected design, technology, and marketing and became an integral part of the development and introduction of the personal computer and the smartphone. He described himself as influenced by Zen and Buddhism. While he was in college he took LSD and described this as "one of the two or three most important things I have done in my life" (Nichols 2016, 332).

Up Close—In Relationships

Some people take small doses, or "microdoses," of hallucinogens. Microdoses are called "sub-perceptual" because they are about one-tenth the size of the dose that causes hallucinations. Microdose users say that hallucinogens improve their productivity, mood, sleep, and relationships with others. Psychologist James Fadiman, an authority on psychedelic drugs and microdosing, writes that this practice does not lead to major therapeutic breakthroughs or mystical experiences, but people feel more energetic, yet relaxed and compassionate (Fadiman and Cohen 2018)

Case Study

Ayelet Waldman, a 52-year-old lawyer, successful novelist, and married mother of four children, was chronically depressed and irritable. Psychotherapy, couples therapy, meditation, and psychiatric medications had not helped her feel better, and she terrified herself when she thought about suicide. Then she read about the work of James Fadiman and microdosing. She was intrigued but nervous about breaking the law to obtain the drug. She had no interest in mystical or spiritual experiences; she just wanted to be able to enjoy her remarkably fortunate life without always feeling tense and alienating her children and husband. She was put in touch with a person who called himself "Lewis Carroll"—he sent her a small bottle of LSD.

She took a microdose of LSD every three days for a month. She had no hallucinations or strange experiences. But she did feel less angry and more optimistic. Pain from a frozen shoulder diminished and her productivity increased. She wrote a book about the experience called *A Really Good Day: How Microdosing Made a Mega Difference in My Mood, My Marriage, and My Life* (2018).

Effects and Costs

Hallucinogens, with the exceptions of phencyclidine, MDMA, and ayahuasca, cause few physical side effects. Phencyclidine has been associated with agitation, suicidality, assaultiveness, and psychosis (National Institute on Drug Abuse 2016; Shalit, Rehm, and Lev-Ran 2019). MDMA has been shown to be neurotoxic (Croft et al. 2001) and can lead to heatstroke and death. It is particularly dangerous when combined with other substances. Ayahuasca is associated with vomiting. No hallucinogens, however, have been associated with fatal overdoses, life-threatening withdrawal, or carcinogenicity. The drugs are not addictive, except possibly for phencyclidine and MDMA.

There has been concern about "flashbacks" or recurrent visual hallucinations, which if persistent and disturbing can lead to a disorder known as hallucinogen persisting perception disorder (HPPD). This has been associated most commonly with LSD. This phenomenon is unusual and seems to be related, at least in some cases, to already existing problems of the user (Halpern, Lerner, and Passie 2018; Krebs and Johansen 2012).

An unusual risk associated with some hallucinogens is associated with mushrooms. Mushrooms can be difficult to identify, and people looking for hallucinogenic mushrooms are at risk of lethal poisoning if they ingest a poisonous mushroom.

The effects of hallucinogens on the pregnant woman and developing fetus are not known. Caution and good sense would suggest that the pregnant or breast-feeding woman should not use hallucinogens. If the pregnant woman also has a chaotic lifestyle, is not getting good prenatal care, and is using other substances, she is putting herself and the unborn baby at more risk.

The costs of hallucinogen use disorder are not known.

Theory and Research

Research into hallucinogens began in the 1950s, much of it taking place at the Spring Grove State Hospital outside Baltimore and funded by the National Institute of Mental Health. But support faded by the mid-1970s because of the association of psychedelic drugs with the counterculture. Some blame Timothy Leary's "antics." Leary was accused of creating a "cult" within the psychology department at Harvard and criticized for his full-throated enthusiasm for the ability of LSD to change the world (Pollan 2018, 140, 185–212). David McClelland, chair of the department of psychology, was scathing about Leary's research: "Many reports are given of deep mystical experiences but their chief characteristic is the wonder at one's own profundity" (quoted in Pollan 2018, 195). By the end of 1966, Sandoz stopped distributing LSD. The FDA stopped all psychedelic research that same year except for research in Maryland, which continued until 1976 (Pollan 2018, 217–218).

Mechanism of Action

The classic hallucinogens (LSD, mescaline, and psilocybin) are thought to work by enhancing a 5-hydroxytryptamine (5-HT) pathway in the brain. Also known as serotonin, 5-HT is a neurotransmitter, or chemical messenger, between nerve cells. At least 14 different serotonin receptors exist along with multiple pathways. Psilocybin, psilocin, and LSD are tryptamines, which are alkaloids formed from the amino acid tryptophan, a precursor to serotonin. These drugs bind strongly to the 5-HT2A receptors, and this activity may be related to their hallucinogenic effects.

Belonging to a family of compounds known as phenethylamines, mescaline has a different structure, but it still binds to serotonin receptors. Some synthetic "designer" psychedelics, such as MDMA are also phenethylamines. MDMA is more stimulant-like than mescaline because it also leads to an increase in two other neurotransmitters, dopamine and noradrenaline (National Institute on Drug Abuse 2018).

The mechanisms of the other substances are not well understood. The psychiatric effects of *Amanita muscaria* may be produced by the amino acid derivatives ibotenic acid and muscimol. Ibotenic acid is structurally related to the amino acid glutamate and activates the N-methyl-D-aspartate (NMDA) receptors (Spinella 2001, 387–390). Phencyclidine and ketamine are thought to work as NMDA antagonists, at least with respect to their dissociative effects. DMT is a tryptamine and thus at least some of its complex effects are probably due to its actions at the 5-HT2A receptors as well as other receptors.

Salvia does not work via the serotonin system but is thought to activate the kappa opioid receptor. (This receptor is distinct from the mu opioid receptor involved with the opioid drugs.) It is not known how anticholinergic compounds found in the solanaceous plants produce their hallucinogenic effects. It may be that people who take these substances develop an anticholinergic delirium, and this is what is distorting their perceptions. (Visual hallucinations are not uncommon in delirium.)

Hallucinogens as Treatments for Addictions and Other Psychiatric Disorders

The therapeutic possibilities of LSD were explored early in its history. Sandoz marketed LSD as a medication with possible clinical applications in psychiatry from 1949 to 1966. These applications were not clearly outlined. Around the same time that Sandoz was trying to find a market for LSD, Tommy Douglas, the premier of Saskatchewan, a pioneer in government-run medical care, was looking for physicians to improve the delivery of mental-health services. He advertised in England. Humphry Osmond, discussed earlier with reference to mescaline, was frustrated by the lack of support in England for his work with this hallucinogen, saw the advertisement, and seized the opportunity. In 1951, he moved to Canada to become deputy director of the Weyburn Mental Hospital in Saskatchewan. He continued to work with psychedelics, but now with LSD supplied by Sandoz. Osmond hypothesized that LSD, by inducing an artificial "delirium tremens," might be therapeutic in the treatment of alcoholic patients. Delirium tremens occurs in cases of severe alcohol withdrawal, is associated with visual hallucinations, and is unpleasant and frightening. In 1954, he and his psychiatric colleague Abram Hoffer began to give LSD to their patients, and to their surprise, saw that people with alcohol use disorders did not have a highly aversive experience. They hallucinated but also had more difficult-to-describe sensations: epiphanies of "a transcendent feeling of being united with the world" and "increased sensitivity to the feelings of others" (Pollan 2018, 150). They felt more empathy for others and more appreciation for philosophy and religion. Importantly, they lost their cravings for alcohol. Osmond and his colleagues treated 2,000 alcoholics with high-dose LSD and reported rates of recovery of nearly 50% (Kaplan 2014, 121). They used LSD in this way for about 13 years, apparently quite uneventfully (Lee and Shlain 1985, 50). Indeed, LSD became a standard treatment option for alcoholism in Saskatchewan (Pollan 2018, 151).

Researchers at UCLA also used LSD in the treatment of alcoholism with good results. LSD became known as "a miracle cure for alcoholism" (Novak 1997, 98). But these successes could not always be replicated. Perhaps this was because LSD and other hallucinogens are more effective when administered by people who believe that they work, and when they are given in a pleasant, comfortable, and relaxing place, perhaps with music and beautiful objects, and in the presence of a "guide." The guide was someone with experience with hallucinogens who could reassure the person if he or she became frightened or overwhelmed. Conversely, hallucinogens are not effective therapeutically if they are administered by skeptics in an unfriendly place (Pollan 2018, 151–152). Despite these failures, a 2012 meta-analysis of six randomized controlled trials found that a single dose of LSD decreased alcohol misuse in 59% of patients; placebo did the same in 38% (Krebs and Johansen 2012).

Other psychedelics may be helpful with addictions to alcohol or other substances. The Native American Church has long used peyote to treat alcoholism (Halpern et al. 2005). An open-label study showed that psilocybin might be useful in the treatment of alcoholism (Bogenschutz et al. 2015). A group from Johns Hopkins showed that, combined with a structured treatment program, two to three doses of psilocybin were associated with smoking abstinence. The subjects were 15 middle-aged men who had tried repeatedly to quit smoking. At follow-up that ranged from 16 months to 57 months, 60% of the subjects had stopped smoking. The study was small and, as is the case with most studies of psychedelic drugs, not double-blind. It is interesting that the effects of psilocybin lasted long after the drug actions had dissipated. The researchers found that the more "mystical" experiences that the subject described, the likelier it was that he would be able to stop smoking (Johnson, Garcia-Romeu, Griffiths 2017).

Europeans and Americans now participate in "ayahuasca tourism" and travel to the Amazon Basin to consume it for various reasons, including the treatment of addictions and post–traumatic stress disorder (PTSD). Anecdotal evidence suggests that when used appropriately, it may be useful and safe in the treatment of addictions to alcohol and cocaine (McKenna 2004). The complexity of the beverage—it contains hundreds of biologically active compounds with great molecular diversity—and the status of DMT as a Schedule I drug make research on ayahuasca difficult. At this point, there is no clear evidence for its effectiveness or safety.

Psychedelic drugs are also used for other psychiatric disorders, some related to addictions. At the Imperial College in London, researchers treated depressed people with psilocybin. After treatment, brain imaging showed reduced blood flow in certain areas of the brain, particularly the amygdala (where fear and stress are processed), and patients reported less depression (Carhart-Harris et al. 2017).

Some of the interest in the hallucinogens as therapeutic agents has to do with their possible modification of the "default mode network." This network is a theoretical description of the work of the brain that takes place even when we are not actively thinking. In the 1950s, neuroscientist Louis Sokoloff and his colleagues noticed that when a person began to think about difficult mathematical issues, metabolism in the brain did not increase. Neurologist Marcus Raichle showed that the brain uses little extra energy when performing mental tasks. In 2001, Raichle used the phrase "default mode" to describe resting-state brain function. Some suggest that the default mode network is overactive in people who have addictions and depression and that such overactivity leads to cognitive rigidity, rumination, and excessive self-referential thought. Psilocybin disrupts communication between the major nodes of the default mode network. This may explain the common description of the "dissolution of the ego" and the oceanic feeling experienced by hallucinogen users (Carhart-Harris et al. 2014).

When used intravenously and at sub-anesthetic doses, ketamine has also been found to reduce suicidal thoughts and act as a rapid antidepressant. The basis for its antidepressant effect is not known but may be related to its activity at opioid receptors (Williams et al. 2018). Strangely, it may also work to block the problematic opioid-induced hyperalgesia described in the opiate chapter (Mion 2017). Some researchers suggest that ketamine may "reset" the default mode network (Carhart-Harris et al. 2017).

Researchers are assessing the value of MDMA as a treatment of PTSD and anxiety in terminally ill patients, and for social anxiety in adults with autism (Bedi 2018; Danforth et al. 2018).

It does not seem, however, that the recreational use of hallucinogens protects against misuse of other substances or psychiatric disorders. People who use hallucinogens are more likely than those who do not to misuse other substances, such as cocaine, alcohol, and nicotine, and to have other psychiatric disorders, although this association is best attributed to confounding by sociodemographic and other factors (Shalit, Rehm, and Lev-Ran 2019). Psychedelic drug use is, however, associated with a reduced risk of opioid abuse and dependence (Pisano et al. 2017).

As many of these drugs are Schedule I, research remains difficult because of the complex approval process needed before a study may begin. Some funding comes from nonprofit organizations such as the Multidisciplinary Association for Psychedelic Studies (MAPS) and the English Beckley Foundation. Another challenge is the difficulty in "blinding" the studies. The subjects and raters will usually be aware that the subjects are taking the active rather than control treatment, and this may well bias their responses. It's also difficult to make quantitative assessments of the mystical or transcendent experiences many have while taking the classical hallucinogens. Because of the unusual nature of the experiences, some authorities recommend that research in psychedelic therapy be conducted in the presence of two experienced guides who are not under the influence of these drugs themselves, further complicating research (Carhart-Harris et al. 2018).

Treatments

The classic hallucinogenic substances (LSD, mescaline, and psilocybin), are not addictive. Medical treatment is sometimes needed for people who are agitated because of phencyclidine or hyperthermic because of MDMA. Cognitive behavioral interventions are recommended for people who are having difficulty stopping their use of hallucinogens. No medications are approved for treatment of hallucinogen use disorder.

Conclusion

Hallucinogens have been used widely by people in various cultures throughout many parts of the world. They have been highly valued by some for their ability to lead to a sense of understanding the cosmos. The early devotees of the hallucinogens, such as Timothy Leary and Aldous Huxley, thought that the use of these drugs could increase our consciousness and lead to world peace. These overblown and naïve ideas were strangely matched by the beliefs of the CIA—that hallucinogens could be used to defeat the enemies of America. Now our hopes are perhaps no less optimistic—that hallucinogens can decrease depression and combat addictions.

Bibliography

American Psychiatric Association. *Diagnostic and Statistical Manual of Mental Disorders (DSM-5)*, 5th ed. Arlington, VA: American Psychiatric Association, 2013.

Bedi, Gillinder. "3,4-Methylenedioxymethamphetamine as a Psychiatric Treatment." *JAMA Psychiatry* 75, no. 5 (2018), 419–420. doi:10.1001/jamapsychiatry.2018.0063.

Bogenschutz, Michael P., Alyssa A. Forcehimes, Jessica A. Pommy, Claire E. Wilcox, PCR Barbosa, and Rick J. Strassman. "Psilocybin-Assisted Treatment for Alcohol Dependence: A Proof-of-Concept Study." *J Psychopharmacol* 29, no. 3 (2015), 289–299. doi:10.1177/0269881114565144.

Brecher, Edward M. *Licit and Illicit Drugs: The Consumers Union Report on Narcotics, Stimulants, Depressants, Inhalants, Hallucinogens, and Marijuana—Including Caffeine, Nicotine, and Alcohol.* Boston: Little, Brown, 1972.

Caporael, Linda. "Ergotism: The Satan Loosed in Salem?" *Science* 192, no. 4234 (1976), 21–26. doi:10.1126/science.769159.

Carhart-Harris, Robin L., Robert Leech, Peter J. Hellyer, Murray Shanahan, Amanda Feilding, Enzo Tagliazucchi, Dante R. Chialvo, and David Nutt. "The Entropic Brain: A Theory of Conscious States Informed by Neuroimaging Research with Psychedelic Drugs." *Front Hum Neurosci* 8 (2014). doi:10.3389/fnhum.2014.00020.

Carhart-Harris, Robin L., Leor Roseman, Mark Bolstridge, Lysia Demetriou, J. N. Pannekoek, Matthew B. Wall, Mark Tanner, et al. "Psilocybin for Treatment-Resistant Depression: fMRI-Measured Brain Mechanisms." *Sci Rep* 7, no. 1 (2017), 13187. Accessed July 29, 2019. https://doi.org/10.1038/s41598-017-13282-7.

Carhart-Harris, Robin L., Leor Roseman, Eline Haijen, David Erritzoe, Rosalind Watts, Igor Branchi, and Mendel Kaelen. "Psychedelics and the Essential Importance of Context." *J Psychopharmacol* 32, no. 7 (2018), 725–731. doi:10.1177/0269881118754710.

Croft, Rodney J., Anthony Klugman, Torsten Baldeweg, and John H. Gruzelier. "Electrophysiological Evidence of Serotonergic Impairment in Long-Term MDMA ('Ecstasy') Users." *Am J Psychiatry* 158, no. 10 (2001), 1687–1692. doi:10.1176/appi.ajp.158.10.1687.

Danforth, Alicia L., Charles S. Grob, Christopher Struble, Allison A. Feduccia, Nick Walker, Lisa Jerome, Berra Yazar-Klosinski, and Amy Emerson. "Reduction in Social Anxiety after MDMA-Assisted Psychotherapy with Autistic Adults: A Randomized, Double-Blind, Placebo-Controlled Pilot Study." *Psychopharmacology* 235, no. 11 (2018), 3137–3148. doi:10.1007/s00213-018-5010-9.

Doblin, Rick. "Dr. Leary's Concord Prison Experiment: A 34-Year Follow-Up Study." *J Psychoactive Drugs* 30, no. 4 (Fall 1998), 419–426. doi:10.1080/02791072.1998.10399715.

Fadiman, James, and Steven Jay Cohen. *The Psychedelic Explorer's Guide: Safe, Therapeutic, and Sacred Journeys.* Old Saybrook, CT: Tantor Media, 2018.

Freudenmann, Roland W., Florian Öxler, and Sabine Bernschneider-Reif. "The Origin of MDMA (Ecstasy) Revisited: The True Story Reconstructed from the Original Documents." *Addiction* 101, no. 9 (2006), 1241–1245. doi:10.1111/j.1360-0443.2006.01511.x.

Halpern, John H., Arturo G. Lerner, and Torsten Passie. "A Review of Hallucinogen Persisting Perception Disorder (HPPD) and an Exploratory Study of Subjects Claiming Symptoms of HPPD." *Curr Top Behav Neurosci.* 36 (2018), 333–360. doi:10.1007/7854 _2016_457.

Halpern, John H., Andrea R. Sherwood, James I. Hudson, Deborah Yurgelun-Todd, and Harrison G. Pope. "Psychological and Cognitive Effects of Long-Term Peyote Use Among Native Americans." *Biol Psychiatry* 58, no. 8 (2005), 624–631. doi:10.1016/j.biopsych.2005.06.038.

Hofmann, Albert. "LSD—My Problem Child." Psychedelic Library. Last modified 1980. http://www.druglibrary.org.

Hudler, George W. *Magical Mushrooms, Mischievous Molds.* Princeton, NJ: Princeton University Press, 2000.

Johnson, Matthew W., Albert Garcia-Romeu, and Roland R. Griffiths. "Long-Term Follow-Up of Psilocybin-Facilitated Smoking Cessation." *Am J Drug Alcohol Abuse* 43, no. 1 (2017), 55–60. doi:10.3109/00952 990.2016.1170135.

Kaplan, Robert M. "Humphry Fortescue Osmond (1917–2004), a Radical and Conventional Psychiatrist: The Transcendent Years." *J Med Biogr* 24, no. 1 (2014), 115–124. doi:10.1177/0967772013479520.

Krebs, Teri S., and Pål-Ørjan Johansen. "Lysergic Acid Diethylamide (LSD) for Alcoholism: Meta-Analysis of Randomized Controlled Trials." *J Psychopharmacol* 26, no. 7 (2012), 994–1002. doi:10.1177/0269881112439253.

Lee, Martin A., and Bruce Shlain. *Acid Dreams: The CIA, LSD, and the Sixties Rebellion.* New York: Grove Press, 1985.

McKenna, Dennis J. "Clinical Investigations of the Therapeutic Potential of Ayahuasca: Rationale and Regulatory Challenges." *Pharmacol Ther* 102, no. 2 (2004), 111–129.

Mion, Georges. "History of Anaesthesia." *Eur J Anaesthesiol* 34, no. 9 (2017), 571–575. doi:10.1097/eja.0000000000000638.

National Institute on Drug Abuse. *Hallucinogens. Drug Facts*. 2016. Accessed January 11, 2019. http://www.drugabuse.gov/publications /drugfacts/hallucinogens.

National Institute on Drug Abuse. *MDMA (Ecstasy/Molly)*. National Institutes of Health: U.S. Department of Health and Services, June 2018. Accessed March 23, 2019. https://www.drugabuse.gov/publications /drugfacts/mdma-ecstasymolly.

Nichols, David E. "Psychedelics." *Pharmacol Rev* 68, no. 2 (2016), 264–355. doi:10.1124/pr.115.011478.

Novak, Steven J. "LSD before Leary: Sidney Cohen's Critique of 1950s Psychedelic Drug Research." *Isis* 88, no. 1 (1997), 87–110.

Pisano, Vincent D., Nathaniel P. Putnam, Hannah M. Kramer, Kevin J. Franciotti, John H. Halpern, and Selma C. Holden. "The Association of Psychedelic Use and Opioid Use Disorders among Illicit Users in the United States." *J Psychopharmacol* 31, no. 5 (2017), 606–613. doi:10.1177/0269881117691453.

Pollan, Michael. *How to Change Your Mind: What the New Science of Psychedelics Teaches Us About Consciousness, Dying, Addiction, Depression, and Transcendence*. New York: Penguin Press, 2018.

Schultes, Richard Evans, Albert Hofmann, and Christian Rätsch. *Plants of the Gods: Their Sacred, Healing and Hallucinogenic Powers*. Rochester, VT: Healing Arts Press, 2001.

Shalit, Nadav, Jürgen Rehm, and Shaul Lev-Ran. "Epidemiology of Hallucinogen Use in the U.S. Results from the National Epidemiologic Survey on Alcohol and Related Conditions III." *Addict Behav* 89 (2019), 35–43. doi:10.1016/j.addbeh.2018.09.020.

Spinella, Marcello. *The Psychopharmacology of Herbal Medicine: Plant Drugs That Alter Mind, Brain, and Behavior*. Cambridge: MIT Press, 2001.

Stevens, Jay. *Storming Heaven: LSD and the American Dream*. New York: Atlantic Monthly Press, 1987.

Substance Abuse and Mental Health Services Administration. *Key substance use and mental health indicators in the United States: Results from the 2017 National Survey on Drug Use and Health (HHS Publication No. SMA 18-5068, NSDUH Series H-53)*. Rockville, MD: Center for Behavioral Health Statistics and Quality, Substance Abuse and Mental Health Services Administration, 2018. Accessed July 29, 2019. http://www.samhsa.gov/data/.

Waldman, Ayelet. *A Really Good Day: How Microdosing Made a Mega Difference in My Mood, My Marriage, and My Life*. New York: Anchor Books, 2018.

Williams, Nolan R., Boris D. Heifets, Christine Blasey, Keith Sudheimer, Jaspreet Pannu, Heather Pankow, Jessica Hawkins, et al. "Attenuation of Antidepressant Effects of Ketamine by Opioid Receptor Antagonism." *Am J Psychiatry* 175, no. 12 (2018), 1205–1215. doi:10.1176/appi.ajp.2018.18020138.

CHAPTER 5

Inhalants

Frances R. Frankenburg

In this book, the term *inhalants* refers to substances that are inhaled for their effects on the mind, even though they were manufactured and intended for different purposes. For example, a common inhalant is glue. Although glue is usually thought of as an adhesive, some young teens will buy it specifically to sniff it and become intoxicated. Substances used as inhalants are either gases or liquids that are easily vaporized at room temperature. The term does not include other misused substances that must be heated or burned before inhaling, such as tobacco, cocaine, or marijuana.

There are various ways of using inhalants. The simplest way is to sniff them. People can sniff fumes directly from a dispenser (such as a glue bottle). Some people put a rag soaked in chemicals around their mouth and "huff" from that. Others put the inhalant in a bag, place the bag over the mouth, mouth and nose, or entire head, and then breathe in the vapors—a method called "bagging." An aerosol, such as computer cleaner, can be sprayed directly into the nose or mouth. Nitrous oxide is sometimes inhaled from a balloon.

Inhalant use disorder is not always noticed because illegal activity is seldom required to obtain inhalants, and there are few telltale or obvious signs of misuse. Routine laboratory tests and urine screens will not detect traces of inhalants.

Of all the drugs or substances misused in the United States, inhalants are the ones misused most commonly by younger adolescents, probably because most are cheap, found at home, and legal. Most teens stop using inhalants by late adolescence or adulthood. Inhalant misusers tend to use a variety of inhalants as well as other substances.

There is no consensus on how to classify inhalants because of their diversity. They can be grouped by function, chemistry, pharmacology, or some combination of these properties. The National Institute of Drug Abuse (NIDA) divides them into four groups based on the forms in which they are usually found: volatile solvents, aerosols, gases, and volatile nitrites.

Volatile Solvents

Volatile solvents, also known as organic solvents, are the most commonly misused inhalants in the Western world. The word *volatile* means the substance is a liquid that vaporizes easily at room temperature. *Solvent* refers to the ability of the substance to dissolve or disperse other substances. Because these substances are hydrocarbons (chemicals made up of hydrogen and carbon), they are often referred to as *organic*. Some of the substances contain aromatic hydrocarbons, which are chemicals containing a benzene structure (six carbon atoms and six hydrogen atoms in a ring) and a characteristic smell. Benzene and toluene are two commonly misused aromatic hydrocarbons. Organic solvents are widely used in industry and manufacture, and for household purposes. They include correction fluids, felt-tip markers, glue, and dry-cleaning fluids. Gasoline, a complex liquid containing over 500 different hydrocarbons and many additives, including alcohol, benzene, ether, and toluene, also belongs in this group.

Aerosols

Aerosols are a suspension of particles in a gas and include commonly used household items, such as vegetable oil sprays, computer cleaning products, hair sprays, deodorant sprays, and spray paints. The aerosol is dispensed by a pressurized propellant liquid or gas, which is the substance that causes the psychoactive effect. In the past, chlorofluorocarbons were used as propellants. The best-known was Freon, which was widely used as a refrigerant and solvent, but it is no longer manufactured because it depletes ozone in the upper atmosphere. Propellants now include hydrofluorocarbons, nitrous oxide, and butane. (The latter two are discussed separately.)

Gases

Several gases can be inhaled for their psychoactive effects. Medical anesthetic gases, including nitrous oxide, ether, and chloroform, can be misused, as can some household or commercial gases.

Nitrous oxide (N_2O) is a colorless gas generally considered to be safe. It is sometimes used by physicians and dentists to induce conscious analgesia or sedation for surgical or dental procedures. Obstetricians may use it to ease the pains of labor and childbirth. Some people get unauthorized access to or steal tanks of this gas to inhale the nitrous oxide for its psychoactive effects.

Nitrous oxide is also used as a propellant in canned whipped cream. Whipped cream is heavy cream, or cream with at least 36% milk fat, that has been whipped, or beaten into froth, with a whisk or food processor to force air into the cream. Milk fat globules surround the resulting air pockets, producing foam. Because of these air bubbles, whipped cream is about twice the volume of the original liquid. Canned whipped cream, by contrast, is made by mixing heavy cream and nitrous oxide gas under pressure. The fat-soluble nitrous oxide permeates the cream. When the can's nozzle is pushed, releasing the pressure, the nitrous oxide and cream mixture rushes out of the can in such a way that the volume of foamed cream is four times the original volume of liquid cream. Alternatively, cream can be put into a dispenser (also known as a siphon); then a *whippit,* a small cartridge filled with nitrous oxide, is attached to a dispenser and discharged. Just as in preparing canned whipped cream, the nitrous oxide is forced into the cream, and when the dispenser's valve is opened, the result is whipped cream. Some people will inhale the nitrous oxide from cans of whipped cream or from the whippits for its psychoactive effects.

Nitrous oxide decompresses as it leaves the whippit or medical-use canister, becoming very cold. If inhaled, it can cause frostbite of the larynx, and the pressure from the gas can injure the throat or lungs. To overcome these potential hazards, users sometimes fill balloons with nitrous oxide and inhale the gas from there, so that the gas is warmer and under less pressure.

Diethyl ether, or ether, is a flammable, colorless, and sweet-smelling liquid that can either be drunk or inhaled. Another anesthetic agent that can be misused is chloroform, which is an anesthetic and a sweet-smelling, volatile liquid. (Both of these liquids are included by NIDA in the gases section, presumably because they are so volatile.)

Butane and propane are highly flammable gases that are used as fuel in cigarette lighters, cooking torches, or camping stoves and as propellants in some products. Propane is also used for home heating or home appliances. They can be used as gases or pressurized and used as liquids and on occasion are misused.

Volatile Nitrites

Volatile nitrites are found in substances such as medications, video head cleaner, room odorizer, leather cleaner, or liquid aroma. The most commonly misused nitrite is amyl nitrite. (Its intended use is to treat the pain of angina, chest pain caused by decreased blood flow to the heart. It has largely been replaced by nitroglycerin.) It is also known as a "popper" because the capsule containing it is "popped" open. Nitrites are different from the other inhalants; in that, they do not act on the central nervous system (CNS). Instead, they are vasodilators, meaning that they relax and expand blood vessels. Nitrites can cause penile vasodilatation and/or relaxation of the anal sphincter—and thus are used to enhance sexual experience. They also can lead to brief sensations of relaxation or euphoria.

Symptoms, Diagnosis, and Incidence

Symptoms

The short-term effects of inhalants are similar to the symptoms of alcohol intoxication: slurred speech, lack of coordination, euphoria, and dizziness. Hallucinations and delusions can occur. As is the case with all inhaled substances, the effects are rapid, because the lungs are so efficient at transporting substances from the air to the bloodstream and then to the brain. The "high" is immediate and brief, lasting for a few minutes. To prolong the effect, the person may repeatedly use the inhalant. Nitrites, in contrast, expand blood vessels and have fewer psychoactive effects.

Because so many inhalant misusers are adolescents, descriptions of the effects are inhalants are not always very clear. However, this passage, written by an Inuit author from Northern Canada, gives a good description of the butane-sniffing experience of a young girl:

> Butane is my drug of choice these days . . . Butane is clean. I like to steal it from the Co-op store and press the nozzle into my front teeth to release the gas, and inhale it deeply. The stars grow sharper and the colours get brighter. Sound elongates. Everything pixelates, blurs and sharpens simultaneously. Echo becomes my world and

the numbness turns into flashes of light while the ground turns into rolling waves. I am a boat. I am a lightning bolt. I belong here in this world where nothing exists. (Tagaq 2018, 42)

Diagnosis

The fifth version of the *Diagnostic and Statistical Manual of Mental Disorders (DSM-5)* (American Psychiatric Association 2013), a manual prepared by the American Psychiatric Association containing descriptions, symptoms, and other criteria for diagnosing mental disorders, describes inhalant use disorder along a continuum. Anyone meeting any two of the criteria described below during the same 12-month period receives a diagnosis of inhalant use disorder. The severity of the inhalant use disorder—mild, moderate, or severe—is based on the number of criteria met: two to three, four to five, or six or more, respectively. People with a severe inhalant use disorder are sometimes said to have an addiction, although that word addiction is becoming old-fashioned.

The criteria are a problematic pattern of use, including: using inhalants in greater amounts or over a longer duration than the person originally meant to; inability to manage one's inhalant use; spending much of one's time procuring, using, or dealing with the after-effects of inhalant use; desperately wanting to use inhalants; inability to carry out one's usual tasks because of inhalant-caused problems; continuing to use inhalants even though they are causing problems with others, such as family members, friends, and teachers and at school; choosing inhalant use over safer or more productive activities; using inhalants even when there are physical hazards, such as cardiac problems or falls or accidents caused by dizziness or lack of coordination; continuing to use inhalants even though they are causing the person problems, such as facial rashes and poor grades; or building up tolerance so the person needs to inhale more to get the desired intoxication. People who stop excessive use of inhalants may have mild withdrawal symptoms, including mood changes, difficulty sleeping, nausea, and loss of appetite. Because withdrawal symptoms, if present, are minimal, withdrawal is not included as a criterion. The disorder is considered severe if the person meets six or more criteria in one year.

Incidence

According to the National Survey on Drug Use and Health (NSDUH), in 2017, just over 9% of respondents ages 12 or over had used inhalants at some point in their lifetime. However, when respondents were asked about use in the last year, the numbers were lower: 0.6 % for all respondents ages 12 or over and 2.3% for respondents between the ages of 12 to 17. For inhalant use in the last month, the numbers were 0.2% for all respondents ages 12 or over and 0.6% for respondents between the ages of 12 and 17 (NIH NIDA 2018). In one study, peak use of inhalants occurred among young adolescents in the eighth grade (Johnston et al. 2018, 16). The data support the clinical impression that inhalant misusers begin at young ages and then stop quickly. Rates of misuse are higher in youngsters involved in the criminal justice system (Howard et al. 2011, 22). There is a wide range of estimates of how many adolescents who begin misuse become addicted, ranging from 4% to 47%, depending on the type of population studied (Howard et al. 2011, 22).

History

Inhalant use may go back to ancient Greece, where people made pilgrimages to the oracle of Delphi on Mount Parnassus to seek advice. A Greek priestess entered a trance-like state and, once in a sufficiently altered state of consciousness, prophesied or offered advice. Some have suggested that the priestess was under the influence of ethylene gases coming from fissures in the ground beneath the temple.

The next significant episodes in the history of inhalant abuse are to do with the anesthetic gases. In 1772, the English chemist Joseph Priestley discovered nitrous oxide by synthesizing it. Young English chemist Humphry Davy later noted its analgesic properties when experimenting with it. For the next 40 years, it was used in traveling medicine shows and carnivals for entertainment because of its intoxicant effects—it became known as laughing gas. American dentist Horace Wells was the first to use it as a dental anesthetic. In 1845, he tried to demonstrate its usefulness at the Massachusetts General Hospital (MGH), but the administration of the gas was flawed, and the patient yelled out in pain during the procedure. Despite this failed demonstration, nitrous oxide has turned out to be a useful anesthetic agent. Some have described mystical experiences with the gas (see Sidebar 5.1).

Known as sweet oil of vitriol, ether (or diethyl ether) was first synthesized in the Middle Ages by distilling ethanol and sulfuric acid, which leads to the dehydration of ethanol. Sixteenth-century Swiss alchemist and physician Paracelsus saw that it anesthetized chickens. (He also invented an early version of laudanum, the famous tincture of opium.)

On October 16, 1846, physician William Morton showed that, when inhaled, ether could be safely used as a general anesthetic. His

Sidebar 5.1 Mystical Consciousness

In the past, inhalants were often seen as benign sources of amusement, and now they are seen as harmful. But there is a third way of perceiving inhalants. Philosopher and psychologist William James inhaled nitrous oxide and described it as one of the most important experiences in his life. He wrote that it made him realize that there are modes of consciousness other than the ones that we usually experience. In *Varieties of Religious Experience*, he wrote:

> Nitrous oxide and ether, especially nitrous oxide, when sufficiently diluted with air, stimulate the mystical consciousness in an extraordinary degree. Depth beyond depth of truth seems revealed to the inhaler. This truth fades out, however, or escapes, at the moment of coming to; and if any words remain over in which it seemed to clothe itself, they prove to be the veriest nonsense. Nevertheless, the sense of a profound meaning having been there persists; and I know more than one person who is persuaded that in the nitrous oxide trance we have a genuine metaphysical revelation. (James 1958, 298)

Bibliography

James, William. *The Varieties of Religious Experience*. New York: Mentor Books, 1958.

demonstration at an MGH operating theater went more smoothly than did Wells's demonstration just a year earlier. October 16 is now known as Ether Day and the MGH theater as the Ether Dome.

In addition to its medical uses, ether has a long history of being used to amuse people. The "ether frolics" of the mid-19th century were parties, sometimes arranged by medical students, where people became intoxicated by sniffing ether. Ether was sometimes drunk in Ireland and in Eastern Europe when alcohol was unavailable; it proved to be as addictive as alcohol. Ether has nonmedical uses as well, as an industrial solvent and a starter fluid. It is highly flammable.

In 1831, three different people synthesized chloroform: Samuel Guthrie, Justus von Liebig, and Eugene Soubeiran. In 1842, English physician Robert Glover showed that it could anesthetize animals. In 1847, Scottish obstetrician James Simpson discovered that inhaling it led to unconsciousness in humans and that it could be used as an anesthetic agent. Unlike ether, chloroform is not flammable, but it can cause cardiac arrhythmias and liver damage.

A few people find the first effects of chloroform to be exhilarating. It can be misused and has on occasion led to addictions. For example, Glover became addicted to chloroform (Defalque and Wright 2004). Horace Wells, the American dentist responsible for introducing nitrous oxide to dentistry, became addicted to chloroform. While living alone in New York in the last few weeks of his life, he used chloroform heavily. He was arrested for the crime of throwing vitriol on prostitutes. He denied the charges but was imprisoned. While in prison, he put a silk handkerchief soaked in chloroform into his mouth. Then he cut his left femoral artery and bled to death (Fenster 2002, 184–185).

The first reported episode of gasoline sniffing seems to have happened in Warren, Pennsylvania, in the late 1940s. Reports of glue sniffing began to appear in 1959. How these two practices began and spread is not clear.

Development and Causes

Most inhalant misusers are young and may also be misusing other drugs. They often come from disadvantaged backgrounds. Adolescents who have difficulty at school or who have friends who misuse inhalants are also more likely to misuse these substances (Ridenour 2005; Nguyen, O'Brien, and Schapp 2016).

In some developed countries, inhalant abusers tend to be from rural or indigenous communities. In the developing world, inhalant abuse is often associated with children or young teenagers who live on the streets.

Up Close—In Society
Inhalant use disorder is often seen as a product of difficult socioeconomic circumstances. Teens who begin to misuse substances may live in communities where there is homelessness, poverty, exploitation of children, and limited opportunities for education. Some of these youth spend much of their time sniffing inhalants and may use other drugs as well. Adolescents who develop inhalant use disorder often develop other substance use disorders.

Case Study
Rosa is a 12-year-old girl living in a city in Central America. She was raped by her father when she was eight, expelled from her house, and has been living on the streets ever since. She went to school for two years while she lived at home but has not gone back since. She supports herself by begging in and around the city's main bus terminal. She spends much

time inhaling glue. Sometimes she soaks a rag in paint thinner, puts the rag on her mouth, and "huffs" or inhales the fumes. When she can, she also uses marijuana, beer, and cocaine. She looks thin and unwell and has a rash around her mouth. She knows that inhalants are not healthy, but she says that the fumes make her a little happier and keep hunger, cold, shame, and bad memories away. Sometimes she thinks about going to a shelter but has heard stories about physical and sexual abuse there. She is afraid of the police for the same reasons.

She has lost touch with her biological family and considers some of the other street children her family. She says of her parents, "They think that I'm no good because of all the sniffing. But I don't have anything else."

Up Close—At Work

Since most inhalant misusers are young teens, there is little in the literature about the effects of these substances at work. However, solvents are used in many occupations such as furniture finishing, dry cleaning, and mechanical and refrigeration system maintenance, and in industries such as textile and leather production. Exposure occurs either by inhalation or by cutaneous contact, typically from unintentional or accidental exposures.

Misuse at work may be rare, but these exposures point to the possible harms from recreational inhalant misuse. For example, the symptoms of a syndrome called "chronic solvent-induced encephalopathy" include long-lasting neuropathies and behavioral problems. Liver and kidney damage may also occur. Another name for this syndrome is "chronic painter's syndrome" because painters are often exposed to solvents. One study showed that women who were exposed to organic solvents as a result of their work in laboratories and factories gave birth to children with higher rates of malformations than did women without exposure to solvents (Khattak et al. 1999, 206). Benzene has been associated with leukemia, and benzene and toluene with brain damage.

Inhalant use disorder does occur among people who work in dentistry, presumably because of the availability of nitrous oxide.

Case Study

Dr. D is a 42-year-old dentist who is married with three children. He works in a group practice in the suburbs of a North American city. He enjoys his work but does not get along well with his colleagues and is sometimes reproached by them for not being more productive. At home, he argues often with his children and wife. One day, he is extracting a decayed filling from one of his more anxious patients. At her request, he administers nitrous oxide to help her tolerate the unpleasant procedure. The patient enjoys the effects of the gas and jokes, "I felt dreamy and relaxed. I wish that I could use that all the time." That evening, after his partners leave the office, Dr. D inhales some nitrous oxide and is relieved not to notice an effect. Nonetheless, he makes an excuse to stay late the next day and use it again. This time he notices a mild euphoria. He begins to stay late every night to use the nitrous oxide and to avoid the tension at home. He tells himself that this is safe, since he uses it for his patients. He is aware that nitrous oxide might interfere with vitamin B_{12} metabolism, so he takes vitamin B_{12} tablets.

His colleagues notice that something is different about him and that they are using up their nitrous oxide supplies faster than usual. Dr. D offers to take over the work of ordering the nitrous oxide to find out what the issues are. Eventually, his colleagues talk to him, airing their suspicions that he is misusing the gas. Dr. D denies it, saying, "Even if I am, so what? It's not illegal. You give it to your patients all the time." He comments on their use of alcohol.

The situation deteriorates, and Dr. D's colleagues eventually refer him to the state's dentist well-being committee.

Up Close–In Relationships
Adolescents who misuse inhalants may come from families where substance use is prevalent and parental supervision or involvement is minimal. Young teens who develop inhalant use disorder may have close relationships with other misusers and conflictual relationships with family members.

Case Study
Joe is a 13-year-old boy whose parents work long hours and drink heavily. Joe spends time with a group of boys who often skip school and sometimes get into trouble shoplifting. One evening Joe's parents notice a rash around his mouth and a chemical odor and ask him what he is doing. He says, "Nothing." Later, some of the parents of the other boys tell Joe's parents that all the boys have been sniffing felt pens and glue, and have been "huffing" computer cleaner for several months. Joe's parents talk to him and are astonished when he admits to this behavior and explains that he wanted to know what it felt like to sniff these substances. He says that it is not harmful, that all his friends do it, and that they would laugh at him if he did not. He tells his parents that he can stop whenever he wants to. He does not tell his parents that he and

another boy in the group have begun to smoke tobacco and marijuana and to steal alcohol from their parents.

Effects and Costs

Most inhalants are thought to achieve their effects by slowing down brain activity. They have been suspected of causing brain damage if used to excess.

Inhalants can lead to pulmonary toxicity, manifested by coughing, wheezing, and trouble breathing. They can also lead to vomiting, and then—if the person is not fully awake—to aspiration, which can lead to pneumonia or death. "Bagging," or using inhalants with a paper or plastic bag over the head, can lead to suffocation. (Nitrous oxide is always supplemented with oxygen when used for analgesia.)

Inhalants can cause an irregular heartbeat, or a cardiac arrhythmia. Animal studies have shown that the mechanism may be sensitization of the heart to input from adrenaline. If a person inhaling substances is suddenly frightened, the combination of adrenaline and a sensitized heart can cause the heart to beat irregularly. If the irregularity is extreme, the heart no longer can pump blood efficiently, leading to what is called "sudden sniffing death" (Shepherd 1989).

Glue sniffing has been associated with perioral dermatitis, or a rash around the mouth and nose, known colloquially as "glue sniffer's rash." Long-term inhalant misuse has been associated with bone-marrow suppression, liver toxicity, and irreversible brain damage. Nitrous oxide can lead to nerve damage or hematological problems through its inactivation of the vitamin cyanocobalamin, or B_{12}.

Pregnant or breastfeeding women risk harming their babies if they misuse inhalants.

The costs of inhalant use disorder are difficult to establish because it so often exists along with other conditions that have their own costs, such as the mistreatment of children.

Theory and Research

Research into inhalant use disorder is sparse perhaps because many substance misuse researchers prefer to study adults who are better able to give informed consent. Also, it is easier to generate specific findings if the subjects are misusing only one substance. Finally, many inhalant misusers live in impoverished or rural settings and have little exposure to urban clinical settings where research often takes place.

Scientists have developed animal models of inhalant use disorder to try to determine how inhalants work and where in the CNS they work. This work is complicated because of the heterogeneity of inhalants. The ability of the organic solvents to enter the brain so quickly is a factor in their toxicity.

Treatments

Can inhalant use disorder be prevented? To be effective, prevention should address the predisposing socioeconomic circumstances, but that is beyond the scope of this chapter. Prevention should also involve education of teens and families as to the harms of inhalants. Because so much inhalant misuse takes place in dysfunctional social systems, this is a difficult task.

Another approach is to reduce the supply of the inhalants. In some states, the sale of glue obviously intended for misuse is restricted. In isolated areas of Australia where gasoline sniffing is common among the indigenous population, the authorities have lowered the aromatic hydrocarbon content of the gasoline to reduce its psychoactive potential. Compulsory warning labels run the risk of making the products easier for adolescents to identify (if they are looking for intoxicants) (Baydala 2010, 446).

Another approach is harm reduction. For example, some experts have recommended that those who do misuse inhalants be taught how to reduce the possibility of asphyxiation: avoid putting plastic bags over their heads, avoid misusing in enclosed spaces, and always have a person nearby who is not inhaling (Howard et al. 2011, 27–28).

Little is known about treatment for inhalant addiction. There are no psychopharmacological remedies. Cognitive behavioral therapy (CBT), brief interventions, and motivational interviewing (MI) may be useful. Family therapy can be considered. Because those who misuse inhalants often have other problems, such as delinquent behavior or other substance misuse and may come from dysfunctional or multiproblem families, residential treatment programs are often suggested (Nguyen, O'Brien, and Schapp 2016).

Bibliography

American Psychiatric Association. *Diagnostic and Statistical Manual of Mental Disorders (DSM-5)*, 5th ed. Arlington, VA: American Psychiatric Association, 2013.

Baydala, Lola. "Inhalant Abuse." *Paediatr Child Health* 15, no. 7 (September 2010), 443–448.

Defalque, Ray J., and Amos J. Wright. "The Short, Tragic Life of Robert M. Glover." *Anaesthesia* 59, no. 4 (2004), 394–400. doi:10.1111/j.1365 -2044.2004.03671.x.

Fenster, J. M. *Ether Day: The Strange Tale of America's Greatest Medical Discovery and the Haunted Men Who Made It.* New York: Perennial, 2002.

Howard, Matthew O., Scott E. Bowen, Eric L. Garland, Brian E. Perron, and Michael G. Vaughn. "Inhalant Use and Inhalant Use Disorders in the United States." *Addict Sci Clin Pract* 6 (July 2011), 18–31.

James, William. *Varieties of Religious Experience.* New York: Mentor, 1958.

Johnston, Lloyd D., Richard A. Miech, Patrick O'Malley, Jerald G. Bachman, John E. Schulenberg, and Megan E. Patrick. "Monitoring the Future National Survey Results on Drug Use, 1975–2017: Overview, Key Findings on Adolescent Drug Use." Ann Arbor: Institute for Social Research, The University of Michigan, 2018. doi:10.3998/2027.42/148123.

Khattak, Sohail, Guiti K-Moghtader, Kristen McMartin, Maru Barrera, Debbie Kennedy, and Gideon Koren. "Pregnancy Outcome Following Gestational Exposure to Organic Solvents." *JAMA* 281, no. 12 (1999), 1106–1109. doi:10.1001/jama.281.12.1106.

Nguyen, Jacqueline, Casey O'Brien, and Salena Schapp. "Adolescent Inhalant Use Prevention, Assessment, and Treatment: A Literature Synthesis." *Int J Drug Policy* 31 (2016), 15–24. doi:10.1016/j. drugpo.2016.02.001.

NIH National Institute on Drug Abuse. *National Survey of Drug Use and Health: Trends in Prevalence of Various Drugs for Ages 12 or Older, Ages 12 to 17, Ages 18–25, and Ages 26 or Older; 2015–2017 (in percent).* 2018. Accessed July 29, 2019. https://www.drugabuse.gov /national-survey-drug-use-health.

Ridenour, Ty A. "Inhalants: Not to be Taken Lightly Anymore." *Curr Opin Psychiatry* 18, no. 3 (2005), 243–247. doi:10.1097/01. yco.0000165593.52811.cd.

Shepherd, R. T. "Mechanism of Sudden Death Associated with Volatile Substance Abuse." *Hum Toxicol* 8, no. 4 (1989), 287–291. doi:10.1177/096032718900800406.

Tagaq, Tanya. *Split Tooth.* New York: Viking, 2018.

CHAPTER 6

Opioids

Caroline A. Arout and Mehmet Sofuoglu

Opioids are the world's most helpful pain-relieving medications and some of the most addictive substances known. They include pain relievers available legally by prescription, such as oxycodone, hydrocodone, codeine, and morphine, and illegal drugs, such as heroin. People can take opioids by mouth, or inject, sniff, snort, or smoke the drugs. Some opioids are used as a transdermal patch or as lozenges or lollipops.

The United States is currently in the throes of an opioid crisis. For the last three decades, the availability and use of prescription and illegal opioids has increased along with rates of opioid use disorders (OUDs), overdoses, and deaths.

Symptoms, Diagnosis, and Incidence

Symptoms

Opioids reduce pain, but unlike other pain-relievers such as aspirin or acetaminophen, they also produce euphoria and reduce anxiety and stress. Some people begin to use opioids searching for the rush of intense pleasure and think that they can use the substances without necessarily becoming addicted to them. Over time, however, these good feelings decrease. Other people who use opioids to treat pain find that they are unable to stop taking them without going through a distressing withdrawal syndrome. In both cases, people continue to use opioids largely because of the misery or fear of withdrawal.

Diagnosis

The 2013 version of the American Psychiatric Association's *Diagnostic and Statistical Manual* (*DSM-5*) (American Psychiatric Association 2013) modified the way we view substance use disorders, from characterizing them by patterns of "abuse" and "dependence" to placing them on a spectrum of use. Use of opioids is problematic when it causes the following: using opioids in greater amounts or using opioids for longer stretches of time than the person had meant to; the inability to reduce opioid use despite trying to do so; having opioid misuse being the predominant activity in one's life; an almost desperate desire for opioids; the inability to complete tasks because of the effects of opioids or the time spent getting them; continuing to use opioids despite it leading to disputes with others; giving up other activities because using opioids takes preference; using opioids despite the risks of overdose; using opioids even though this worsens the person's health (for example, getting infections); the development of a tolerance (needing higher doses); and developing withdrawal symptoms (described later in this chapter) when not using opioids.

Anyone meeting 2 of the 11 criteria during the same 12-month period receives a diagnosis of OUD. A person with two or three symptoms has a mild OUD, someone with four or five symptoms a moderate OUD, and someone with six or more symptoms a severe OUD, known, to use a word that is falling out of favor, as an addiction. Perhaps the best-known symptom of OUD is the characteristic opioid withdrawal syndrome that users experience either upon abrupt cessation of opioid use or after receiving an opioid antagonist such as naloxone to treat an overdose.

Incidence

The 2015 National Survey on Drug Use and Health (NSDUH) surveyed prescription opioid use in 72,600 civilian, noninstitutionalized adults over the age of 18. Of the 51,200 that responded to the survey, 38% reported having used prescription opioids in the past year, and of these people, 13% misused them. Misuse and use disorders were disproportionately reported by those who were unemployed, uninsured, reported low income, and diagnosed with co-occurring mental health conditions. Sixty percent of those who reported misuse of prescription opioids reported nonprescription use of opioids as well, and 41% got them for free from friends or family for their most recent episode of misuse (Han et al. 2017).

In 2017, nearly 50,000 Americans died because of an overdose on prescription opioids, heroin, or fentanyl. (Fentanyl is a potent synthetic opioid that comes in a variety of forms and is prescribed for severe or chronic pain. But illicit fentanyl is now widely available and, because it is so strong, is associated with many overdose deaths.) About 1.7 million people in the United States had substance use disorders related to prescription opioid pain relievers, and 652,000 suffered from a heroin use disorder. These groups of people overlap (National Institute of Drug Abuse 2019). Opioid use tends to be more problematic in rural areas, where there is less access to preventative addiction education and substance use treatment (Leonardson et al. 2014).

History

Recreational opioid use began as early as 3000 BCE in Egypt and Asia. The Sumerians were among the first to farm poppies, naming them the *hul gil*, or "plant of joy." Around 1500 BCE, descriptions of the medicinal use of opium appeared. Because potency varied, physicians were hesitant at first to use it. But by the 13th century CE, the use of opium was widespread across Europe, and manuscripts describing abuse and addiction began to appear. Despite growing evidence of dangerous side effects, efforts to ban opium were unsuccessful.

Around 1806, German pharmacist Friedrich Sertürner isolated the active ingredient in opium from the dried juice of the unripe seedpods of the poppy plant and named it "morphium" after the god of dreams, Morpheus. By the 1850s, physicians were using morphine intravenously for surgical procedures and the management of pain. However, with increasing use came reports of side effects, such as addiction, respiratory depression, and analgesic tolerance. In the unsuccessful search for a safer alternative pain medication, it became common to use other opioids, though each of these substances turned out to be addictive. For example, in 1898, the Bayer pharmaceutical company introduced heroin as a less addictive alternative to morphine. After a few years, the addictive properties of heroin became obvious. While other medications such as aspirin, acetaminophen, and gabapentin have been developed to treat pain, opioids are still considered one of the most effective classes of medications for treatment of *acute* pain (see Sidebar 6.1 for an explanation of the nomenclature).

Sidebar 6.1 Opiate or Opioid?

Though the terms *opiate* and *opioid* are often used interchangeably, they have slightly different definitions. *Opiate* refers to the natural substances derived from the poppy plant (*Papaver somniferum*). Opium is the dried milky latex collected from the immature seedpods of this plant and contains natural substances such as morphine and codeine. *Opioid* refers to these substances *and* to synthetic (man-made) and semi-synthetic forms of opium. Synthetic opioids are manufactured in laboratories and include drugs such as fentanyl and methadone. Semi-synthetic opioids are made by modifying natural opiates and include such drugs as heroin and oxycodone. The term *opioid* is most often used, since it includes all these substances. Opioids are ligands, which are substances that bind to receptors. A receptor is a protein in the membrane of a cell that responds to specific molecules from outside the cell. Because of their binding to opioid receptors, opioids relieve pain, make people feel relaxed, and are addicting.

Discovery of the Opioid Receptors

In the 1940s, scientists began using agonists and antagonists in an effort to understand how drugs work at receptors in the nervous system. Agonists are compounds that are structurally nearly identical to the primary ligand, or substance that binds to the receptor of interest. The receptor is the cell membrane protein that is poised to set a series of events into action when the ligand binds to it. Agonists bind to the receptor and have effects like those of the primary ligand. Morphine is an example of an opioid agonist; it binds to opioid receptors to produce euphoria and analgesia. Antagonists, in contrast, are compounds that are also structurally similar to a receptor's natural ligand but bind to the receptor *without* activating it and by *blocking* the spot for an agonist to bind and activate the receptor. An antagonist works like a Canadian quarter in an American slot machine. It fits into the slot for a quarter, but does not allow the key to be turned. Naloxone is an opioid antagonist and blocks the effects of morphine. Because of these actions, naloxone can be lifesaving. It also induces withdrawal.

Some compounds have opioid-like effects, but simultaneously interrupt the effects of other opioids. For example, the mixed agonist–antagonist nalorphine blocks the effects of morphine while also having its own analgesic effect.

In 1973, by using antagonists and agonists, three separate groups of investigators independently discovered the mu-opioid receptor (Pert and Snyder 1973; Simon 1973; Terenius 1973). Two years later, endorphins—the natural, or endogenous, ligands for opioid receptors—were found. Endorphins bind to the opioid receptors and serve as the body's natural pain reliever. By the early 1980s, four classes of endogenous chemicals that bind to opioid receptors had been described: endorphins, enkephalins, dynorphins, and prepronociceptin. These molecules are not as potent as exogenous opioids but do exert noticeable effects. For example, a "runner's high" is due to the release of endorphins.

Studies of the neurophysiological and behavioral effects of the opioids led to the discovery of several opioid receptor subtypes. Subsequently, three different receptors were named after the opioid that was discovered to bind to each one: mu for morphine, kappa for ketocyclazocine, and delta for deltorphins and enkephalins. Later, a fourth "opioid-like" receptor was found and named ORL_1, or the nociception/orphanin FQ (N/OFQ) receptor (Mollereau et al. 1996). Most opioids that are clinically used or abused are pure mu-opioid receptor agonists.

Regulatory History of Opioids

Prior to the 20th century, opioids were regulated in the United States primarily at the city or state level. Around this time, opium was the main opioid, and "opium dens" were quite popular, particularly in China and Southeast Asia. Opium dens were establishments where people could purchase and smoke opium and buy related paraphernalia. During the California Gold Rush (1848–1855), many Chinese immigrants came to the United States and some brought opium, and opium dens, with them. (The history of opium in China involves British imperialism and exploitation centered on a trade triangle of opium from India to China, tea and Chinese goods from China to England, and textiles and machinery from England to India, which led to the Opium Wars.) These dens were initially frequented only by the Chinese who introduced them, but eventually others used them also. In 1875, the San Francisco Opium Den Ordinance made it a misdemeanor to own or go to opium dens, because the dens were associated (perhaps inaccurately) with crime and addiction. This ordinance was one of the first attempts to regulate opium and set a precedent as the nation's first anti-drug law. Over the following two decades, several states enacted laws banning the use of opioids without a prescription. In 1890, the federal government began levying taxes on morphine and opium, initiating its role in the regulation of opioids.

In the 1800s, drugs containing alcohol, morphine, opium, and cannabis did not have to be labeled as such. Consequently, many seemingly innocent and popular household remedies contained opioids, perhaps the best known being soothing syrups for babies. Some cures marketed for opioid addiction included opioids, and in most of these cases, the consumer did not know that these substances contained opioids. In 1906, Congress passed the Pure Food and Drug Act, outlawing the manufacture, sale, or transportation of adulterated or poisonous food or mislabeled drugs. Due to its focus on consumer protection, this act is considered by many to mark the unofficial beginning of the Food and Drug Administration (FDA).

Opioids themselves were not outlawed and were used by all social classes, the difference being the method of ascertainment and opioid of choice. Physicians prescribed morphine to treat middle-class women with gynecological ailments, such as menstrual cramps or pregnancy-related complications. Lower-class men smoked opium or snorted heroin they bought on the streets. In 1914, the Harrison Narcotics Tax Act was passed, requiring all those importing, exporting, manufacturing, and distributing opium products and cocaine to register with the federal government and pay taxes on their products. This act did not apply to prescribing physicians, even though overprescription was blamed for the high rates of opioid use. However, physicians were not allowed to prescribe opioid maintenance to treat addiction (not then considered an illness), which meant those who were addicted to opioids were cut off from a legal prescription supply. Because physicians were no longer able to prescribe opioids for addicts, and they were no longer as easy to obtain legally, there was an increase in the illicit use of opioids, such as heroin, and a subsequent rise in drug-related crime. The U.S. Drug Addiction Treatment Act of 2000 now allows the prescription of opioids for maintenance to treat addiction with a waiver. (See Treatment.)

Development and Causes

The cause of the current OUD epidemic, unlike other substance use disorders, is best discussed within the context of prescribing practices. The usual precipitating and predisposing factors are much as described in other chapters—family history of substance use, difficult childhood, difficulty regulating emotion, and misuse of other substances—but these factors are now overshadowed by the events of the last three decades. Pain and prescription opioids lead to OUDs. The current opioid crisis dates back to the 1990s with the beginning of what is now seen as the overprescription of opioid medications, caused by physicians being encouraged to address what they were told was the inadequate treatment of pain. Although pain is subjective, it became the fifth *vital sign*. The four original vital signs, all of which can be objectively measured, are temperature, respiratory rate, pulse, and blood pressure. In 2001, the use of pain as a vital sign became a benchmark used to evaluate the performance of health-care professionals; this practice has since been ended. Pharmaceutical companies aggressively marketed the newly formulated opioids, which were not supposed to be addicting when used for pain. But it turns out that even when prescribed to treat pain, the new opioids were addicting for some people.

The result of this increased attention to pain has been an increase in the number of opioid prescriptions, overdoses, and deaths in the United States. In a population of over 76,000 Medicaid patients under the age of 65, the majority of opioid-related fatalities occurred in those with a history of chronic noncancer pain, many of whom were prescribed opioids (Olfson et al 2018). Opioid prescribing rates are still quite high, despite reports questioning the efficacy of long-term use for chronic pain and evidence supporting a dose-dependent risk in misuse, addiction, overdose, and death (Reuben et al. 2015; Sullivan and Howe 2013).

One study showed that 90% of patients presenting to a pain management center were already on an opioid regimen (Manchikanti et al. 2004), suggesting inadequate pain relief, addiction, or both. As many as 35% of patients with chronic pain may also have a comorbid OUD (Boscarino et al. 2011). From the viewpoint of the patient with OUD, one study found that about 40% of patients who were diagnosed with OUD had a chronic pain diagnosis that preceded their opioid use (Hser et al. 2017).

Cicero et al. (2014) compared a typical opioid misuser in the 1960s to a typical misuser in the early 2000s. The earlier misusers were more likely to be urban male teenagers who initiated their use with heroin. A current opioid misuser has a relatively equal chance of being a man or a woman, is more likely to be white, from a less urban area, and to be over 20 years old. The opioid misuser of 2019 is more likely to have begun with a prescription opioid and then transitioned to heroin after no longer receiving opioids from a physician.

Once developed, OUD can be lifelong. For example, 600 criminal offenders addicted to heroin were enrolled in a compulsory drug treatment program, the California Civil Addict Program, between 1962 and 1964 and followed for over 33 years. At the end of the study, 21% were confirmed by positive urine toxicology to still be using heroin, 14% were back in prison, and another 10% refused the drug test. Many of the subjects were using tobacco, alcohol, marijuana, and stimulants. Though the mean age of those interviewed was only 57.4 years old, nearly 50% of the sample had died (Hser et al. 2001).

Up Close—In Society
Even if people who misuse opioids begin because of prescription medications, opioid misuse and addiction are still stigmatized.

Case Study
Jo is a 28-year-old woman in early remission from an opioid use disorder. At the age of 20, she married and had a son. Her husband became abusive and often beat her, once breaking her arm. She was prescribed 21 days of oxycodone for this injury. A day after she stopped taking the medication, she developed anxiety, diarrhea, tremors, sweating, and abdominal pain. She borrowed some oxycodone from a friend and then began to buy pills on the street. Her arm healed, but she had developed an addiction. Her husband discovered that she was buying drugs and left her, saying that he would not live with an addict. Jo was unable to pay the rent and became homeless. Eventually, Jo got help for her OUD. She was treated with naltrexone by mouth and then monthly naltrexone injections. She was approved for government assistance to help her get a home for her and her son but still struggled to find a place to live. The problem was finding a landlord who accepted her benefits—even though her reason for receiving benefits was not disclosed, many landlords are aware that most people receiving such benefits are in drug recovery programs.

Up Close—At Work
Opioid addiction complicates employment and can be dangerous if the person operates heavy equipment or works with children, patients, the elderly, or other vulnerable populations. In the 1990 Americans with Disabilities Act (ADA), addiction is covered as a disability. The ADA covers people who are properly using prescribed medications for medical conditions, but it does not protect people who misuse drugs, whether they be licit or illicit opioids.

The 2010 Affordable Care Act (ACA) requires health insurance plans to cover substance use disorder treatment, a benefit that had previously been hard to come by for those seeking treatment. If this requirement is changed in the future, those receiving addiction treatment may encounter increasing hurdles to this benefit.

Managing a normal life as an employee with an OUD is not easy. One of the most difficult struggles is maintaining a job during an active addiction, as drug-seeking and drug-taking often consume a person's day (one of the criteria of the disorder). Once a person decides to seek treatment for opioid use disorder, that very treatment may prove difficult while trying to maintain a job due to side effects of the medication, time constraints with dosing schedules (see Treatments), and explaining positive drug tests to one's employer.

Case Study

Scott is a 34-year-old man who tore his left meniscus while playing basketball. He needed surgery to repair the injury, and as part of the postoperative pain management, the surgeon sent Scott home with a one-time prescription of twenty 5-mg oxycodone tablets to last a week, with instructions to take one tablet every six hours as needed for the pain. After a few days, Scott began to feel that one tablet did not control his pain, and he began taking two tablets, and then he began to reduce the time between doses. He soon ran out of his oxycodone, but the surgeon would not refill his prescription, telling him to try over-the-counter pain relievers. Scott started buying hydrocodone pills off the street and progressed to snorting heroin and then using it intravenously.

He said: "I was terrified to use needles. But the heroin was so much cheaper than the pills, and using it by needle—shooting it up—is better and cheaper than snorting it. I was thinking about nothing but heroin. That was all I cared about. And a couple of times I overdosed. Each time it was an accident. Maybe I got heroin with fentanyl. Anyway, each time someone found me. They called 911 and gave me a Narcan spray both times. I was lucky. And then I went to find some more heroin."

After a year, he decided to seek treatment. He found a clinic and was started on buprenorphine maintenance. He relapsed twice, selling the buprenorphine on the street and using heroin again. But now he has been "clean" for a year. He says that the buprenorphine curbs his cravings for opioids, and he has a month-long prescription for sublingual films, so his treatment does not interfere with his job. He goes to Narcotics Anonymous (NA) and sees a counselor every week.

Up Close—In Relationships

Addiction can be part of relationships, friendships, and "good times" people have together while using. People often use with another person and will sometimes say that one of the factors in continuing use of a drug was a relationship forged by that very drug. It is difficult to stop misusing substances in the midst of misuse by others.

If two people in a relationship have an OUD, perhaps only one person may be ready to seek treatment. If the other person feels obligated to seek treatment based on his or her relationship, treatment is less likely to succeed. If someone is hiding an active addiction from a partner, the situation can become fraught. Anger and disappointment may result. Coping with an addiction requires substantial social support, and dishonesty with others complicates and hinders progress.

Case Study

John and I hit it off from our very first date. He was a funny guy who seemed smart and kind. But about five months into dating, he accidentally left his phone at my house one morning. For about an hour, text messages kept coming through from a name I didn't recognize. Thinking it may be an emergency, I checked the phone; the whole conversation was about "blues" and how badly they needed them. I asked him about the texts, and he admitted to struggles with oxycodone over the previous months. This was extremely hard for me to accept. He had been hiding it from me.

About two weeks later, he called me from an inpatient detoxification unit. He had been using heroin and had decided to get "clean." I couldn't believe it—he had been lying to me even more than I knew. And he was a good liar. I thought that I would have known for sure if my boyfriend was using heroin. After detox, he went into an inpatient rehabilitation facility. I don't know why, but I visited him once a week, and he wrote me letters every day. He moved into a sober living facility for six months. I started attending meetings with him, which helped me understand the reasons why people suffering from addiction need social support. I was scared about the drugs. I was hurt from all the deceptions, but gradually I saw that wasn't really him. I knew about all his good qualities, and they just became even clearer once he gave up the drugs.

Fast-forward six years: a marriage and a puppy. Being the partner of a person with an OUD isn't an easy choice to make. We have been fortunate that he has maintained his sobriety. We don't brush it under the rug, and we don't pretend it didn't happen. The lying has stopped. We are open about his past, his slip-ups, and his triggers. You are never "cured" of addiction; you just learn to cope. John is thinking about become a drug counselor. I hope he does—he could help others.

Effects and Costs

Pain Relief

For centuries, opioids have been a front-line and effective treatment for moderate to severe *acute* pain. They are used to control intraoperative pain and in postoperative pain management regimes. However, the rates of chronic pain diagnoses have surged over recent decades, with more than 25 million adults diagnosed with chronic pain each year (Reuben et al. 2015). Opioids have become a mainstay for the treatment of chronic pain, even though there is little to no evidence that they are effective for pain that persists for more than three months (i.e., chronic pain) (Chou et al. 2015). A study of patients being treated with opioids for noncancer conditions from 2000 to 2005 found that patients receiving high doses of opioids for more than 90 days were at higher risk for developing an OUD than those who received lower doses or a shorter course of opioids (Edlund et al. 2014). Duration and dose of opioid therapy predict the development of OUD.

Side Effects

As well as relieving pain and anxiety, opioids can cause side effects such as sedation, constipation, cardiac arrhythmia, sexual dysfunction, itchiness, and hyperthermia. People who sniff or snort heroin can damage the tissue inside the nose.

The most serious side effect of opioids is their effect on breathing. When opioids bind to the mu-opioid receptors, they suppress the brain activity that controls breathing, and they also depress the brain's ability to respond to increasing levels of carbon dioxide. Thus, they depress respiration, causing death in opioid overdoses. (As is described in the sedative hypnotic chapter, benzodiazepines are implicated in about a third of opioid overdoses.)

Another complication of opioid misuse, not directly related to the drug, is damage caused by injections. People who inject the substance and share needles with others are at risk for getting HIV, hepatitis B and/or C, or life-threatening heart infections. Sometimes they can develop abscesses on their skin. Intravenous opioid users may develop "track marks," which can indicate scarred veins that may not heal.

Opioids and Pregnancy

The number of women who use opioids during pregnancy is increasing. They may be using opioids prescribed for pain or may be undergoing treatment for OUD and thus be taking an agonist. However, they also may be misusing prescription opioids or illegal opioids. Some women who are using opioids illicitly may also have a chaotic lifestyle and be using other substances, and therefore be less likely than nonsubstance misusing women to get proper antenatal care, increasing the risk of harm to the fetus.

A pregnant woman with an OUD will need medical care. Withdrawal from opioids during pregnancy can be difficult for both mother and baby. On the other hand, if a woman uses opioids throughout her pregnancy, she risks giving birth to a baby who develops neonatal abstinence syndrome (NAS). A baby with NAS is at risk for low birth weight, seizures, and breathing difficulties and usually will have to stay in the hospital, perhaps in a neonatal intensive care unit, for a prolonged period. Some states will notify child-care agencies if a baby is diagnosed with NAS even if this is due to prescribed methadone or buprenorphine/naloxone.

Dependence, Tolerance, and Withdrawal

Following exposure to opioids for weeks or months, individuals develop physical dependence, the key elements of which are *tolerance* and *withdrawal*. Tolerance is a need to take higher doses of a substance to experience pain relief or euphoria. Tolerance *selectively* and *differentially* develops to opioid effects quite quickly—this means that higher doses are needed to produce a positive *subjective* effect (i.e., the "high") or alleviate withdrawal symptoms. However, there may be less tolerance for the respiratory depressing effects of opioids, resulting in overdose risk if the person increases their opioid usage.

In physically dependent individuals, abstinence from opioids (or significant reduction in opioid intake) leads to symptoms of opioid withdrawal, including both physical (e.g., nasal discharge, tears from eyes, fever, abdominal pain, vomiting, diarrhea, enlarged pupils, restlessness, goose bumps, pain, and chills) and affective (e.g., dysphoria, anxiety, irritability, and craving) symptoms. The colloquial term for restlessness is "kicking the habit" and for goose bumps is "cold turkey." Although very uncomfortable, opioid withdrawal syndrome is not life-threatening and subsides within one to two weeks. The higher the dose, the worse the withdrawal.

Costs

Prescription opioid misuse cost the United States about $78.5 billion in 2013 (Florence, Luo, Xu, and Zhao 2016). About a third of these costs were due to excess health costs, such as emergency-room visits, ambulance costs, hospitalizations, substance use treatment, education, and medications used during overdose and treatment, such as naloxone, buprenorphine, and methadone. Lost productivity and costs associated with the criminal justice system accounted for most of the rest of the costs. If the costs of nonprescription opioid misuse were included, the costs would be even higher.

Theory and Research

The primary reason opioids are addictive is their reinforcing and euphoric subjective effects, attributed to increased dopamine levels in the mesolimbic dopamine, or "reward," pathway. Dopamine is a neurotransmitter associated with reward, anticipation, and learning as well as pleasure, released in response to drugs or natural rewards, such as food. The reward pathway originates from the ventral tegmental area (VTA) of the midbrain and projects to several limbic and cortical areas, including the nucleus accumbens, amygdala, and prefrontal cortex. Mu-opioid receptors are located on GABAergic cells in the VTA, which inhibit VTA dopamine neurons. Opioids act at the mu receptors to switch off the GABAergic cells, thus leading to increased dopamine release in the nucleus accumbens (Klitenick, DeWitte, and Kalivas 1992). Mu-opioid receptors are the main target for typically misused opioid drugs (e.g., morphine, heroin, oxycodone) as well as endogenous opioids like endorphins.

Much of the current research is focused on finding solutions to the opioid crisis, with various states experimenting with different solutions. Some states have controlled long-term prescriptions of opioids. For example, in 2018, New Jersey passed a law prohibiting the prescription of more than a five-day regime of opioids at a time. Another approach is to establish prescription-monitoring programs that allow physicians to view all the dispensed controlled substances an individual has received from other providers. Rates of opioid prescriptions are now decreasing, with 214 million prescriptions dispensed in 2016, compared to 255 million prescriptions in 2012 (Schuchat, Houry, and Guy 2017).

There are a range of consequences to these changes. Patients who feel that they need opioids to control their chronic pain and do not misuse them are resentful that they are being made to feel like "addicts." Patients in severe acute pain may not be treated adequately if the treating prescriber is concerned about the possibility of misuse. Finally, the decreasing rate of opioid prescriptions may drive users more quickly toward using nonprescribed opioids, such as heroin and illicit fentanyl. And indeed, there may be increased use of the high-potency synthetic opioid fentanyl in response to increasingly limited access to prescription opioids, and the desire for a stronger high than what heroin offers. Fentanyl is 30 to 50 times more potent than heroin. Many batches of heroin have been found to be tainted by illicitly manufactured fentanyl from China, leading to accidental fatal overdoses. About half of the opioid overdose deaths in 10 states between July and December 2016 were thought to involve fentanyl or fentanyl analogues (O'Donnell et al. 2017). (Fentanyl analogues are drugs that were developed to imitate fentanyl; some are legal but most are not. They may not be detected by some drug tests and are often much stronger than fentanyl.)

Another phenomenon that is receiving increasing attention and could be playing a major role in the development and maintenance of OUDs is a state known as opioid-induced hyperalgesia (OIH). OIH is a paradoxical state of increased pain sensitivity to normally innocuous stimuli, found to occur in animals (Arout et al. 2015a; Waxman et al. 2009) and humans receiving short- or long-term doses of opioids (Chu, Clark, and Angst 2006; Compton, Athanasos, and Elashoff 2003; Compton et al. 2012; Compton, Charuvastra, and Ling 2001). OIH is typically evident following administration of moderate to high doses of opioids and is often misinterpreted as analgesic tolerance when in fact it is the opioid itself that is potentially making the patient's pain worse. With tolerance, increasing the dose of opioid relieves the pain, but with OIH, increasing the dose increases the pain. Researchers are currently investigating the potential underlying mechanisms of OIH, to identify medications to be used alongside opioids to optimize pain management (Arout et al. 2015b).

Another variable is whether a person uses pills or administers the drug intravenously. As of 2019, prescription pills are sometimes more expensive and difficult to obtain than illicit drugs. Using heroin or fentanyl intravenously may be the cheapest and most dangerous way to misuse opioids, since the user has no way of knowing the purity or the composition of the substances.

Treatments

Once a person with an OUD decides to seek treatment, the person needs to stop taking opioids. (Reduction of the dose is rarely successful.) Withdrawal from opioids is difficult, and if the opioids were used to treat pain, that pain may worsen during withdrawal, regardless of whether the opioid use was short term or long term (Angst et al. 2003; Rieb et al. 2018).

A person who withdraws from opioids intentionally, often with help from others, is said to be going through *detoxification*, or as it is commonly called, "detox." Sometimes detoxification is done under medical supervision using a regime of low-dose opioids, such as buprenorphine and methadone, as well as adjunctive medications to relieve the withdrawal symptoms. Detox may take place in an inpatient program, where the person will be offered a variety of treatments, such as one-on-one cognitive behavioral or supportive therapy, group therapy, and pharmacological treatments (discussed later in this chapter). Following detox, people sometimes enter an inpatient rehabilitation facility for a period of several weeks or even months. Longer detox programs are associated with better outcomes.

People often use other drugs in combination with opioids, so it is important to evaluate what other drugs or medications the person may have been taking, so that other potential withdrawal symptoms and dangers can be addressed (Kristensen et al. 2006).

The individual should be evaluated for comorbid medical and psychiatric conditions such as infections, depression, and anxiety disorders.

Immediately following detoxification, the person may still crave opioids and is at a high risk for relapse. If a person relapses using the same dose he or she was using before detox, the result can be a fatal overdose because of decreased tolerance to the opioid's depressant effects on respiration.

Ongoing therapy and support groups like NA are helpful. NA is a free, peer-support, community-based group that is run by people who have struggled with OUD. This organization is like Alcoholics Anonymous. NA follows the 12-step program and encourages frequent attendance at group support meetings where those struggling with substance use can share their experiences with each other.

Pharmacological Treatment Options

Those who choose to detox from opioids but not go on to take medications designed to treat OUD often relapse. In one study of outcomes after a short-term inpatient stay, over 60% of patients treated without medication relapsed within one month. Maintenance medication reduced this rate. The authors suggest that detox should always be followed by medication-assisted treatment (MAT) (Nunes et al. 2018). Options include methadone, buprenorphine/naloxone, and naltrexone. A great deal of support is also needed.

Methadone is a Schedule II drug, a mu-opioid receptor agonist, and can only be dispensed by a specialized methadone clinic for opioid use disorder treatment purposes, which a patient typically must visit daily for the first three months. Then the patients may be given a supply to take home if that seems safe. Methadone works well as maintenance medication, because its half-life is 18–24 hours and can be taken once a day, so the person does not have to be preoccupied with when he or she can next take the drug. Its onset of action is slow and it rarely leads to euphoria.

Buprenorphine/naloxone is a Schedule III drug and so can be prescribed by any physician, physician assistant, or nurse practitioner—with certain restrictions. It is a combination of an opioid receptor partial agonist (buprenorphine) and an antagonist (naloxone). The buprenorphine binds to opioid receptors but does not fully activate them, thus producing only minimal subjective effects. The activation is enough to relieve withdrawal symptoms and to control cravings. The binding is so strong that it blocks other opioids from binding. The naloxone is an opioid receptor antagonist that is not absorbed when taken in sublingual form, but if a person injects buprenorphine/naloxone, trying to get "high," the naloxone will be absorbed and block the effects of any opioid agonists. Buprenorphine/naloxone can be started in a person who is in mild-to-moderate withdrawal; it is typically given in weekly to monthly prescriptions, depending on the provider's protocol and the progress of the patient. One challenge with buprenorphine/naloxone is that prescribers must go through eight hours of training and obtain a "waiver" to prescribe it, and they are only permitted to treat a certain number of patients at a time. The waiver refers to an exception in the Drug Addiction Treatment Act of 2000 that will allow prescription of the drug. Some prescribers are reluctant to get this waiver, fearing that they will not be able to manage what they perceive as a difficult task.

Both methadone and buprenorphine/naloxone do have some subjective effects and can be misused. While physicians will usually try buprenorphine/naloxone first, if the person still craves opioids, the prescriber may then try methadone because of its higher potency. Some patients will switch from methadone to buprenorphine/naloxone because of the greater convenience of buprenorphine/naloxone and the smaller likelihood of experiencing a "high" from it. These problems do not arise when naltrexone is used. Naltrexone, also used to treat alcohol use disorders, is an opioid antagonist. Patients on naltrexone do not experience positive subjective effects from opioids and have fewer cravings. Naltrexone can be given orally or as a monthly injection. A person must go through withdrawal before beginning naltrexone treatment because the medication will precipitate withdrawal if given to a person with opioids in his or her system. Naltrexone can be prescribed by any prescriber and, unlike methadone and buprenorphine/naloxone, is not associated with withdrawal, diversion, or misuse. Success rates are similar when buprenorphine/naloxone and monthly injections of naltrexone are compared, although it is more difficult to start naltrexone (Lee et al. 2018).

MAT is a controversial treatment option, as many think that opioid maintenance with methadone or buprenorphine/naloxone is replacing an addiction to drugs like heroin and fentanyl with an addiction to a prescribed opioid medication for an indefinite period of time. While naltrexone is not addictive, it still is a medication that should be taken long-term. Nevertheless, MAT is quite successful in reducing illicit opioid use and in improving overall treatment retention; addiction experts recommend it.

Bibliography

American Psychiatric Association. *Diagnostic and Statistical Manual of Mental Disorders (DSM-5)*, 5th ed. Arlington, VA: American Psychiatric Association, 2013.

Angst, Martin S., Wolfgang Koppert, Ilka Pahl, David J. Clark, and Martin Schmelz. "Short-Term Infusion of the μ-opioid Agonist Remifentanil in Humans Causes Hyperalgesia during Withdrawal." *Pain* 106, no. 1 (2003), 49–57. doi:10.1016/s0304-3959(03)00276-8.

Arout, Caroline A., Megan Caldwell, Grace Rossi, and Benjamin Kest. "Spinal and Supraspinal N-methyl-d-aspartate and Melanocortin-1 Receptors Contribute to a Qualitative Sex Difference in Morphine-Induced Hyperalgesia." *Physiol Behav* 147 (2015a), 364–372. doi:10.1016/j.physbeh.2015.05.006.

Arout, Caroline A., Ellen Edens, Ismene L. Petrakis, and Mehmet Sofuoglu. "Targeting Opioid-Induced Hyperalgesia in Clinical Treatment: Neurobiological Considerations." *CNS Drugs* 29, no. 6 (2015b), 465–486. doi:10.1007/s40263-015-0255-x.

Boscarino, Joseph A., Margaret R. Rukstalis, Stuart N. Hoffman, John J. Han, Porat M. Erlich, Stephen Ross, Glenn S. Gerhard, and Walter F. Stewart. "Prevalence of Prescription Opioid-Use Disorder Among Chronic Pain Patients: Comparison of the DSM-5 vs. DSM-4 Diagnostic Criteria." *J Addict Dis* 30, no. 3 (2011), 185–194. doi:10.1080/10550887.2011.581961.

Chou, Roger, Rick Deyo, Beth Devine, Ryan Hansen, Sean Sullivan, Jeffrey G. Jarvik, Ian Blazina, Tracy Dana, Christina Bougatsos, and Judy Turner. "The Effectiveness and Risks of Long-Term Opioid Treatment of Chronic Pain." *Ann Intern Med* 162, no. 4 (February 2015), 276–286. doi:10.23970/ahrqepcerta218.

Chu, L., D. Clark, and M. Angst. "Opioid Tolerance and Hyperalgesia in Chronic Pain Patients After One Month of Oral Morphine Therapy: A Preliminary Prospective Study." *J Pain* 7, no. 1 (2006), 43–48. doi:10.1016/j.jpain.2005.08.001.

Cicero, Theodore J., Matthew S. Ellis, Hilary L. Surratt, and Steven P. Kurtz. "The Changing Face of Heroin Use in the United States." *JAMA Psychiatry* 71, no. 7 (2014), 821–826. doi:10.1001/jamapsychiatry.2014.366.

Compton, Peggy, Peter Athanasos, and David Elashoff. "Withdrawal Hyperalgesia after Acute Opioid Physical Dependence in Nonaddicted Humans: A Preliminary Study." *J Pain* 4, no. 9 (2003), 511–519. doi:10.1016/j.jpain.2003.08.003.

Compton, Peggy, Catherine P. Canamar, Maureen Hillhouse, and Walter Ling. "Hyperalgesia in Heroin Dependent Patients and the Effects of Opioid Substitution Therapy." *J Pain* 13, no. 4 (2012), 401–409. doi:10.1016/j.jpain.2012.01.001.

Compton, Peggy, V. C. Charuvastra, and Walter Ling. "Pain Intolerance in Opioid-Maintained Former Opiate Addicts: Effect of Long-Acting Maintenance Agent." *Drug Alcohol Depend* 63, no. 2 (2001), 139–146. doi:10.1016/s0376-8716(00)00200-3.

Edlund, Mark J., Bradley C. Martin, Joan E. Russo, Andrea Devries, Jennifer B. Braden, and Mark D. Sullivan. "The Role of Opioid Prescription in Incident Opioid Abuse and Dependence among Individuals with Chronic Non-Cancer Pain." *Clin J Pain* 30, no. 7 (July 2014), 557–564. doi:10.1097/ajp.0000000000000021.

Florence, Curtis S., Feijun Luo, Likang Xu, and Chao Zhou. "The Economic Burden of Prescription Opioid Overdose, Abuse, and Dependence in the United States, 2013." *Med Care* 54, no. 10 (2016), 901–906. doi:10.1097/MLR.0000000000000625.

Han, Beth, Wilson M. Compton, Carlos Blanco, Elizabeth Crane, Jinhee Lee, and Christopher M. Jones. "Prescription Opioid Use, Misuse, and Use Disorders in U.S. Adults." *Ann Intern Med* 167, no. 5 (2017), 293–301. doi:10.7326/M17-0865.

Hser, Yih-Ing, Valerie Hoffman, Christine E. Grella, and M. D. Anglin. "A 33-Year Follow-up of Narcotics Addicts." *Arch Gen Psychiatry* 58, no. 5 (2001), 503–508. doi:10.1001/archpsyc.58.5.503.

Hser, Yih-Ing, Larissa J. Mooney, Andrew J. Saxon, Karen Miotto, Douglas S. Bell, and David Huang. "Chronic Pain among Patients with Opioid Use Disorder: Results from Electronic Health Records Data." *J Subst Abuse Treat* 77 (2017), 26–30. doi:10.1016/j.jsat.2017.03.006.

Klitenick, Mark A., Paula S. DeWitte, and Peter W. Kalivas. "Regulation of Somatodendritic Dopamine Release in the Ventral Tegmental Area by Opioids and GABA: An In Vivo Microdialysis Study." *J Neurosci* 12, no. 7 (1992), 2623–2632. doi:10.1523/jneurosci.12-07-02623.1992.

Kristensen, Øistein, Terje Lølandsmo, Åse Isaksen, John-Kåre Vederhus, and Thomas Clausen. "Treatment of Polydrug-Using Opiate Dependents during Withdrawal: Towards a Standardisation of Treatment." *BMC Psychiatry* 6, no. 1 (2006), 54. doi:10.1186/1471-244x-6-54.

Lee, Joshua D., Edward V. Nunes, Patricia Novo, Ken Bachrach, Genie L. Bailey, Snehal Bhatt, Sarah Farkas, et al. "Comparative Effectiveness of Extended-Release Naltrexone versus Buprenorphine-Naloxone for Opioid Relapse Prevention (X:BOT): A Multicentre, Open-Label, Randomised Controlled Trial." *Lancet* 391, no. 10118 (2018), 309–318. doi:10.1016/s0140-6736(17)32812-x.

Lenardson, Jennifer D., David Hartley, John A. Gale, and Karen B. Pearson. "Substance Use and Abuse in Rural America. In J. C. Warren and K. B. Smalley (Eds.), *Rural Public Health: Best Practices and Preventive Models*, 95–114. New York: Springer Publishing Company, 2014.

Manchikanti, Laxmaiah, Kim S. Damron, Carl D. McManus, and R. C. Barnhill. "Patterns of Illicit Drug Use and Opioid Abuse in Patients with Chronic Pain at Initial Evaluation: A Prospective Observational Study." *Pain Physician* 7, no. 4 (October 2004), 431–437. doi:10.1186/1471-2253-5-10.

Mollereau, C., M. J. Simons, P. Soularue, F. Liners, G. Vassart, J. C. Meunier, and M. Parmentier. "Structure, Tissue Distribution, and Chromosomal Localization of the Prepronociceptin Gene." *Proc Nat Acad Sci* 93, no. 16 (1996), 8666–8670. doi:10.1073/pnas.93.16.8666.

National Institute on Drug Abuse. *Opioid Overdose Crisis*. Revised January 2019. Accessed March 22, 2019. http://www.drugabuse.gov.

Nunes, Edward V., Michael Gordon, Peter D. Friedmann, Marc J. Fishman, Joshua D. Lee, Donna T. Chen, Mei C. Hu, Tamara Y. Boney, Donna Wilson, and Charles P. O'Brien. "Relapse to Opioid Use Disorder after Inpatient Treatment: Protective Effect of Injection Naltrexone." *J Subst Abuse Treat* 85 (2018), 49–55. doi:10.1016/j.jsat.2017.04.016.

O'Donnell, Julie K., John Halpin, Christine L. Mattson, Bruce A. Goldberger, and R. M. Gladden. "Deaths Involving Fentanyl, Fentanyl Analogs, and U-47700—10 States, July–December 2016." *MMWR* 66, no. 43 (2017), 1197–1202. doi:10.15585/mmwr.mm6643e1.

Olfson, Mark, Melanie Wall, Shuai Wang, Stephen Crystal, and Carlos Blanco. "Service Use Preceding Opioid-Related Fatality." *Am J Psychiatry* 175, no. 6 (2018), 538–544. doi:10.1176/appi.ajp.2017.17070808.

Pert, Candace B., and Solomon H. Snyder. "Opiate Receptor: Demonstration in Nervous Tissue." *Science* 179, no. 4077 (January 1973), 1011–1014. doi:10.1126/science.179.4077.1011.

Reuben, David B., Anika A. Alvanzo, Takamaru Ashikaga, G. A. Bogat, Christopher M. Callahan, Victoria Ruffing, and David C. Steffens. "National Institutes of Health Pathways to Prevention Workshop: The

Role of Opioids in the Treatment of Chronic Pain." *Ann Intern Med* 162, no. 4 (2015), 295–300. doi:10.7326/m14-2775.

Rieb, Launette M., Wendy V. Norman, Ruth E. Martin, Jonathan Berkowitz, Evan Wood, Michael J. Milloy, and Ryan McNeil. "Linking Opioid-Induced Hyperalgesia and Withdrawal-Associated Injury Site Pain." *Pain Rep* 3, no. 3 (2018), e648. doi:10.1097/pr9.0000000000000648.

Schuchat, Anne, Debra Houry, and Gery P. Guy. "New Data on Opioid Use and Prescribing in the United States." *JAMA* 318, no. 5 (2017), 425–426. doi:10.1001/jama.2017.8913.

Simon, Eric J. "In Search of the Opiate Receptor." *Am J Med Sci* 266, no. 3 (1973), 160–168. doi:10.1097/00000441-197309000-00001.

Sullivan, Mark D., and Catherine Q. Howe. "Opioid Therapy for Chronic Pain in the United States: Promises and Perils." *Pain* 154 (2013), S94–S100. doi:10.1016/j.pain.2013.09.009.

Terenius, Lars. "Stereospecific Interaction between Narcotic Analgesics and a Synaptic Plasma Membrane Fraction of Rat Cerebral Cortex." *Acta Pharmacol Toxicol* 32, no. 3 (1973), 317–320.

Waxman, Amanda R., Caroline Arout, Megan Caldwell, Albert Dahan, and Benjamin Kest. "Acute and Chronic Fentanyl Administration Causes Hyperalgesia Independently of Opioid Receptor Activity in Mice." *Neurosci Lett* 462, no. 1 (2009), 68–72. doi:10.1016/j. neulet.2009.06.061.

CHAPTER 7

Sedatives

Amanda U. von Horn and Anna Terajewicz LaRose

Sedative hypnotics are substances primarily used for their sedating and tranquilizing effects. They consist of different classes of medications, such as benzodiazepines, non-benzodiazepine hypnotics, barbiturates, muscle relaxants, and anti-epileptics. The U.S. Food and Drug Administration (FDA) approves them for the treatment of insomnia, anxiety, alcohol withdrawal, seizures, and as premedication and amnestic agents for anesthesia. These drugs increase the effects of gamma-aminobutyric acid (GABA), a neurotransmitter that inhibits brain activity. This inhibitory effect makes sedative hypnotics useful medications, but they can interfere with cognition, movements, and breathing. They also carry a risk of physiological and psychological dependence. Worsened anxiety and insomnia may occur when the medications are stopped suddenly; on rare occasions, seizures may occur. In this chapter, the misuse of these medications will be discussed with a focus on addiction.

Sedative hypnotics is a term used to refer to a large class of medications with multiple names. Sedatives, also known as anxiolytics, or agents that reduce anxiety, are used to calm people or to induce sleep, and include the nonbenzodiazepine "Z-drugs," such as zopiclone and zolpidem, benzodiazepines such as alprazolam, clonazepam, diazepam, and lorazepam, some muscle relaxants, and barbiturates. The word *hypnotic*, from the Greek word for sleep, *hypnos*, refers to a medication that induces sleep and includes the medications mentioned in the previous sentence as well as benzodiazepines that are specifically prescribed for insomnia, including flurazepam, temazepam, and triazolam. The word *tranquilizer* is sometimes used to describe these medications. There is much overlap between these terms and categories. The fifth edition of the American Psychiatric Association's *Diagnostic and Statistical Manual (DSM-5)* (American Psychiatric Association 2013) refers to these substances as one group: sedatives, hypnotics, or anxiolytics.

Most of this chapter will focus on the many benzodiazepines, which differ with respect to their rapidity of onset of action, half-life (how quickly they are cleared from the body), potency (dose needed to achieve a certain effect), active metabolites (breakdown products that have similar effects), and abuse potential. For example, alprazolam has a shorter half-life than clonazepam, and lorazepam is more potent than diazepam. Diazepam is particularly long lasting because the liver metabolizes it into three active drugs, nordiazepam, temazepam, and oxazepam. The more lipid soluble benzodiazepines, such as alprazolam, are more addictive than other benzodiazepines, perhaps because lipid-soluble drugs reach the brain quickly and rapidly lead to a sense of calm.

Symptoms, Diagnosis, and Incidence

Symptoms

The response to sedative hypnotics varies between individuals and depends on factors such as age, gender, medical conditions, and genetics—all of which affect the metabolism, or clearance, of the drug from the body. Even at recommended doses, intoxication or side effects can occur.

Sedative hypnotic intoxication can appear as drowsiness, slurred speech, impaired motor (muscle) coordination, slowing of cognition and reaction time, and impaired impulse control and judgment. The motor coordination defects may include ataxia (unsteadiness) and decreased reflexes, which can lead to falls and injuries. Impaired judgment can also lead people to place themselves into unsafe situations, putting them at risk for physical harm and sexual assault. The combination of impaired motor coordination and judgment can make driving a car or operating machinery dangerous.

One of the most hazardous side effects of sedative hypnotic intoxication is slowed breathing. This side effect is more common if sedative hypnotics are used in conjunction with other central nervous system (CNS) depressants, such as alcohol or opioids.

Certain sedative hypnotics are associated with anterograde amnesia, an inability to learn new information or make new memories. This characteristic is useful in anesthesia during surgeries, as the patient will rarely remember the discomfort felt during the procedure. However, it has also led to the use of sedative hypnotics in sexual assaults. Flunitrazepam and gamma-hydroxybutyric acid (GHB), in particular, are known as "date-rape drugs."

Some individuals take more of these medications than prescribed, and then are more likely to experience side effects and intoxication. *Hazardous use* is a pattern of substance use that increases the risk of injurious physical, mental, or social consequences. *Harmful use* is a pattern of substance use that causes damage to health. *Physiological dependence* (also known as tolerance) happens when the brain and other organs become accustomed to the substance so that an individual must take higher amounts to achieve the same effect, or when the individual has withdrawal symptoms such as anxiety, tremor, or seizures when stopping the drug. Some individuals who misuse sedative hypnotics may become addicted.

Diagnosis

Sedative, hypnotic, or anxiolytic use disorder is the term used in *DSM-5* (American Psychiatric Association 2013) to describe misuse of these medications. A person who meets two or more of the following criteria within a year receives a diagnosis of sedative-hypnotic use disorder: using more of the medication than initially intended (or prescribed); trying but failing to cut down or stop using the medication; spending much time obtaining the medication, being sedated from it, or recovering from using it; a strong desire to take the medication; missing important social, school, or work activities because of medication-related intoxication, sedation, or recovery; continued use of the medication even if causes arguments with others; medication use despite physical hazards, such as driving dangerously due to sedation; taking the medication instead of becoming involved in other activities; development or exacerbation of medical problems related to the medications, such as sedation-related falls; development of tolerance (needing to take more to have the same effects); and having withdrawal symptoms, such as increased anxiety, insomnia, and tremors, when stopping. The greater the number of criteria an individual meets, the more severe the sedative-hypnotic use disorder. People with a mild sedative-hypnotic use disorder (in contrast to the more severe disorders) will not necessarily need the same amount of treatment and can often stop taking the drug on their own. An individual with a severe sedative hypnotic use disorder (or to use a term falling out of favor, addiction), that is, someone who meets more than six criteria, will likely need medical and psychiatric support.

The timing of the progression (if it develops) from misuse of medications to frank addiction is difficult to predict. Some people may remain in the hazardous use pattern for years before escalating to harmful use, while others may quickly progress from hazardous use to a severe substance use disorder. Other people may misuse the medications but still be able to carry on their relationships and work. These people are sometimes referred to as "functional addicts" and are unlikely to begin treatment unless they develop more severe consequences of misuse.

Incidence

Despite the adverse effects and addictive potential of sedative hypnotics, they remain some of the most widely prescribed medications in the United States. In 2012, almost 38 prescriptions per 100 patients were written by U.S. physicians for benzodiazepines (Lembke, Papac, and Humphreys 2018). According to a review of all medication-related insurance claims in 2016, the most frequently prescribed psychoactive medications are sedative hypnotics. In 2015, of those individuals over the age of 12 in the United States, about one in five used tranquilizers or sedatives that year (Hughes et al. 2016).

According to the 2016 National Survey on Drug Use and Health, 21.6% of the U.S. population over the age of 12 used sedatives or tranquilizers in the past year but only 2.9% of the population misused these substances. The estimated lifetime prevalence of a sedative hypnotic use disorder (addiction) is estimated to be around 1% of the general population (Center for Behavioral Health Statistics and Quality 2017).

History

Before the 1800s, the best-known substances that exerted sedative or hypnotic effects were alcohol and opium. Chloral hydrate, the first synthesized sedative hypnotic, was developed in 1832. Mary Todd Lincoln, wife of President Abraham Lincoln, might have been prescribed chloral hydrate for her severe insomnia in her later years. (Chloral hydrate dissolved in alcohol was known as a "Mickey Finn" and used to sedate and then rob customers in Chicago restaurants and bars in the late 1800s and early 1900s.) Chloral hydrate has been largely replaced by the barbiturates and benzodiazepines but is still used to sedate children before dental or medical procedures, although that practice is becoming increasingly uncommon.

Barbiturates are a separate class of sedative hypnotic substances based on barbituric acid, a compound synthesized in 1864 by Adolf von Baeyer. (In 1905, he won the Nobel Prize in Chemistry.) In 1903, barbital became the first marketed barbiturate, synthesized by chemists Emil Fischer and Josef von Mering, who were both employees of Bayer Pharmaceuticals. Barbital was used to induce anesthesia for various surgeries and procedures, as well as to treat anxiety or "hysteria." (The word *hysteria*, derived from the Greek for "uterus" is an outdated and somewhat pejorative term describing excitability or extreme emotionality, especially in women.) Phenobarbital was synthesized in 1912 and used as a treatment for anxiety and insomnia. The dangers of accidental overdose on these medications quickly became obvious, as they are long acting, sedating, and have a narrow therapeutic index, meaning that there is little difference between a therapeutic and a toxic dose. Barbiturates were implicated in the deaths of several celebrities, including Marilyn Monroe, Judy Garland, and Jimi Hendrix. By the 1970s, phenobarbital was declared a controlled substance under the Controlled Substances Act of 1970 and its use decreased as safer medications, such as benzodiazepines, were developed. (See Sidebar 7.1.) Barbiturates are still used today as anti-epileptic medications, intravenous agents to induce anesthesia, more rarely in the treatment of alcohol withdrawal and migraines, and in assisted suicide.

Meprobamate, or Miltown, was another early tranquilizer. Synthesized in the 1940s, meprobamate was brought to market in 1955 by two chemists, Frank Milan Berger and John Ludwig. Marketed as a "minor" tranquilizer, meprobamate quickly rose to fame, as it provided seemingly miraculous relief of a wide variety psychiatric symptoms, particularly anxiety and insomnia:

> When it was finally released, Miltown proved a commercial sensation ... it became the first psychotropic blockbuster and the fastest-selling drug in US history . . . By 1957, Americans had filled 36 million prescriptions for Miltown, more than a billion tablets had been manufactured, and tranquilizers accounted for a staggering one-third of all prescriptions. (Tone 2009, xvi)

The popularity of meprobamate among Hollywood celebrities solidified its status as a hallmark of 1950s popular culture. It even inspired the creation of jewelry and cocktails:

> In 1956, Tiffany jewelers reported brisk sales of "ruby and diamond-studded pill coffers for those who wished to glorify their

new-found happiness." Cartier sold a bracelet charm shaped like a pill with enough room for two peace pills for $20, and a $148 gold box with sapphires and rubies that held six. . . . The Miltown cocktail was a Bloody Mary (vodka and tomato juice) spiked with a single pill, and the Guided Missile . . . consisted of a double shot of vodka and two Miltowns. More popular still was the Miltini, a dry martini in which a Miltown replaced the customary olive. (Tone 2009, 59)

Celebrities such as author Aldous Huxley and television comedian Milton Berle said that the drug was essential to their craft, and pills were often distributed at Hollywood parties, along with the less popular amphetamines and barbiturates. The U.S. military distributed meprobamate to pilots to treat their insomnia, and professional athletes were prescribed the drug for performance anxiety (Tone 2009, 113–114).

The phenomenon of meprobamate's quick rise to fame as a "miracle" anti-anxiety agent changed the culture of mental health treatment in the United States. Anxiety became accepted as a legitimate psychiatric illness, and interest in research to investigate the neurobiology of anxiety soared. Pharmaceutical companies, eager to benefit from this newly profitable market of tranquilizers, began to develop similar agents, especially after concerns were raised in the late 1950s about the addictive potential and long-term adverse effects of meprobamate.

When it was first introduced, meprobamate was marketed as a relatively safe and not habit-forming medication. However, studies of its safety and efficacy revealed a high rate of physiological and psychological dependence, as well as detrimental effects on cognition and motor functioning. In 1970, meprobamate became a controlled substance (Schedule IV) (see Sidebar 7.1) due to the evidence of psychological and physical dependence, and the search for a safer and more effective sedative hypnotic continued. Meprobamate is still FDA approved for anxiety but is rarely used.

Benzodiazepines were the next group of sedative hypnotic and anxiolytic agents to be developed. Benzodiazepines were named for their chemical structure, specifically a heterocyclic ring (a ring structure made of more than one kind of element) system that is a fusion between benzene (a ring containing six carbon atoms and six hydrogen atoms) and diazepine (a ring containing seven atoms, two of which are nitrogen) ring systems. The first benzodiazepine, chlordiazepoxide, was synthesized by Leo Sternbach in 1956 and approved by the FDA in 1960. Diazepam was approved in 1963. The benzodiazepines quickly became some of the most widely prescribed medications due to their impressive effectiveness in relieving anxiety and inducing sleep. (The 1966 Rolling Stones' song "Mother's Little Helper" might refer to diazepam.) In the late 1960s, dependence on these substances began to become apparent. Despite the misuse, benzodiazepines are still prescribed regularly by primary care physicians, psychiatrists, and neurologists for a variety of conditions, including anxiety, insomnia, seizures, and panic disorder.

"Z-drugs," nonbenzodiazepine sedative hypnotics, were developed in the 1980s and 1990s as the search continued for effective anxiolytics and hypnotics without addictive potential. Zopiclone was the first of the Z-drugs, synthesized in the 1980s as a treatment for insomnia. Zolpidem was developed in the early 1990s and induces sleep quickly for some people. Two other similar drugs, zaleplon and eszopiclone, were brought to market in 1999 and 2005, respectively. Z-drug use has been associated with unusual behaviors, such as walking, driving, and eating while asleep, and memory loss. Just as with other classes of sedative hypnotics, misuse, tolerance, and dependence can occur. All forms of Z-drugs are classified as Schedule IV substances under the Controlled Substances Act. Currently, Z-drugs are most often prescribed for insomnia.

Gamma-hydroxybutyrate (GHB) is a sedative hypnotic that has gained notoriety for its use in facilitating sexual assault, hence its reputation as

---

Sidebar 7.1 Drug Schedules

Before the 20th century, drug manufacturing and possession were largely unregulated, and drugs such as cocaine and opium were used in over-the-counter tonics and tinctures. In 1906, Congress passed the Food and Drug Act that began to regulate food and drugs. Over time, more laws were enacted to limit the manufacture, sale, and possession of certain drugs that had addiction potential or those that had no medical purpose and were being used recreationally. By the 1970s, it had become obvious that other drug classes, including sedative hypnotics, should be regulated as well. The Controlled Substances Act of 1970 categorized and regulated the manufacturing, possession, and/or use of controlled substances. In the United States, controlled substances are assigned a Schedule from I to V, with Schedule I substances being the most tightly regulated and monitored. Substances are assigned to their respective schedule based on whether there is a currently accepted medical use of the substance, the relative abuse potential, and likelihood of causing dependence when abused. Currently, most benzodiazepines are Schedule IV substances in the United States, meaning that they are considered to have some abuse potential, and prescribing practices are monitored by the Drug Enforcement Administration (DEA).

a "date-rape drug." It is a naturally occurring substance in the human brain but was first synthesized and introduced into the medical community in the 1960s. It was initially used as an anesthetic, as well as a treatment for narcolepsy. It produces euphoria followed by sedation and can be lethal when combined with alcohol or other CNS depressants. Currently, GHB is a Schedule I controlled substance. Sodium oxybate, a salt of GHB, is approved for the treatment of narcolepsy in the United States and is a Schedule III substance.

Development and Causes

As noted earlier, most individuals who use a sedative hypnotic for insomnia or anxiety will not misuse the drug or develop an addiction. However, over the last 20 years, there has been a steady increase in the number of sedative hypnotic (particularly benzodiazepine) prescriptions written by physicians and a corresponding increase in the number of adverse medical outcomes associated with these medications, including overdose and death when combined with other substances of abuse. As more people become exposed to these medications, it is important to understand the factors predisposing an individual to addiction.

Biological factors and genetics play a large role in the development of a substance use disorder. Family, adoption, and twin studies suggest that addiction to sedatives is somewhat heritable, although addiction to opioids or cocaine has a stronger heritable component (Ducci and Goldman, 2012).

Having a comorbid psychiatric illness is a significant risk factor for developing a substance use disorder. The psychiatric illnesses closely associated with substance use disorders include panic disorder with agoraphobia, bipolar disorder, post–traumatic stress disorder (PTSD), and certain personality disorders (Grant et al. 2016). Effective treatment of these comorbid illnesses is vital in structuring a comprehensive treatment plan for those with substance use disorders.

If an individual has poor distress tolerance, he or she may seek out immediate comfort in the form of drugs or alcohol. Biological aspects of personality affect how someone handles stress. Adverse childhood experiences—such as physical, emotional, or sexual abuse, neglect, exposure to domestic violence, or having family members who are abusing substances—may predispose the person to developing maladaptive coping strategies, physical and mental illness, disability, and addiction (Centers for Disease Control 2016).

The concept of personal choice in addiction has always been thorny. Many point out that an addiction can only develop after an individual chooses to use or misuse these drugs, and that the addiction is a direct product of poor life choices. However, many people are initially exposed to these drugs through prescriptions. Some people likely have a genetic predisposition to develop misuse and addiction to these drugs. Those with a previous history of alcohol use disorder are more at risk for developing sedative hypnotic use disorders. In addition, those individuals who feel more euphoria after taking these medications, likely secondary to genetic differences in their neuronal receptors, will also be at higher risk.

Up Close—In Society

By the 1960s, meprobamate had become one of the most frequently prescribed prescription medications in history, and an icon in popular culture. It is interesting to consider which societal and cultural forces contribute to a generation's vulnerability to addiction to a specific substance. In the case of sedative hypnotics, the generational attitudes toward women and their societal role may have contributed to the drugs' rising popularity. According to Jonathan Metzl, a professor of sociology and psychiatry at Vanderbilt University, there was a surge in articles published between 1955 and 1959 that recommended pharmaceutical cures for everyday women's problems:

> *Health columns such as Henry Safford's regular "Tell Me Doctor" section in* Ladies Home Journal *and Walter Alvarez's Ask the Doctor in* Cosmopolitan *explained how, thanks to psychopharmacology, "emotional" problems could be cured by simply visiting a doctor, obtaining a prescription and taking a pill . . . psychopharmaceuticals came of age in a post-war consumer culture intimately concerned with the role of mothers in maintaining individual and communal peace of mind. As a result, the 1950s set precedents connecting women and psychopharmaceuticals that lay the foundation for Mother's Little Helpers in the decades to come. (Metzl 2003, 241)*

While the view of women as emotionally frail has changed over the last 60 years, the long-held belief that the female gender has a unique inability to tolerate stress may linger. Data published in 2014 show that benzodiazepines are prescribed to women twice as often as men (Drug Abuse Warning Network 2014). Women are less likely to use illegal drugs, perhaps due to greater adherence to cultural norms and less risk-taking behavior than men, and are more likely to use and misuse prescription drugs.

Case Study

Alice is a 27-year-old college student with depression, panic disorder, and trouble sleeping. She comes to the school mental health clinic after being arrested for theft. Her primary-care physician had prescribed alprazolam to treat her panic attacks and zolpidem to treat her insomnia, but she overused them and ran out before she could refill the prescription. She then stole some alprazolam from another student.

Alice has no medical problems and does not take any other medications. She has a family history of alcohol use disorder in her father and opioid use disorder (heroin addiction) in her mother. She was raised by her grandmother, who was verbally and emotionally abusive throughout her childhood. She began to misuse the alprazolam and zolpidem because they improved her mood and made her feel more confident.

Because she is living on student loans, she cannot afford therapy. She feels guilty and ashamed about her drug abuse and wants to stop. She has tried to quit on her own without success: she becomes anxious and experiences palpitations, sweating, and insomnia when she stops completely. She is worried about the legal consequences of stealing others' medications.

At the student health clinic, a psychiatrist prescribes antidepressant medications for Alice and slowly tapers down the alprazolam and zolpidem. She begins to see a therapist at the free school clinic. Her anxiety and depression improve. During exam time, her anxiety increases and she considers buying alprazolam off the street, but instead she talks about her anxiety with her friends and therapist and gets a tutor. Due to her participation in treatment, the courts put her on probation.

Up Close—At Work

Substance use disorders can diminish productivity by leading to lost work days or inefficiency due to impairment in concentration and focus. As addiction progresses, an individual may become increasingly preoccupied with the substance and spend more time acquiring and using it. In industries like construction, which require manual labor or operation of heavy machinery, workplace safety can also be compromised if employees are using substances; injuries or even fatalities may result.

Many companies mandate drug testing to monitor and discourage substance abuse, during both the hiring process and employment. If prospective employees test positive, they may not be hired or only hired on the condition that they get treatment. If a current employee tests positive, he or she may be subject to termination or mandatory treatment. Employees who are prescribed benzodiazepines are advised to tell their employer about the prescription and perhaps be prepared to show the employer a physician's letter. Many companies have employee assistance programs to help workers with personal problems, including substance use disorders. These types of programs seek to minimize lost productivity, absenteeism, and overall monetary cost to both the employee and employer.

Drug testing usually involves testing urine (or hair, saliva, blood, or sweat) specimens for substances and/or metabolites. Benzodiazepines are commonly tested for because they are the most widely prescribed and misused sedative hypnotics. Benzodiazepine metabolites can be present in the urine for anywhere between 36 hours to 30 days after ingestion of the substance, depending on the dose taken, the particular drug's half-life, and the extent to which it is metabolized. For example, diazepam is a long-acting benzodiazepine with a half-life of 20 to 80 hours; it has active metabolites that can be detected in the urine for up to 30 days after ingestion. Lorazepam, which is short acting with a half-life of 10 to 20 hours, is only detected in the urine for three days after ingestion. Most assays test for oxazepam and nordiazepam, which are the primary metabolites of many of the benzodiazepines. Initial testing uses an enzyme-linked immunosorbent assay and is not specific. Confirmatory testing, using mass spectroscopy, can identify the specific benzodiazepine as well as levels of the benzodiazepine in the urine.

Because sedative hypnotics can impair cognitive and motor functioning, it is dangerous and unlawful to operate a motor vehicle while under their influence. There have been several studies showing a dose-dependent relationship between benzodiazepine use and traffic collision risk (Thomas 1998). If police pull over an individual because they suspect impaired driving and then find benzodiazepines in his or her urine, that person is at risk of being charged with driving under the influence (DUI) even if the individual is prescribed these medications. Depending on various circumstances, as well as specific state legislation, consequences can range from probation to jail time.

Case Study

Jim is a 66-year-old physician in a group practice who has been prescribed lorazepam for many years by his own physician to help him sleep. In May, he had dental surgery and was prescribed Percocet (oxycodone and acetaminophen). Despite the medications, he was still in pain and had difficulty sleeping. He asked his dental surgeon for more Percocet for his pain and clonazepam to help him sleep at night. His dental surgeon gave him a limited supply of both and told him that those would be the last prescriptions that he would write for him.

Throughout the summer, Jim's office staff noticed that he did not seem like himself. Once or twice he fell asleep during the middle of the day, and occasionally he seemed slightly confused.

In October, Jim asked one of his older patients to bring in all her medications to count them to make sure that she was taking them correctly. During this visit, a nurse thought that she might have seen Jim take three of his patient's lorazepam tablets, and she told another physician her suspicions. This physician talked to Jim, but he denied it and said: "You are treating me like I'm an addict!" However, he did tell his colleague that he was experiencing a resurgence of anxiety with marked insomnia, that his dental surgery has not gone well, and that he was still in pain. He thought that his insomnia was interfering with his work and that he needed more medication to help him with his pain and his sleep.

Jim's colleagues became concerned and called the physician's health program (PHP) in his state to evaluate Jim. The PHP determined that Jim needed treatment for anxiety, insomnia, and benzodiazepine and possible opioid misuse. The program warned him of the danger of combining benzodiazepines and opioids. The state medical licensing board instructed Jim that to renew his medical license and treat patients, he needs to follow the recommendations of the PHP.

Up Close—In Relationships
The devastating nature of addiction is most obvious in its effects on the family and relationships. Due to genetic and environmental factors, children of people with addiction have a higher likelihood of developing substance use and mental health disorders than do others. Children may copy both their parents' attitudes toward drugs and alcohol and their maladaptive coping skills. Living in a home where addiction is present can also be confusing for children. The parent may be intoxicated and mildly confused or drowsy, or withdrawing and irritable. These unpredictable mood swings may interfere with the development of children's ability to regulate their own moods. The children might also blame themselves for the parent's behavior, become anxious or depressed, or feel that they have no control over their lives. When children have these emotional problems, it affects their behavior and can result in poor school performance, disturbed relationships with their peers, or getting into trouble with authority figures. If the person misusing sedative hypnotic substances is not honest about this habit with his or her spouse, the deceitfulness will usually become apparent and take a toll on the marriage.

The occupational, financial, and legal consequences of substance abuse affect the whole family. Resentment and anger may build over time and undermine the intimacy and trust needed for the maintenance of relationships. The person with a substance use disorder cannot find pleasure in the usual rewarding activities, such as enjoying a good meal or bonding with others. The drug has taken over the part of the brain that ties reward and pleasure into "normal" behaviors, and the person becomes primarily motivated to take the drug. Getting the individual and the family into treatment can be helpful, but it may take time for the relationships to heal.

Case Study

Mary's mother has just died from breast cancer, and she has been having a difficult time dealing with her grief. Mary gets a prescription for lorazepam from her own doctor to help her manage her sadness and the stresses at work. The lorazepam helps, but is not enough. Mary talks about this with her closest friend who gives Mary some of her own lorazepam. Mary is also having trouble sleeping. She begins to drink alcohol first to help her sleep, and then to supplement her lorazepam. Now she is often intoxicated. Her husband does not want her to drive to the liquor store when she is intoxicated, so when she finishes a bottle and wants more, he goes out to buy the liquor. When she combines alcohol with lorazepam, she sleeps so heavily that she cannot get up to eat breakfast with her family. She has stopped attending her children's sporting events. Her family talks to her about her use of lorazepam and alcohol. Mary begins to cry and tells them that they just don't understand how difficult her life is. She blames them for not helping around the house and adding to her stresses.

Mary's friend and husband have good intentions, but sharing medications and buying alcohol for her is not helpful. They are helping Mary misuse the substances, a practice known as *enabling*. Mary's husband and children may want to find a therapist for themselves to help them cope with Mary's addiction. They can also seek out support groups for family members of people who struggle with addiction. For example, Mary's husband could benefit from Al-Anon, and her children might benefit from Alateen. Only Mary can make the decision to get treatment, but until she makes that decision, her family can model appropriate coping skills and get the support they need.

Effects and Costs

While the consequences of addiction to street drugs like heroin, methamphetamine, or cocaine are well publicized, the effects of misuse of prescription medications like sedative hypnotics are more insidious. Because these drugs are legal and prescribed by doctors, they may seem to be safe, but this is not always the case. Repeatedly taking drugs, even legal drugs, conditions the brain to require drugs to deal with daily stress. It stops people from building resilience and developing the skills necessary to overcome adversity. Over time, the individual starts taking the substance for minor anxiety-provoking situations and using more drugs to overcome the struggles of daily life. This cycle becomes harder to break as the person becomes psychologically and physically dependent on the substance.

In addition to the personal costs associated with addiction to sedative hypnotics, there are significant health-care and societal costs to consider as well. Emergency department visits for complications secondary to benzodiazepine misuse (such as overdose or accidents) almost doubled over a period of seven years, from just over 46,000 in 2005 to over 89,000 in 2011 (Drug Abuse Warning Network 2014).

Benzodiazepines also are associated with short-term impairment in memory, learning, attention, and visuospatial ability, all of which lead to transient cognitive impairment that might not reverse once benzodiazepines are stopped (discussed later in this chapter).

The side effects of sedative hypnotics can be dangerous in older adults, who generally are more sensitive to adverse effects of medications. Benzodiazepines can be associated with sedation and impaired gait and sense of balance, all of which increase the risk for falls and fractures in the elderly. Fractures in the elderly can have significant consequences. One third of older adults with hip fractures die within a year of the injury (Markota et al. 2016). These side effects and their complications affect the wellbeing of the elderly person, and also can be costly in terms of emergency room visits and hospitalizations. Family members living with or caring for the person will also feel the impact of these problems and events.

Early studies in the 1980s showed an association between benzodiazepine use during pregnancy and physical dysmorphia (cleft palate), growth aberrations, and CNS defects like those seen in fetal alcohol syndrome, raising concerns that benzodiazepines might cause malformations in a developing embryo and fetus. However, more recent studies have not found evidence that benzodiazepines are teratogenic but have found that they are associated with low birth weight, an increased risk for preterm birth, and the "floppy infant syndrome," in which babies are abnormally limp when born. The newborn baby may develop neonatal abstinence syndrome (NAS), caused by withdrawal of the benzodiazepines, and need intensive care for management of this syndrome.

The American College of Obstetricians and Gynecologists (ACOG) has classified medications with respect to safety in pregnancy. Category A, no evidence of risk; Category B, no demonstrated risk in animals and no studies in humans; Category C, harm in animal studies but no studies in humans; Category D, a small risk of fetal injury; Category X, evidence of harm; should not be used. Benzodiazepines are listed as Category D, meaning that they can be prescribed if the benefits seem to outweigh the risks. (ACOG 2007). Therefore, some physicians do prescribe benzodiazepines for pregnant women suffering with severe anxiety.

Managing addiction to sedative hypnotics during pregnancy is difficult. If a pregnant woman attempts to stop using benzodiazepines abruptly, withdrawal can cause an elevated heart rate, high blood pressure, and seizures. The emotional stress of withdrawal carries significant risks, such as extreme mood fluctuations, worsening anxiety, and even increased risk of suicidal thoughts (ACOG 2007).

Theory and Research

GABA is the chief inhibitory neurotransmitter in the CNS and is synthesized from the amino acid glutamate. GABA binds to specific receptors embedded in the plasma membrane of neurons. The GABA (A) and GABA (B) receptors are found throughout the brain and CNS. When GABA binds to the GABA (A) receptor, it hyperpolarizes the membrane by allowing negative chloride ions into the cell. This hyperpolarization inhibits membrane depolarization and thus neurotransmission in the CNS.

The GABA (A) receptors are usually made of five subunits arranged around a channel. There are seven subunits (alpha, beta, gamma, delta, epsilon, rho, and pi), each of which has different isoforms that are numbered. In the brain, the most common GABA (A) receptors are made up of one gamma subunit and two alpha and two beta subunits. The different subtypes are thought to modulate different effects. For example, when a benzodiazepine binds to GABA (A) receptors that contain the alpha 1 subunit isoform, it is thought that this results in the sedating, memory-lessening, and anti-seizure properties of that benzodiazepine, while binding to receptors containing the alpha 2 subunit isoform is likely responsible for the effects of lessening anxiety and muscular relaxation. The alpha 1 subunit isoform is probably also responsible for the addictive property of benzodiazepines. Experimental benzodiazepines affect specific subtypes and have different properties than currently available benzodiazepines (Tan, Rudolph, and Lüscher 2011).

Benzodiazepines modulate the GABA (A) receptor by binding to separate sites on the receptor and enhancing the ability of the GABA molecules to open the chloride channel, resulting in hyperpolarization of the neurons and depression of neuronal activity. Benzodiazepines are thus known as *positive allosteric modulators* (indirect agonists) of the GABA receptor. Benzodiazepines can be blocked by a synthetic drug called flumazenil. Flumazenil also binds to the GABA receptor but is an antagonist of the GABA receptor. In the past, it was used to treat benzodiazepine overdose but because of the risk of inducing seizures is no longer used.

Barbiturates also affect GABA. At lower doses, barbiturates modulate the GABA (A) receptor via the same mechanism as benzodiazepines. At higher concentrations, barbiturates act as direct agonists at the GABA (A) receptor, directly binding to and activating the GABA receptors, having the same action as GABA. They prolong the opening of the chloride channel, allowing more negatively charged chloride ions into the cell, enhancing neuronal hyperpolarization and inhibiting neurotransmission. Barbiturates are more dangerous than benzodiazepines, however, as they are toxic at doses slightly above therapeutic doses. In addition, the actions of barbiturates in the nervous system cannot be reversed by any currently available medication.

The Z-drugs, like the benzodiazepines, are positive allosteric modulators of the GABA receptor. The Z-drugs differ from benzodiazepines in that they bind to different subunits of the GABA receptor. They have more variable effects—one might be more sedating, while another might be better at reducing anxiety, depending on which subunits they bind to and the strength of the binding.

Because of the significant side effects and abuse potential of most sedative hypnotics, there have been efforts over the past 10 to 20 years to develop safer alternatives with similar effects. Cyclobenzaprine, gabapentin, and pregabalin are sometimes used to decrease anxiety or, in the case of cyclobenzaprine, muscle tension second to anxiety. Growing clinical experience suggests that these medications may also be addictive and have many of the same side effects as the sedative hypnotics that were developed earlier. Because the common pathway for many of the sedative hypnotics is modulation of the GABA receptor, any future drugs that affect the receptor may have similar side effects and potentially lead to abuse.

The neurobiology of sedative hypnotic addiction has not been as thoroughly studied as the neurobiology of addiction to other drugs, such as alcohol, cocaine, heroin, or nicotine. The central neurobiological theory of addiction involves the reward pathway of the brain, also known as the mesolimbic dopamine pathway, located deep in the brain. Dopamine is a neurotransmitter associated with pleasure and reward. Its release, normally triggered by activities that improve survival or reproduction, such as eating satisfying food or sexual activity, reinforces these important behaviors. But addictive drugs trigger the release of dopamine at higher levels, thus superseding the normal function of the pathway.

Although sedative hypnotics do not directly affect dopamine, the neurotransmitter associated with addiction, it is thought that the benzodiazepines may decrease inhibitory interneuron activity on dopamine-releasing cells, thus leading to the presence of more dopamine in the system (Tan et al. 2010). Further research is needed to clarify the role of dopamine in sedative hypnotic addiction.

If a sedative hypnotic is used regularly, the brain will equilibrate to the increase in GABA activity caused by the drug. The user will then need greater amounts of the sedative hypnotic to have the same effects on anxiety or sedation. This phenomenon is known as *tolerance*. If the drug is used long term, the brain will adapt to the substance and will need it to function normally; this is called *physiological dependence*. Without the sedative hypnotic, the brain becomes overactive, which can result in withdrawal symptoms, including an increase in blood pressure and pulse, anxiety, insomnia, and possibly the development of hallucinations and seizures. To stop safely, the person using the sedative hypnotic must reduce the dose slowly, probably with the help of a physician.

Recent research is increasing our knowledge of the dangers of sedative hypnotics, including overdose deaths and cognitive problems. The National Institute on Drug Abuse reported a steady increase in the number of overdose deaths involving benzodiazepines, from around 2,000 in 2002 to over 10,000 in 2016. In many of these cases, benzodiazepines had been combined with other substances, most commonly opioids. Benzodiazepines are involved in more than 30% of opioid overdoses (National Institute on Drug Abuse 2018).

The problem is not entirely new. Over 20 years ago, Darke et al. (1994) warned of the dangers of combining benzodiazepines with intravenous (IV) drugs such as cocaine and heroin. Individuals using both benzodiazepines and IV drugs were more likely to share injection equipment than those just using IV drugs, which increased the risk of transmission of HIV and hepatitis B and C. The authors suggested that unemployment, comorbid psychiatric illnesses such as anxiety and depression, and more severe social dysfunction predicted benzodiazepine use with IV drugs. In a later study, benzodiazepine use was shown to be a reliable predictor of infection with hepatitis C in people using IV drugs (Bach et al. 2016).

The number of individuals prescribed benzodiazepines and the amounts of benzodiazepines being prescribed have increased since the 1990s (Lembke, Papac, and Humphreys 2018). There are now prominent warnings, known as "black box warnings," on package inserts for prescription opioids and benzodiazepines, highlighting the dangers of coprescribing these classes of medications.

Recent studies have investigated the long-term adverse effects of sedative hypnotics. A meta-analysis pooling various studies found that long-term use can affect all areas of cognition (Barker et al. 2003). There is also some evidence that long-term benzodiazepine use is linked to an increased risk of Alzheimer's disease. For example, one group of researchers found a significantly higher risk of Alzheimer's disease in those using benzodiazepines, with the risk directly increasing with the length of exposure (Billioti de Gage et al. 2014), although another study did not find this association (Imfeld et al. 2015).

More recently, a new subtype of benzodiazepines has emerged: designer benzodiazepines. These are "drug candidates" produced by pharmaceutical companies in the process of drug development that have not been approved for medical use. Pure powder forms are available for purchase online without a prescription and can be dangerous, as many are highly potent and can cause sedation even at small doses. They have also become popular "party drugs," often used as "downers" after abuse of stimulants. This pattern of use carries a significant risk of accidental overdose and development of addiction. It is not clear if designer benzodiazepines are covered by controlled substances legislation; therefore, it has been difficult to minimize access to the public (Moosmann, King, and Auwärter 2015).

Treatments

Most people who develop problematic use of these medications will have obtained them from their physicians. When prescribing these medications, physicians should discuss the abuse potential, side effects, and overdose potential with their patients. Physicians can check whether patients are getting duplicate prescriptions from other providers, early refills, or other medications like opioids that are dangerous in combination through state-run prescription monitoring programs. These programs monitor all controlled substance prescriptions (Schedule II–V) in their states. To deter misuse, some physicians remind their patients that they should take medications as prescribed, keep medications locked up and/or in a place where they cannot be easily accessed by children or others, and not share medications. Some physicians perform random pill counts or do random urine drug screens to make sure the medications are being taken as prescribed and not diverted. The urine drug screen is also to check that the medication is not being combined with other dangerous drugs such as opiates. Finally, it is standard in some medical practices to ask the patient to sign a treatment contract indicating understanding and acceptance of these expectations.

If someone does develop a sedative hypnotic use disorder, there are several phases of treatment. The first phase is when an individual may be actively misusing sedative hypnotics but is ambivalent about change. Ambivalence is a normal response when considering any kind of behavioral change, whether that is exercising more, eating a balanced diet, or cutting down on drug or alcohol use. During this "contemplative" phase, many studies have shown that motivational interviewing (MI), a style of counseling meant to elicit changes in behavior, can be highly effective. MI allows individuals to discuss the pros and cons of their current behaviors with a clinician who is skilled at eliciting from people why they might want to change and then helping them identify how the change will align with their overall life goals.

Once an individual has made the decision to stop using sedative hypnotics, he or she will need help to do this safely. Some individuals might need treatment to withdraw from the medications. As reviewed earlier, when sedative hypnotics are abruptly discontinued, people can have heightened anxiety, insomnia, restlessness, tremors, and at times delirium, psychosis, or seizures. For these reasons, the treatment for withdrawal involves the careful administration of medications, usually a benzodiazepine such as lorazepam or diazepam, and a subsequent slow taper of the dose to ease the individual through the withdrawal phase, which can last anywhere from a few days to weeks, depending on which substance it is and how long the individual was taking it.

The final phase of recovery is the maintenance of abstinence. The end of acute withdrawal does not necessarily correspond to a cessation of cravings or a decrease in the anxiety that led to sedative hypnotic addiction in the first place. The neurological changes and adaptations that occur because of longstanding drug use take a long period of sustained sobriety to reverse. During this time of reequilibration, or protracted withdrawal, people might have trouble sleeping and dealing with stress.

It can be difficult to determine if the person is still going through withdrawal, suffering from "rebound" anxiety, or experiencing a reappearance of the original problem for which the medication was prescribed. Some people might need alternative medications for insomnia and/or anxiety. Psychotherapy to address any underlying anxiety disorder, panic disorder, or PTSD can be useful. There also might be social issues contributing to use, such as lack of primary or social supports, unemployment, and homelessness. Intervention from social workers or involvement of family members can be helpful.

Some individuals who stop using drugs or alcohol also find community support groups, such as Alcoholics Anonymous (AA), Narcotics Anonymous (NA), or Smart Recovery, to be valuable resources. These are peer-run "fellowships" of individuals with addiction that provide support and sometimes mentorship.

Mindfulness, a type of meditation in which people focus on awareness of self, emotions, and the environment so that they can be fully present in each moment and react in a balanced way in times of stress or turmoil, may aid in the prevention of relapse. Mindfulness-based relapse prevention is a manualized therapy that integrates mindfulness and cognitive behavioral therapy (Witkiewitz, Marlatt, and Walker 2005). Other forms of meditation and exercise might also be effective for stress management, a key component of relapse prevention.

People who misuse sedatives or hypnotics along with other drugs present challenges in treatment. It is not unusual for people who have abused alcohol and/or opiates to say to their physician that they need benzodiazepines to stay away from those two substances. Some clinicians will indeed prescribe benzodiazepines in those situations, thinking that the toxicity, lethality, and other adverse health consequences of sedative hypnotics are minor in comparison to those associated with alcohol and opiates. Other clinicians will not, arguing that people with a propensity for addiction should never be prescribed drugs with any abuse potential, except for special circumstances, such as alcohol withdrawal. In the case of alcohol withdrawal, benzodiazepines are often administered to combat the dangerous symptoms of withdrawal, such as seizures, caused by the sudden absence of alcohol, which leads to a decrease in GABA activity and excitation of the CNS. Over a few days, the dose of the benzodiazepine can slowly be decreased then discontinued. Use of benzodiazepines for alcohol withdrawal is standard practice, though sometimes barbiturates are also used in severe cases.

Bibliography

ACOG (American College of Obstetricians and Gynecologists). "ACOG Practice Bulletin No. 87: Use of Psychiatric Medications During Pregnancy and Lactation." *Obst Gynecol* 110, no. 5 (2007), 1179–1198. doi:10.1097/01.aog.0000291559.02462.7f.

American Psychiatric Association. *Diagnostic and Statistical Manual of Mental Disorders (DSM-5)*, 5th ed. Arlington, VA: American Psychiatric Association, 2013.

Bach, Paxton, Geoffrey Walton, Kanna Hayashi, M-J Milloy, Huiru Dong, Thomas Kerr, Julio Montaner, and Evan Wood. "Benzodiazepine Use and Hepatitis C Seroconversion in a Cohort of Persons Who Inject Drugs." *Am J Public Health* 106, no. 6 (2016), 1067–1072. doi:10.2105/ajph.2016.303090.

Barker, Melinda J., Martin Jackson, Kenneth M. Greenwood, and Simon F. Crowe. "Cognitive Effects of Benzodiazepine Use: A Review." *Aust Psychol* 38, no. 3 (2003), 202–213. doi:10.1080/00050060310001707217.

Billioti de Gage, Sophie, Yola Moride, Thierry Ducruet, Tobias Kurth, Helene Verdoux, Maire Tournier, Antoine Pariente, and Bernard Begaud. "Benzodiazepine Use and Risk of Alzheimer's Disease: Case-control Study." *BMJ* 349 (September 2014), g5205. doi:10.1136/bmj .g5205.

Center for Behavioral Health Statistics and Quality. *2016 National Survey on Drug Use and Health*. Rockville MD: Substance Abuse and Mental Health Services Administration, 2017.

Centers for Disease Control and Prevention. "Adverse Childhood Experiences (ACEs)." Last modified 2016. https://www.cdc.gov/violence prevention/acestudy/index.html.

Darke, Shane, Wendy Swift, Wayne Hall, and Michael Ross. "Predictors of Injecting and Injecting Risk-Taking Behaviour among Methadone Maintenance Clients." *Addiction* 89, no. 3 (1994), 311–316. doi:10.1111/j.1360-0443.1994.tb00897.x.

Drug Abuse Warning Network. *The DAWN (Drug Abuse Warning Network) Report: Benzodiazepines in Combination with Opioid Pain Relievers or Alcohol: Greater Risk of More Serious ED Visit Outcomes*. Rockville, MD: Substance Abuse and Mental Health Services Administration, Center for Behavioral Health Statistics and Quality, 2014.

Ducci, Francesca, and David Goldman. "The Genetic Basis of Addictive Disorders." *Psychiatr Clin North Am* 35, no. 2 (2012), 495–519. doi:10.1016/j.psc.2012.03.010.

Grant, Bridget F., Tulshi D. Saha, W. J. Ruan, Risë B. Goldstein, S. P. Chou, Jeesun Jung, Haitao Zhang, et al. "Epidemiology of DSM-5 Drug Use Disorder: Results from the National Epidemiologic Survey on Alcohol and Related Conditions. II." *JAMA Psychiatry* 73, no. 1 (2016), 39–47. doi:10.1001/jamapsychiatry.2015.2132.

Hughes, Arthur, Matthew R. Williams, Rachel N. Lipari, Jonaki Bose, Elizabeth A. Copello, and Larry A. Kroutil. *Prescription Drug Use and Misuse in the United States: Results from the 2015 National Survey on Drug Use and Health*. NSDUH Data Review, 2016. Accessed July 29, 2019. http://www.samhsa.gov/data/.

Imfeld, Patrick, Michael Bodmer, Susan S. Jick, and Christoph R. Meier. "Benzodiazepine Use and Risk of Developing Alzheimer's Disease or Vascular Dementia: A Case–Control Analysis." *Drug Safety* 38, no. 10 (2015), 909–919. doi:10.1007/s40264-015-0319-3.

Lembke, Anna, Jennifer Papac, and Keith Humphreys. "Our Other Prescription Drug Problem." *New Engl J Med* 378, no. 8 (2018), 693–695. doi:10.1056/nejmp1715050.

Markota, Matej, Teresa A. Rummans, John M. Bostwick, and Maria I. Lapid. "Benzodiazepine Use in Older Adults: Dangers, Management, and Alternative Therapies." *Mayo Clin Proc* 91, no. 11 (2016), 1632–1639. doi:10.1016/j.mayocp.2016.07.024.

Metzl, Jonathan M. "'Mother's Little Helper': The Crisis of Psychoanalysis and the Miltown Resolution." *Gender Hist* 15, no. 2 (2003), 228–255. doi:10.1111/1468-0424.00300.

Moosmann, Bjoern, Leslie A. King, and Volker Auwärter. "Designer Benzodiazepines: A New Challenge." *World Psychiatry* 14, no. 2 (2015), 248. doi:10.1002/wps.20236.

National Institute of Drug Abuse. *Benzodiazepines and Opioids*. National Institute of Health, Revised March 2018. Accessed July 29, 2019. www.drugabuse.gov /drugs-abuse/opioids/benzodiazepines-opioids.

Tan, Kelly R., Matthew Brown, Gwenaël Labouèbe, Cédric Yvon, Cyril Creton, Jean-Marc Fritschy, Uwe Rudolph, and Christian Lüscher. "Neural Bases for Addictive Properties of Benzodiazepines." *Nature* 463, no. 7282 (2010), 769–774. doi:10.1038/nature08758.

Tan, Kelly R., Uwe Rudolph, and Christian Lüscher. "Hooked on Benzodiazepines: GABAA Receptor Subtypes and Addiction." *Trends Neurosci* 34, no. 4 (2011), 188–197. doi:10.1016/j.tins.2011.01.004.

Thomas, Roger E. "Benzodiazepine Use and Motor Vehicle Accidents. Systematic Review of Reported Association." *Can Fam Physician* 44 (April 1988), 799–808.

Tone, Andrea. *The Age of Anxiety: A History of America's Turbulent Affair with Tranquilizers*. New York: Basic Books, 2009.

Witkiewitz, Katie, G. A. Marlatt, and Denise Walker. "Mindfulness-Based Relapse Prevention for Alcohol and Substance Use Disorders." *J Cogn Psychother* 19, no. 3 (2005), 211–228. doi:10.1891/jcop.2005 .19.3.211.

CHAPTER 8

Stimulants

Frances R. Frankenburg and Amy Yule

Stimulants are a group of medications, both natural and manmade, that produce their effects by increasing levels of monoamine neurotransmitters, such as dopamine, serotonin, and noradrenaline. Dopamine is an important molecule that mediates pleasure and motivation in the reward pathway. Serotonin is involved in many psychological processes, particularly those having to do with mood. Noradrenaline is active in the sympathetic or noradrenergic system and leads to increases in heart rate, vasoconstriction, and attention.

Stimulants have some legal medical uses, but they are often used illegally to produce short-term increases in mood and physical and/or mental energy. While stimulant misuse is not as common as the misuse of other drugs such as marijuana or alcohol, it causes significant morbidity and mortality. Misuse most often follows illegal use of stimulants.

Natural stimulants have been used for many centuries. Ma huang (*Ephedra sinica*) is a shrub grown in China whose extract has been used in traditional Chinese medicine for over 5,000 years to induce sweating and to treat the symptoms of viral illnesses such as colds and influenza. The leaf of the coca plant was used in the Andes as a stimulant in pre-Incan and Incan times. These natural products were not, as far as is known, problematic or misused, until scientists isolated the active ingredients. These chemical advances allowed the active substances to be used more efficiently, with a quicker onset of action—and increased potential for addiction.

In 1887, Lazăr Edeleanu, a Romanian chemist, synthesized amphetamine at the University of Berlin. It seemed to have no value until pharmacologist Gordon A. Alles experimented with it in the 1920s as a treatment for asthma and noticed its stimulant properties. In 1934, the large pharmaceutical company Smith, Kline & French marketed amphetamine as a decongestant inhaler under the trade name Benzedrine.

Meanwhile, in 1885, the Japanese chemist Nagai Nagayoshi had isolated ephedrine, the active ingredient in Ma huang. In 1893, he synthesized methamphetamine from ephedrine. Later, people worked out ways of synthesizing methamphetamine from a closely related molecule, pseudoephedrine, a commonly used nasal decongestant.

The active alkaloid of the coca plant, cocaine, was synthesized in the late 1800s and became a powerful, potentially addictive stimulant.

Congress passed the Comprehensive Drug Abuse Prevention and Control Act in 1970, which, among other actions, classified amphetamine, cocaine, and methamphetamine as Schedule II drugs, restricting their prescription. These drugs have a high potential for abuse, possibly leading to severe psychological or physical dependence and other harms.

This chapter is divided into three parts. Yule covers prescription stimulant medication, and Frankenburg reviews methamphetamine and cocaine. Each part has one case study.

Prescription stimulants (part A), including amphetamines and methylphenidate, are approved by the Food and Drug Administration (FDA) to treat attention deficit hyperactivity disorder (ADHD), a disorder marked by impulsivity, hyperactivity, and difficulty sustaining attention. Methylphenidate also has a role in treating depression and apathy, particularly in the elderly and medically ill.

Methamphetamine (part B) is legal but rarely used as a prescription drug; it is more often manufactured illicitly and used in an illegal manner. Its most notorious form, "crystal meth," is associated with paranoia, violence, and serious medical problems.

Cocaine (part C) is used legally in some circumstances as a topical anesthetic agent. When snorted, smoked, or injected to get "high," cocaine is illegal and has no therapeutic purpose. Because of its rapid entry into the brain, it is addicting.

Part A

Prescription Stimulants

Prescription stimulants, such as amphetamines and methylphenidate, are most commonly prescribed to treat attention deficit hyperactivity disorder (ADHD), a neurobehavioral disorder that, in most individuals, begins in childhood and continues into adulthood. When prescription stimulants are used to treat ADHD and are taken as prescribed, they are safe and effective. Prescription stimulants can be misused, however, and nonmedical use (NMU) of prescription stimulants includes not taking the medication as prescribed or taking the medication without a prescription. Because these stimulants *are* prescribed, young people and parents often do not identify their NMU as risky or problematic when compared to the misuse of other drugs (Partnership for Drug-Free Kids 2013). However, there has been increasing concern regarding NMU of prescription stimulants, particularly among college students. When NMU is severe or problematic, it can meet the criteria for a stimulant use disorder; but because NMU is more common than stimulant use disorder, this part of the chapter will focus on NMU of prescription stimulants.

Symptoms, Diagnosis, and Incidence

Symptoms

Within the two classes of prescription stimulant medications, amphetamines and methylphenidate, there are several formulations that differ in duration of action and release pattern. As with other misused substances, the faster the prescription stimulant reaches the brain, the more reinforcing the substance is. Prescription stimulants that are "immediate release" (IR), such as mixed amphetamine IR or methylphenidate IR, quickly reach maximum concentration in the brain and have a short duration of action (three to four hours). Immediate-release prescription stimulants are more likely to be misused than are medium- and long-acting prescription stimulants. Individuals with no history of a substance use disorder felt more of an effect, and liked it more, when they took immediate-release methylphenidate than when they took a long-acting methylphenidate formulation (Spencer 2006, 391). When prescription stimulants are misused, they are most commonly ingested orally or intranasally. They are rarely smoked or injected intravenously (White, Becker-Blease, and Grace-Bishop 2006, 264).

NMU of prescription stimulants, particularly at high dosages, can be associated with increased anxiety including panic attacks, increased difficulty sleeping, aggression, paranoia, and perceptual disturbances (hallucinations).

Diagnosis

Unlike the other disorders in this book, NMU is not a *DSM-5* diagnosis. NMU includes using prescription stimulant medication without a prescription, using more than prescribed, or using the medication in a way other than what the doctor intended (Compton et al. 2018, 742). (Criteria for *DSM-5* stimulant use disorder are outlined in the Methamphetamine section.)

Incidence

In 2016, 2.1% of Americans aged 12 years and older admitted to NMU of a prescription stimulant at least once during the past year, and 0.2% met criteria for a prescription stimulant use disorder (Compton et al. 2018, 743). Rates of past-year NMU of prescription stimulants were highest among young people aged 18 to 25 years (7.5%), with lower rates in adolescents aged 12 to 17 years (1.7%) and adults aged 26 years and older (1.3%). Among young people, annual NMU of prescription stimulants is higher in those who are attending college compared to those who are not attending college. Studies of lifetime NMU of prescription stimulants among college students have ranged from 5% to 35%, and a recent meta-analysis estimated 17% of college students had a lifetime history of NMU of prescription stimulants (Benson et al. 2015). Among college students, higher rates of NMU of prescription stimulants have been seen among students involved in fraternities and sororities (Weyandt et al. 2016, 402).

History

One of the first amphetamines to reach the market was Benzedrine (amphetamine sulfate), which was used in the 1930s to treat nasal congestion. The company that developed the drug noticed it had "stimulating effects on brain function" and encouraged further study of the medication. In 1937, a psychiatrist named Charles Bradley found that, when he gave Benzedrine to children with behavioral disorders to treat severe headaches, it improved attention and decreased hyperactivity. In the 1930s, ADHD had not been well characterized or described, and research on the use of stimulant medication did not develop further until the mid-1950s when psychiatrists began to prescribe methylphenidate to treat hyperactivity. In 1968, the diagnosis of hyperkinetic reaction of childhood was included in the *DSM-II* (Epstein and Loren 2013, 455). It was not, however, until the publication of the *DSM-III* in 1980 that the diagnosis of ADHD, including problems related to attention, impulsivity, and hyperactivity, was created. With an established diagnosis and studies demonstrating the effectiveness of stimulant medication for the treatment of ADHD, prescriptions for prescription stimulants steadily increased through the 2000s (Castle et al. 2007, 336–339; Renoux et al. 2016, 860–861).

Development and Causes

Most individuals with NMU of prescription stimulants, particularly if they are college students, obtain the medication from friends or family for free (Murphy et al. 2018, 71). Among college students who had ADHD and were prescribed stimulant medication, 56% were asked by peers to share or sell their medication (Rabiner et al. 2009, 148), 53% had given the medication away for free, and 39% had sold it (DeSantis, Anthony, and Cohen 2013, 449). Some individuals will share their prescription stimulant medication with others in exchange for other substances or some other social nonmonetary gain, such as friendship, concert tickets, or meals (Murphy et al. 2018, 71–72).

Only a small percentage of individuals report NMU of prescription stimulants to get "high." Instead, most people report they misuse prescription stimulants to improve school or work performance (Murphy et al. 2018, 71). But NMU of prescription stimulants has been associated with poorer academic performance (Weyandt et al. 2016, 403). It may be, however, that individuals with neuropsychological deficits are more likely to misuse prescription stimulants. For example, one study compared college students with and without a history of NMU of prescription stimulants; it found that students who misused prescription stimulants performed worse on neuropsychological testing in the domains that involved attention and impulsivity than those who did not misuse them (Wilens et al. 2017, 381–384). Other substance use may also influence NMU of prescription stimulants in college students. When college students with NMU of prescription stimulants were compared to those without NMU of prescription stimulants, they were found to be three times more likely to have a substance use disorder (Wilens et al. 2016, 943). Another study that followed college students longitudinally found that those with alcohol and cannabis use disorders began skipping class, which was associated with a decline in grades. These students subsequently reported NMU of prescription stimulants (Arria et al. 2013).

Up Close—In Society

Since prescription stimulant medications are associated with a risk for misuse, they are classified as Schedule II medications by the U.S. Drug Enforcement Agency (DEA). Consequently, individuals who divert their medication, either by sharing or by selling it, could face criminal charges. Colleges have become increasingly concerned about NMU and diversion of prescription stimulants. Some view NMU of prescription stimulants as "cheating" and a violation of the honor code, carrying with it the possible consequence of expulsion (Abelman 2017). Other colleges have restricted prescriptions for these drugs or have banned student-health clinicians from diagnosing ADHD and/or prescribing stimulant medication to treat ADHD. Although NMU is a significant problem on college campuses, restricting access to care for individuals with ADHD has its own drawbacks because untreated ADHD is associated with poor academic performance (Uchida 2015). Furthermore, as detailed earlier, NMU of prescription stimulants is a sign that a student is struggling and would benefit from a thorough assessment of his or her substance use and psychiatric symptoms. College administrators should put systems in place that challenge students' positive beliefs associated with NMU of prescription stimulants and decrease peer pressure for students to divert their ADHD medication.

Case Study

Mr. B is a 20-year-old man with ADHD who has been prescribed a long-acting stimulant medication since mid-adolescence. He did well in a small high school with academic accommodations and organizational support and coaching from his parents. Mr. B and his parents were excited and proud when he was awarded an academic scholarship to a large out-of-state private school. Mr. B was eager to transition to college and decided to pledge a fraternity in his first semester. He began binge-drinking every weekend and using cannabis regularly. While at a fraternity event, a friend gave him a prescription stimulant pill to help him stay awake while drunk. Mr. B then told his friend that he was already prescribed prescription stimulant medication. The next day, the two of them, along with some other friends, discussed their use of these pills.

Mr. B found it difficult to focus in his large classes. As midterms approached, he began to feel overwhelmed by his coursework. He had extra dosages of his prescription stimulant medication on hand since he had often skipped his medication on the days after he used substances heavily and slept in. Mr. B began taking two to three times his prescribed dose of medication to stay up to study. Other members of his fraternity asked him to share his medication. In turn, he sometimes borrowed pills from his friends when they refilled their prescriptions, which were written by off-campus physicians. The night before his last midterm, Mr. B took five times his prescribed dose of stimulant medication. His heart rate increased, he became very anxious, and he drank shots of hard liquor to try to calm down. His resident advisor found him in the bathroom intoxicated and minimally responsive and brought him to the emergency room for further evaluation.

Up Close—At Work
Most of the research on NMU of prescription stimulants has been focused on college-age students, since misuse rates are high in this population. Research regarding NMU in older people and in the workplace is limited.

Up Close—In Relationships
Most people who misuse prescriptions get these medications for free from peers. Young people prescribed prescription stimulant medication may struggle when approached to share their medication. These difficult interactions complicate friendships.

Effects and Costs

Medical Side Effects

NMU of prescription stimulants can be associated with decreased appetite and, more seriously, with cardiovascular side effects, including an increase in blood pressure or heart rate. Although intravenous use of prescription stimulants is less common, it can be associated with the blockage of small blood vessels due to insoluble fillers in the tablets that are more common in longer-acting formulations (Canadian 2016a, 1).

Costs

NMU of prescription stimulants among adolescents is associated with increased difficulties in adulthood, which is costly for society. A recent study, which followed adolescents with NMU of prescription stimulants into middle age, found that they were less likely to obtain a two-year or four-year college degree when compared either to adolescents who were prescribed a stimulant medication and did not misuse it or to adolescents with no history of NMU of prescription stimulants (McCabe et al. 2017). Furthermore, in this study, adolescents with NMU of prescription stimulants were also more likely to have symptoms of a substance use disorder in adulthood.

As previously noted, NMU of prescription stimulants can be associated with adverse medical outcomes, which is also costly for society. A study of calls about exposure to ADHD medication to poison control centers between 2000 and 2014 found that 50% of adolescents who called had intentionally ingested a high dose of a prescription stimulant, either for misuse or to intentionally end their life (King et al. 2018). Among the 37,000 poison control calls for adolescent exposure to stimulant medication, 18% resulted in serious medical outcomes, including two deaths related to intentional misuse.

There is little research about the safety of prescription stimulants in pregnancy and breastfeeding. Amphetamine is considered a Class C drug for pregnant women, meaning that there are potential risks. Pregnant and breastfeeding women are advised not to use amphetamines.

Theory and Research

Because prescription stimulants are effective in the treatment of ADHD, much research is ongoing to create formulations of the medications with less risk for misuse.

Treatments

Most studies of the treatment of stimulant use disorders have focused on individuals with cocaine and/or methamphetamine use disorders. With limited research on treatment for prescription stimulant use disorders available, and given the shared mechanism of action of all stimulants, clinicians can consider using psychosocial treatments that have been effective for the treatment of cocaine and methamphetamine use disorders.

For individuals with NMU of prescription stimulants and/or a prescription stimulant use disorder, it is important to ask about misuse of other substances and disorders that can impact academic performance, such as ADHD, given the high comorbidity associated with NMU of prescription stimulants. If an individual with ADHD is diagnosed with a current prescription stimulant use disorder, stimulant medication is generally contraindicated. Nonstimulant medications for ADHD, such as atomoxetine or guanfacine, should probably be tried first. Furthermore, increased academic support should be provided to high school or college students with a current prescription stimulant use disorder and ADHD.

Certain strategies may decrease NMU of prescription stimulants, such as challenging the beliefs of college students concerning NMU of prescription stimulant medication. For example, some students believe that the NMU of prescription stimulants is helpful academically, safe, and common (Canadian 2016b, 9–11). One randomized controlled trial in college students at high risk for NMU of prescription stimulants evaluated the impact of an intervention that refuted the belief that prescription stimulants help with studying (Looby, De Young, and Earleywine 2013). The intervention was effective at first, but rates of NMU of prescription stimulants were the same between the group that did and the group that did not get the intervention at six-month follow-up.

Because most individuals with NMU of prescription stimulants get them for free from friends or family, increased efforts have focused on teaching providers who prescribe prescription stimulants how to educate children, adolescents, and families about the importance of taking the medication as prescribed and storing their medication safely (Harstad and Sharon 2014, e297–298).

Part B

Methamphetamine

Methamphetamine differs from amphetamine only in that it has an extra methyl group. Like amphetamine, it has some medical uses and is sometimes still prescribed for the treatment of ADHD, narcolepsy, or obesity. But its medical use is rare; it is considered more addictive than amphetamine. Like amphetamine and cocaine, methamphetamine is a Schedule II stimulant. In some ways, cocaine and methamphetamine are complementary drugs, in that each tends to be used in areas where the other is not—cocaine in urban areas, methamphetamine in rural areas. Most of the methamphetamine misused has been illicitly manufactured.

Symptoms, Diagnosis, and Incidence

Symptoms

The acute effects of methamphetamine, sometimes known as the "rush," are an intense increase of energy and alertness combined with euphoria. Libido increases and appetite for food disappears. After 5 to 30 minutes, the rush passes, but a person will still feel euphoria for up to 12 hours. In order to maintain these feelings, the person will take more of the drug. Users of methamphetamine often have episodes of bingeing, lasting from hours to days, sometimes known as "meth runs." A "meth run" may end in an unpleasant state sometimes known as a "tweak," in which the person is uncomfortable, feels miserable, and is unable to be still.

Methamphetamine is usually smoked or "snorted," and less commonly, injected or taken by mouth. Smoking and injecting methamphetamine are the quickest ways of delivering the drug into the brain, and are thus the most likely methods to lead to addiction (Radfar and Rawson 2014, 147). Once addiction has developed, the person may need to take higher doses of the drug or take it more often for it to have the same effects.

As addiction develops, euphoria may be replaced by paranoia or undue suspiciousness. Misusers of methamphetamine might develop persecutory delusions, believing that other people are following or trying to hurt them. These delusions can be associated with violence. They might also experience auditory, visual, and tactile hallucinations. The psychotic symptoms associated with methamphetamine occur in about 40% of users (Glasner-Edwards and Mooney 2014).

Withdrawal from methamphetamine, known as "crashing," is characterized by fatigue, somnolence, disturbed sleep, anxiety, depression, irritability, and craving. During this time, the person will experience prolonged anhedonia—the inability to experience pleasure. There are none of the physical withdrawal signs that are so prominent in withdrawal from benzodiazepines, alcohol, and opiates.

Diagnosis

According to the American Psychiatric Association's diagnostic manual, DSM-5 (American Psychiatric Association 2013), methamphetamine use meets criteria for a stimulant use disorder if the person meets two or more of the following criteria within a 12-month period: taking the stimulant in larger amounts or over a longer period despite original intentions; inability to control one's use of the stimulant; spending much time on stimulant-related activities that have become the focus of one's life; feeling a strong, almost irresistible desire to use the stimulant; inability to carry out one's usual tasks, usually because of being under the influence of the stimulant or recovering from its effects, although some claim that their job performance is improved by the stimulant; continuing to use the stimulant even though it is causing problems (often legal); giving up other activities because using the stimulant is more pleasurable and seems more urgent; using the stimulant even when it is associated with physical hazards; continuing to use the stimulant even though use is causing medical or psychological problems, such as heart problems; building up tolerance and needing to take higher doses of the stimulant to get the desired "rush," or having withdrawal symptoms when not using it. The disorder can be considered an addiction (a word that is being used less these days) or a severe disorder if the person meets six or more criteria.

Incidence

The 2017 National Survey on Drug Use and Health (NSDUH) reported that 1.1% of the U.S. population between the ages of 18 and 25 and

0.6% of those aged 26 or over had used methamphetamine in the last year (Substance Abuse and Mental Health Services Administration 2018). The first methamphetamine "epidemic" happened on the West Coast in the early 1980s. Since then, use of methamphetamine has remained more common in rural areas throughout the West and Midwest compared to other areas of the country. Unlike other drugs, methamphetamine is used by almost as many women as men. One group of people who seem to have higher rates of methamphetamine misuse than others is men who have sex with men (MSM).

Methamphetamine may be more likely to be used by Caucasians, Hispanics, Native Americans, and Asian-Pacific Islanders than by African Americans (Weisheit and White 2009, 19).

History

In 1885, the Japanese chemist Nagai Nagayoshi isolated the molecule ephedrine, and then in 1893, he synthesized methamphetamine from that molecule. Another form of synthesis was worked out in 1919, again in Japan. When methamphetamine became available in other parts of the world, it was used as a treatment for narcolepsy and as a weight-loss drug.

Methamphetamine was used as a stimulant in World War II by both the Allies and the Axis. Its use in Germany has been extensively described (see Sidebar 8.1).

Methamphetamine was used intravenously in the late 1950s and early 1960s by a few physicians as a treatment for heroin addiction (Weisheit and White 2009, 31). Illicit manufacturing of the drug may have begun in the United States in California in the early 1960s. By the late 1960s, intravenous methamphetamine was being used, along with other drugs, in California and some urban centers. It became associated with violence and psychosis. By the 1970s, most of the methamphetamine sold on the street in the United States had been illicitly manufactured (Weisheit and White 2009, 119).

There are several ways of synthesizing methamphetamine, some involving hazardous household chemicals and some involving other chemicals, such as anhydrous ammonia, a substance used as fertilizer in commercial agriculture. When methamphetamine is made in a certain way, it is a solid crystal that looks like shards of glass. This is known as "crystal meth" or "ice," and it can be ground into a powder and then snorted, swallowed, smoked, or injected. Beginning in the 1980s, people known as methamphetamine "cooks" synthesized methamphetamine in

Sidebar 8.1 Stimulant Use in Germany in World War II

In the days of the Weimar Republic, the German pharmaceutical industry was a leading producer and exporter of many drugs, including opioids and stimulants. Berlin in the 1920s was infamous for its excesses, nightlife, and liberal use of heroin, morphine, and cocaine. When Adolf Hitler first came to power, he declared drug abusers to be criminally insane, and people were encouraged to report them to the authorities. They could be imprisoned indefinitely, and some were sent to concentration camps. The image that Hitler presented of himself was of someone who did not smoke tobacco or drink alcohol or coffee and who disapproved strongly of mind- or mood-altering agents. However, he changed his mind as the Nazis discovered some uses for these drugs. In 1937, the Germans mastered their own synthesis of methamphetamine, naming it Pervitin. Millions of Pervitin pills were distributed to the German armed forces in 1940; and some have claimed that the overwhelming speed and endurance of the German army during the Blitzkrieg at the start of World War II was due, at least in part, to the use of methamphetamine. The increasingly bizarre behavior of Hitler at the end of World War II has been attributed to the use of many substances—administered by his physician—including opioids, cocaine, and methamphetamine, which he took by mouth and by injection (Ohler 2018).

Bibliography

Ohler, Norman, and Shaun Whiteside. *Blitzed: Drugs in the Third Reich.* New York: Mariner Books, 2018.

---

small "mom-and-pop" laboratories throughout the Midwest. For some years "meth labs" were implicated in explosions, fires, and the generation of toxic waste in the areas around the labs.

Because the common nasal decongestant pseudoephedrine was used in the manufacture of methamphetamine, in 2005, Congress passed the Combat Methamphetamine Epidemic Act, placing restrictions on the purchase of that drug. (There were already regulations limiting the availability of ephedrine.) Federal regulations require that the drug not be available on pharmacy shelves but only sold behind the pharmacy or service counter. Regulations vary between states, but the general purpose is to restrict the purchase of large amounts of the drug. No prescription is needed in most states.

Following the passage of this act, the number of small methamphetamine labs decreased, the price of methamphetamine increased, and purity of the drug decreased. An unintended consequence of this precursor control was that powerful international drug-trafficking operations began supplying more of the product. Now, much methamphetamine is made in "super labs" in Mexico and smuggled across the Mexican border.

Although it is rarely prescribed, methamphetamine is still approved by the FDA for the treatment of ADHD and obesity. It is sold as Desoxyn, and the prescriptions are not refillable to prevent overuse.

Development and Causes

The transition from using methamphetamine and "liking" the effects to intense craving for the drug is not fully understood.

Up Close—In Society
Methamphetamine is more prevalent in rural areas where its use is particularly problematic because of limited access to health-care and treatment facilities. People living in rural areas are also likely to begin using methamphetamine at a younger age than their urban counterparts. Rural use is more likely to be intravenous, which is particularly concerning since people in these areas have less access to clean needles, and sharing needles is associated with the transmission of infectious diseases (Dombrowski et al. 2016).

Methamphetamine is associated with violence, domestic violence, and child neglect. Whether the association is due to methamphetamine itself is difficult to determine because of the psychosocial stressors that may precede the drug use and because of comorbid drug use, especially alcohol, all of which independently may be associated with violence.

Case Study
Mr. A is a 25-year-old roofer who has been admitted to an inpatient unit with suicidal thoughts. Recently, he has had trouble keeping a job and is about to lose his health insurance. He says that crystal meth is his "drug of choice." He smokes or injects it and often drinks alcohol at the same time. He says that methamphetamine is the only drug that makes him feel as though life is worthwhile and that he can't stop using it. While on the unit, he has assaulted other patients and has smuggled in illicit drugs in his shoes. He accuses hospital staff of mistreating him and stealing his belongings. He tells them that he is worried he might have hepatitis C because his friend, with whom he uses drugs, has recently been given that diagnosis. Hospital staff suggest to him that he go to a long-term treatment facility, but he refuses, saying that he knows that such

programs do not work and that he cannot afford it anyway. He plans to ask an outpatient doctor for a prescription for a long-acting amphetamine, which he has heard will treat his cravings for methamphetamine. Hospital staff talk to him about the importance of staying healthy by no longer using methamphetamine; if he does continue injecting it, he should use new needles every time he injects.

Up Close—At Work

Methamphetamine may be used preferentially in occupations such as truck-driving or manufacturing. Anecdotal reports suggest that some people use it to help them concentrate and be more productive at work. Whether or not this happens, when addiction takes over, the person becomes lost in a cycle of being "high," "crashing," and needing higher and higher doses of the drug. A person who is dependent on methamphetamine will have difficulty being reliable at work. The use of methamphetamine at work is associated with absenteeism, violence, distractibility, and loss of jobs (Weisheit and White 2009, 21–22, 87–98).

Up Close—In Relationships

Many of the effects of a methamphetamine use disorder—such as preoccupation with getting the drug, going through withdrawal, and paranoia—make sustaining relationships difficult. As previously noted, methamphetamine is associated with domestic violence and child neglect. One of the effects of methamphetamine is increase in libido. For some MSM, methamphetamine has become an important part of their sexuality, and the prospect of sexual activity in a drug-free state can be unappealing.

Effects and Costs

Medical Effects

Chronic users of methamphetamine may suffer the death of nerve cells, although this effect has not yet been established definitively. Some neuroimaging studies have shown structural and functional changes in the brain that may explain memory loss and mood disturbances. Proebstl et al. (2018) reviewed the literature and concluded that methamphetamine use is associated with metabolic changes in the dopaminergic system and, possibly because of these and other changes, impaired memory, attention, and concentration. Whether these changes remit with abstinence from methamphetamine is not known.

The most serious health effects of methamphetamine are cardiovascular and cerebrovascular. Users can develop high blood pressure, cardiac arrhythmias, heart attacks, and cardiomyopathy. Methamphetamine use is associated with hemorrhagic strokes, even in young people (Huang et al. 2016; Lappin, Drake, and Farrell 2017).

As noted earlier, methamphetamine can be injected, and if the person does not use clean needles, that individual will be at increased risk of contracting HIV and/or hepatitis B or C. Snorting methamphetamine may also increase the risk of contracting these diseases (Fernandez et al. 2016).

In their work with MSM, Halkitis, Mukherjee, and Palamar (2008) note that methamphetamine decreases inhibitions and increases sexual arousal, leading sometimes to multiple partners and unprotected sex. The combination of risky sexual behaviors and drug injections puts these methamphetamine users at particularly high risk of contracting HIV and/or hepatitis B and C.

Dental problems, resulting in "meth mouth," may be related to methamphetamine-caused dry mouth and tooth grinding. Other factors associated with methamphetamine, such as poor nutrition and inadequate dental hygiene, may also contribute to tooth decay and gum problems.

Sometimes people who use methamphetamine develop itching, a sensation of bugs crawling on them, or feeling something under their skin. They may begin to pick at their skin, and skin infections or abscesses can develop. Some people develop repetitive motor activity and pick their skin repeatedly, worsening their skin problems.

Methamphetamine is associated with increased mortality. In a Taiwanese study of over 1,200 subjects with methamphetamine dependence, the risk of unnatural deaths was more than 25 times what would have been expected in women and ten times what would have been expected in men (Kuo et al. 2010).

Pregnant or breastfeeding women should avoid misusing methamphetamine. Because of the possible dangers of methamphetamine during pregnancy and the difficulty of withdrawal, the pregnant woman misusing methamphetamine should contact her clinician for help. Other problems often associated with methamphetamine misuse such as poor diet and infections can also adversely affect pregnancy.

Because of the complexity of these problems, some authorities suggest that pregnant women with a methamphetamine use disorder get care at a residential treatment center where they can receive comprehensive care and social support services.

Cost

According to a 2009 RAND study that reviewed data from 2005, methamphetamine use might have cost the United States about $23.4 billion in that year, although the bounds of this figure are between $16.2 billion to $48.3 billion. Most of this cost is due to "intangible burdens" such as premature death, but it also includes estimates of legal costs, lost productivity, child endangerment, treatment, and hazards resulting from methamphetamine production (Nicosia et al. 2009).

Theory and Research

Methamphetamine is structurally similar to amphetamine and dopamine. It blocks the reuptake of monoamine neurotransmitters (such as dopamine, serotonin, or noradrenaline), as does cocaine, and it increases the release of dopamine. Methamphetamine leads to higher concentrations of dopamine in the synaptic cleft (the space between neurons) than cocaine and lasts longer in the body. Most of the effects of methamphetamine are thought to be due to the increase of dopamine in the synaptic cleft and the subsequent temporary increase in dopamine signaling. (The effects of disrupted dopamine are described elsewhere.) Methamphetamine also increases levels of noradrenaline, which may explain the cardiovascular activation.

Treatments

Treatment for methamphetamine use disorder is often mandated by the criminal justice system or child protection services (Weisheit and White 2009, 214). Withdrawal does not present with medical problems or need medical monitoring, but the somnolence, anhedonia, and craving for food can be almost intolerable and lead to reuse of the drug.

Behavioral treatments for methamphetamine use disorder include contingency management. In this approach, abstinence from methamphetamine or attendance at certain meetings or activities is reinforced by rewards, such as money or vouchers. The "matrix model" is an intensive 16-week outpatient program that uses a combination of behavioral approaches such as cognitive behavioral therapy (CBT) and motivational interviewing (explained in other chapters) in individual and group settings (Obert et al. 2000).

No medication has been clearly found to be helpful for the treatment of methamphetamine use disorder, and none is approved by the FDA.

Trials of antidepressants bupropion or mirtazapine show some modest utility (Colfax et al. 2011; Stoops and Rush 2013).

Another way of treating this disorder is to consider harm reduction. Supplying people who use methamphetamine with clean needles and encouraging condom use may decrease the risk of HIV and hepatitis B and C transmission (Radfar and Rawson 2014, 150).

Some tentative approaches to treatment include the use of cognitive-enhancing agents (important if methamphetamine does indeed lead to cognitive damage), deep brain stimulation (Kish 2008, 1682) and perhaps naltrexone (Roche et al. 2017).

Ancillary services, such as social work, vocational counseling, and family therapy, are essential. Mutual-aid societies, such as Crystal Meth Anonymous, which is based on Alcoholics Anonymous, can be helpful.

Part C

Cocaine

Cocaine, found in the coca leaf, is a natural substance that has been used for centuries in the Andes as a mild stimulant. When cocaine was extracted or isolated from the coca leaf, it became easier to use. It is now an addictive drug and increasingly dangerous because it is sometimes combined with the potent synthetic opioid fentanyl.

Symptoms, Diagnosis, and Incidence

Symptoms

When coca leaves are chewed or drunk in the form of a tea, cocaine is delivered to the brain slowly, leading to a mild increase in energy and/or the ability to tolerate altitude sickness. When cocaine powder is snorted, it is absorbed immediately into the blood vessels of the nasal membranes and then rapidly transported to the brain. Cocaine is absorbed fastest, however, when it is injected as a powder dissolved in water or when it is smoked as crack cocaine. The faster the brain uptake, the more intense is the "rush" and the more likely it is to lead to addiction.

Snorting, injecting, or smoking cocaine leads at first to euphoria. But this euphoria can quickly change to irritability, suspiciousness, and rage. Cocaine can also be associated with hallucinations, that is, hearing, seeing, or feeling things that are not there. Injected cocaine and smoked crack cocaine are the two routes most commonly associated with the development of paranoia and hallucinations.

Some of those who use high doses of cocaine by snorting, injecting, or smoking it become addicted. Withdrawal, known colloquially as "crashing," has none of the dangerous medical problems seen in withdrawal from benzodiazepines and alcohol, such as seizures, or, as with alcohol, delirium tremens or death, but individuals with cocaine use disorders experience intense misery, somnolence, and craving for cocaine when not using it. They may also have trouble sleeping, increased appetite, agitation, and prolonged anhedonia—the inability to experience pleasure. More clearly than with the other misused substances, these symptoms are related to changes in brain pathways that may take months to readjust.

Diagnosis

Cocaine use meets criteria for an American Psychiatric Association (2013) *DSM-5* substance use disorder if it meets the criteria outlined in the Methamphetamine section.

Incidence

The 2014–2015 NSDUH estimates that about 5% of people aged 18 to 25 in the United States used cocaine in the last year. The use varies geographically, from 2% in Mississippi to 11% in New Hampshire (Hughes et al. 2016). Most cocaine use is by young urban men.

The number of people with cocaine use disorder is considerably lower. In reviewing the data from the 2000–2001 National Household Surveys on Drug Abuse (NHSDA), O'Brien and Anthony (2005) found that between 5% and 6% of those who use cocaine will become dependent on it within two years. The risk was higher among females and those who smoked crack cocaine or injected cocaine.

The estimated annual prevalence of cocaine use disorder in the United States is about 0.4% among individuals 12 years and older (Substance Abuse and Mental Health Services Administration 2018).

History

Erythroxylon coca (sometimes spelled *Erythroxylum coca*), or coca, is a revered long-lived evergreen shrub that grows in the valleys of the Andean Mountains in Peru, Bolivia, Ecuador, and Colombia. Coca leaves have been chewed for several thousand years in South America.

Coca is associated with the Incas, a tribe in the Cusco area (now in Peru) that formed an empire from about 1200 to 1600 CE, comprising at one point 12 million people and stretching out along the Pacific Coast of South America from present-day Ecuador to Chile. Runner-messengers and laborers who built Machu Picchu chewed coca leaves to energize themselves. Coca was also an important part of Incan rituals.

Coca leaf, in the pre-Incan and Incan eras and in much of Andean South America today, is chewed with lime-rich materials so that the cocaine alkaloid can be freed from the rest of the leaf. Coca leaf is sometimes steeped in hot water to form coca tea, a beverage containing small amounts of cocaine that may help overcome altitude sickness.

In the 15th century, Spanish soldiers explored, conquered, and exploited parts of the Americas looking for gold, silver, and spices. The Andean use of the coca leaf shocked the Spanish, and the bishop of Cusco declared coca to be an agent of the devil. (In a similar way, King James I of England had declared nicotine to belong to the devil.) But after the Spanish realized that they could tax coca leaf—and get more work (and silver) from the Andeans and provide them with less food if they gave them coca leaf to chew—the bishop withdrew his disapproval.

The Prussian geographer and naturalist Alexander von Humboldt encountered coca leaf during his travels to South America from 1799 to 1804 and described its remarkable ability to help its users withstand fatigue and hunger. In 1860, the president of the British Royal Geographical Society and Incan historian and linguist, Sir Clements Markham, also explored South America and chewed coca leaf to keep up with his porters.

In 1875, Sir Robert Christison, the president of the British Medical Association and personal physician to Queen Victoria, used coca leaf to help him climb mountains at the age of 75. English race walkers chewed coca leaves to improve their performance (Karch 1998, 19).

In the late 1860s, Angelo Mariani, a chemist from Corsica, created a bestselling beverage, Vin Mariani, by marinating coca leaves in Bordeaux wine. John Stith Pemberton, an American pharmacist, created a similar beverage using wine, coca leaf, and kola nut extracts containing caffeine. He marketed French Wine Coca as a patent medicine that could treat morphine addiction. In 1886, Pemberton removed the alcohol from French Wine Coca, added sugar, more caffeine, and carbonation—and created Coca-Cola.

German chemists Friedrich Gaedcke and Albert Niemann separately identified the active ingredient of the coca leaf, Niemann coming up with the name *cocaine*. This chemical advance made cocaine a more commercially attractive substance because it was easier to ship cocaine to Europe than the mold-susceptible coca leaf—and easier to standardize. Parke-Davis and Merck, American and German pharmaceutical companies, respectively, began to sell cocaine products.

A German army physician, Dr. Theodor Aschenbrandt, used Merck cocaine to improve the performance of soldiers. This report attracted the attention of neurologist and founder of psychoanalysis Sigmund Freud, who thought that cocaine was a safe way to increase energy and treat addiction to opiates. Freud told one of his colleagues, Carl Koller, a young Viennese doctor studying ophthalmology, about this drug.

Ophthalmologists who removed cataracts needed a safe numbing drug that acted quickly and briefly. Koller had tried many different drugs with no success, until he experimented with cocaine. The ability to remove cataracts painlessly was a breakthrough in medicine. William Halsted, an American surgeon, expanded the uses of cocaine further by inventing nerve-blocking anesthesia. (Halsted became addicted to cocaine and then opiates.)

In the late 1800s and early 1900s, coca leaf and cocaine were used in Europe and North America as tonics or cures for addictions, colds, or hay fever. Cocaine was even used briefly to treat asthma. (Cocaine may constrict the blood vessels in the mucosa of the nose and lungs, reducing any swelling and thus improving airflow.)

Parke-Davis sold coca cheroots (a type of cigar) and coca cigarettes. The cheroots and cigarettes were never very popular, probably because smoking cocaine powder destroys most of it. The company also sold syringes and cocaine powder together to make cocaine injections convenient for the customer.

In the early 20th century, snorting cocaine powder became fashionable among the wealthy and the unconventional in Europe and the United States. Cocaine then became less popular, possibly because of the arrival of the cheaper amphetamines. The use of cocaine as a local anesthetic was largely replaced by synthetic drugs such as procaine.

After World War II, large amounts of cocaine began to be smuggled out of South America by gangsters and politicians, such as Manuel Noriega, military dictator of Panama from 1983 to 1989. Pablo Escobar, the creator of the Medellín drug cartel, smuggled cocaine paste through Panama into the United States with the help of Noriega. The corruption funded by the profits of cocaine, the armed conflicts, and the complicated involvement of the CIA have been extensively described (Cockburn and St Clair 1998; Streatfield 2001).

In the 1960s, cocaine powder was being snorted on Wall Street and in Hollywood, but it was not considered to be a very addictive drug. However, the public and drug experts became more alarmed in the late 1970s when free-base cocaine appeared.

Cocaine powder is a salt, cocaine hydrochloride, which can be changed into a base by the removal of the hydrochloride molecule. This can be done in several ways. One way is with ether, but this method is dangerous because ether is flammable. In the early 1970s, people began to use baking soda (or sodium bicarbonate) to process the cocaine powder into a base. If cocaine powder and baking soda are heated together, chunks of free-base cocaine form. In the 1980s, this preparation became known as *crack cocaine* because of the crackling sound that it makes when heated and smoked. Crack cocaine was cheap, easy to prepare and smoke, and highly addictive.

Cocaine powder can be smoked, but at high temperatures the powder burns, the cocaine molecule degrades, so the powder loses much of its potency. Free-base or crack cocaine, in contrast, turns into a vapor at the temperature at which it is smoked. Vaporized free-base cocaine is unchanged, reaching the brain in a few seconds and leading to a rapid and intense "high."

Development and Causes

Although the causes of cocaine use disorder are not known, some risk factors can be described. People at the highest risk for using cocaine are unemployed men who are in their twenties, high school graduates, and living in urban areas. Cocaine misuse is highly correlated with the misuse of other substances, particularly cigarettes and alcohol.

As previously noted, the development of a cocaine use disorder is more likely if people are heavy users or inject or smoke the drug because the drug gets to the brain so much faster than other ways. (Coca tea drinkers are not likely to develop a cocaine use disorder.) Studies of fraternal or identical twins suggest that there may be a genetic vulnerability to cocaine use disorder (Ducci and Goldman 2012).

Up Close—In Society

As a result of the "War on Drugs" and the emphasis on the dangers of crack cocaine, the United States has one of the highest incarceration rates in the world. The incarcerations are mainly among the black population, even though there are few if any differences between the races in rates of drug use and selling (Alexander 2012, 6–7). The high rates of incarceration have been disastrous for the inner cities and the African American population (see Sidebar 8.2).

Up Close—at Work

Cocaine is sometimes used as a "party drug" on weekends as a "reward" for a week at work. If the person develops a cocaine use disorder, it is likely that his or her performance at school or work will suffer.

Sidebar 8.2 Legal and Race Issues

The development of crack cocaine in the late 1970s was particularly harmful for the African American population. Easily available and cheap, crack cocaine became associated with inner cities, minorities, and violence, while powder cocaine was associated with wealth and irresponsibility. The federal government publicized the problems with crack cocaine to support its "War on Drugs." In 1986, the American Anti-Drug Abuse Act was passed, with the hope that tough laws and mandatory minimum sentencing would stop the epidemic of crack cocaine use. Possession (with intent to distribute) of 500 grams of powder cocaine or 5 grams of crack cocaine meant a five-year mandatory minimum sentence. Possession of 5,000 grams of powder cocaine or 50 grams of crack cocaine meant a 10-year mandatory minimum sentence.

Because of the 100-to-1 sentencing disparity between powder cocaine and crack cocaine, poor people with small amounts of crack cocaine made up a disproportionate share of those jailed for drug offenses (Alexander 2012). Eventually, in 2010, Congress partially addressed these problems by passing the Fair Sentencing Act, which reduced the powder–crack disparity in sentencing from 100 to 1 to 18 to 1 and eliminated the 5-year mandatory minimum sentence for simple possession of crack cocaine.

Prosecutorial discretion exacerbates this inequity. For example, prosecutors can make case-by-case decisions as to whether a person will be prosecuted in a state or federal court. Prosecutors may more often allow white Americans to be sentenced according to the more lenient state guidelines, while African Americans are sentenced according to the harsh federal guidelines. Prosecutors also more frequently charge black juveniles in adult court than white juveniles, where penalties are more severe (Alexander 2012, 115–118).

Bibliography

Alexander, Michelle. *The New Jim Crow: Mass Incarceration in the Age of Colorblindness*. New York: The New Press, 2012.

Case Study

Sam is a 35-year-old financial analyst. Since the age of 13, he has drunk alcohol and smoked cigarettes. Ten years ago, he began to go to parties on the weekend, where he snorted cocaine powder but worried that he might be damaging his nose. One day he was given crack cocaine to smoke. He preferred this route and found that the effects were stronger, so his cocaine consumption increased. He enjoyed it so much that he could not believe that it was harmful.

Sam's weekends began to be dominated by his cocaine misuse, and after a few weeks, it began to affect his work. He was irritable with his coworkers and developed a persistent cough. He thought that his coworkers had told the police that he was using drugs and that the police were surveilling him. He moved into a cheaper apartment, hoping to get away from the police and to save money. He wanted to quit his job but needed his salary to pay for his drugs. To have more money to spend on cocaine, he attempted to embezzle money from his workplace but was eventually caught and fired. He was unable to pay his taxes and started getting letters from the IRS.

Occasionally, Sam would realize that his problems were due to his use of cocaine, and he would quit. He would feel much better after a few weeks—but then celebrate by resuming his habit. If he had a particularly bad day—for example, if another letter from the IRS arrived—he would use more cocaine.

Up Close—In Relationships
As with other substance use disorders, the person with a cocaine use disorder will have difficulty with relationships, as the need for the drug displaces other needs.

Effects and Costs
Medical Complications of Cocaine

Cocaine blocks sodium ion channels—this is how it works as an anesthetic, and this might be why it leads to cardiac arrhythmias. Because it also leads to increased neurotransmitter release, including adrenaline, cocaine constricts, or narrows, the blood vessels, leading to high blood pressure, decreased blood supply to the heart, and a faster heartbeat. Cocaine has been associated with heart attacks. Cocaine use is also associated with ischemic stroke within 24 hours of use in people under the age of 49 (Cheng et al. 2016). The combination of alcohol and cocaine leads to the formation of the compound cocaethylene in the liver, which is more toxic to the heart than either substance alone.

Despite its earlier use as a treatment for asthma, cocaine is now thought to harm the lungs and trigger asthma attacks. Smoking crack cocaine can lead to pulmonary symptoms, such as cough, shortness of breath, and wheezing. Cocaine use can also lead to gastrointestinal and kidney problems. People who inject cocaine are at risk for contracting HIV and/or hepatitis B or C. People who snort cocaine may also be at risk contracting hepatitis C because of damage to nasal blood vessels (Fernandez et al. 2016).

The person using cocaine may feel that bugs or parasites are crawling under his or her skin, a sensation known as "formication." Users sometimes pick at their skin, trying to get rid of the hallucinated "cocaine bugs." Some users also develop repetitive and compulsive behaviors (known as "punding") or extreme anxiety.

By snorting cocaine powder, one can damage several parts of the nose, including the turbinates and nasal septum; and because cocaine has anesthetic effects, the damage may not be noticed very quickly. The damage is due to blood vessel constriction, caused by the cocaine, and exacerbated by chemical irritation from adulterants. The cocaine may also impair the movement of the cilia, tiny hair-like structures that move the mucus blanket along the interior of the nose, leading to a frequent runny nose. Misusing other substances increases the cocaine-associated harms, particularly if the substance used with cocaine is fentanyl. Rates of drug overdose deaths involving cocaine increased by 52% between 2015 and 2016 (Seth et al. 2018).

In the past, medical authorities warned that children born to women using crack cocaine during pregnancy could later suffer from low intelligence and poor social skills. These warnings about the "crack babies" are now thought to have been grossly exaggerated. Nonetheless, as with methamphetamine, cocaine use during pregnancy and breastfeeding should be avoided because, among all the other problems associated with its misuse, it can be dangerous to both the pregnant woman and her baby. Pregnant women using cocaine are themselves at increased risk for having seizures, high blood pressure, miscarriages, preterm birth, and difficult deliveries. Some babies may be born dependent on cocaine and be "jittery" and experience growth delay. Experts suspect that as these babies grow older, they may develop learning difficulties and have subtle problems in adolescence with language and memory.

Cocaine misuse is often associated with other conditions that are harmful, such as misuse of other substances, poor nutrition, inadequate prenatal care, and difficult socioeconomic conditions. Cocaine-using pregnant women should receive appropriate medical care and social support.

Costs

Surprisingly, there has been little research into the costs of cocaine misuse.

Theory and Research

Cocaine is one of the best understood addictive substances, thanks in part to many experiments with rodents. In some well-known experiments, rats will press levers to obtain cocaine to the exclusion of most other activities. In most of these experiments, the rats are housed in single wire cages. Canadian psychologist Bruce Alexander was interested in the environments of these rats and created an environment known as "Rat Park" in which 20 to 30 rats of both genders lived in a large enclosure with cedar shavings, tin cans for hiding and nesting, and poles, balls and wheels for play. The Rat Park rodents showed less drive for morphine than rats housed in cages (Alexander et al. 1981). Other researchers have also shown that rats have less craving for cocaine in enriched environments (Chauvet et al. 2009).

Ventral tegmental area (VTA) neuron axon terminals release dopamine into the nucleus accumbens. Cocaine blocks the dopamine reuptake pumps (or transporters) and the resulting temporary increase of nucleus accumbens dopamine is thought to lead to the intense pleasure that the drug causes. Cocaine disrupts the normal functioning of other parts of the brain involved in executive functioning (described in greater detail elsewhere). VTA projections to the hippocampus and amygdala are probably involved in establishing associations between cocaine and pleasure, and for "teaching" the person to link cocaine with pleasure.

Treatments

Many behavioral treatments for cocaine addiction are used. Contingency management programs reward people who abstain from cocaine (and/or other drugs) with a voucher or prize. (Abstinence is confirmed by a "clean" urine screen.) Vouchers can be used for a variety of rewards such as movie tickets or meals at restaurants.

Another approach is CBT, in which cocaine use disorder is seen as a learned maladaptive behavior that can be modified by teaching the person different patterns of thought and behavior. Some people who use cocaine are referred to live-in therapeutic communities for up to 12 months. Participation in Cocaine Anonymous, a mutual-aid group based on Alcoholics Anonymous, can be helpful.

Harm-reduction strategies, such as a needle exchange program, where individuals can receive new, clean needles for free and safely dispose of used needles, are controversial but thought to be helpful in reducing the spread of infectious diseases such as hepatitis B and C and/or HIV among people who use drugs intravenously.

No medications have been approved by the FDA to treat cocaine use disorder. The antidepressant bupropion is a weak dopamine agonist that increases extracellular dopamine levels in the nucleus accumbens by binding to the dopamine transporter and inhibiting dopamine uptake. This medication may be helpful when combined with behavioral treatment (Stoops and Rush 2013). Trials of amphetamine-like medications, including sustained-release methamphetamine, have shown some success (Stoops and Rush 2013). The treatment of ADHD in patients with cocaine use disorder with extended-release mixed amphetamine salts at "robust" doses combined with CBT and close monitoring was safe and effective and led to a reduction in cocaine use (Levin et al. 2015). There is some interest in other medications, such as disulfiram, methylphenidate, and modafinil (Soyka and Mutschler 2016).

Researchers are currently testing medications that act at the dopamine D_3 receptor or substances that affect glutamate or gamma-aminobutyric acid (GABA) transmission. There is interest in a cocaine vaccine, in which the vaccine stimulates the immune system to produce antibodies to the cocaine molecule (Heekin, Shorter, and Kosten 2017). Whatever the treatment, ongoing support or aftercare is essential to help people avoid relapse.

Bibliography

Abelman, Dor D. "Mitigating Risks of Students Use of Study Drugs through Understanding Motivations for Use and Applying Harm Reduction Theory: A Literature Review." *Harm Reduct J* 14, no. 1 (2017), 68. doi:10.1186/s12954-017-0194-6.

Alexander, Bruce K., Barry L. Beyerstein, Patricia F. Hadaway, and Robert B. Coambs. "Effect of Early and Later Colony Housing on Oral Ingestion of Morphine In Rats." *Pharmacol Biochem Behav* 15 (1981), 571–576.

Alexander, Michelle. *The New Jim Crow: Mass Incarceration in the Age of Colorblindness.* New York: The New Press, 2012.

American Psychiatric Association. *Diagnostic and Statistical Manual of Mental Disorders: Fifth Edition.* Arlington, VA: American Psychiatric Association, 2013. doi:10.1176/appi.books.9780890425596. 744053.

Arria, Amelia M., Holly C. Wilcox, Kimberly M. Caldeira, Kathyrn B. Vincent, Laura M. Garnier-Dykstra, and Kevin E. O'Grady. "Dispelling the Myth of 'Smart Drugs': Cannabis and Alcohol Use Problems Predict Nonmedical Use of Prescription Stimulants for Studying." *Addict Behav* 38, no. 3 (2013), 1643–1650.

Benson, Kari, Kate Flory, Kathyrn L. Humphreys, and Steve S. Lee. "Misuse of Stimulant Medication among College Students: A Comprehensive Review and Meta-Analysis." *Clin Child Fam Psychol Rev* 18 (2015), 50–76.

Canadian Centre on Substance Abuse. "Canadian Drug Summary: Prescription Stimulants" (2016a).

Canadian Centre on Substance Abuse. "Prevention of Prescription Stimulant Misuse among Youth" (2016b).

Castle, Lon, Ronald E. Aubert, Robert R. Verbrugge, Mona Khalid, and Robert E. Epstein. "Trends in Medication Treatment for ADHD." *J Att Dis* 10, no. 4 (2007), 335–342.

Chauvet, Claudia, Virginie Lardeux, Steven R. Goldberg, Mohamed Jaber, and Marcello Solinas. "Environmental Enrichment Reduces Cocaine Seeking and Reinstatement Induced by Cues and Stress but Not by Cocaine." *Neuropsychopharmacology* 34, no. 13 (2009), 2767–2778. doi:10.1038/npp.2009.127.

Cheng, Yu-Ching, Kathleen A. Ryan, Saad A. Qadwai, Jay Shah, Mary J. Sparks, Marcella A. Wozniak, Barney J. Stern, et al. "Cocaine Use and Risk of Ischemic Stroke in Young Adults." *Stroke* 47, no. 4 (2016), 918–922. doi:10.1161/strokeaha.115.011417.

Cockburn, Alexander, and Jeffrey St. Clair. *Whiteout: The CIA, Drugs and the Press*. New York: Verso, 1998.

Colfax, Grant N., Glenn M. Santos, Moupali Das, Deirdre M. Santos, Tim Matheson, James J. Gasper, Steven Shoptaw, and Eric Vittinghoff. "Mirtazapine to Reduce Methamphetamine Use." *Arch Gen Psychiatry* 68, no. 11 (2011), 1168–1175. doi:10.1001/archgenpsychiatry.2011.124.

Compton, Wilson M., Beth Han, Carlos Blanco, Kimberly Johnson, and Christopher M. Jones. "Prevalence and Correlates of Prescription Stimulant Use, Misuse, Use Disorders, and Motivations for Misuse among Adults in the United States." *Am J Psychiatry* 175 (2018), 741–755.

DeSantis, Alan D., Kathryn E. Anthony, and Elisia L. Cohen. "Illegal College ADHD Stimulant Distributors: Characteristics and Potential Areas of Intervention." *Subst Use Misuse* 48, no. 6 (2013), 446–450.

Dombrowski, Kirk, Devan Crawford, Bilal Khan, and Kimberly Tyler. "Current Rural Drug Use in the US Midwest." *J Drug Abuse* 2, no. 3 (2016), 22.

Ducci, Francesca, and David Goldman. "The Genetic Basis of Addictive Disorders." *Psychiatr Clin North Am* 35, no. 2 (2012), 495–519. doi:10.1016/j.psc.2012.03.010.

Epstein, Jeffrey N., and Richard E. Loren. "Changes in the Definition of ADHD in DSM-5: Subtle but Important." *Neuropsychiatry* 3, no. 5 (2013), 455–458.

Fernandez, Noelle, Craig V. Towers, Lynlee Wolfe, Mark D. Hennessy, Beth Weitz, and Stephanie Porter. "Sharing of Snorting Straws and Hepatitis C Virus Infection in Pregnant Women." *Obst Gynecol* 128, no. 2 (2016), 234–237. doi:10.1097/aog.0000000000001507.

Glasner-Edwards, Suzette, and Larissa J. Mooney. "Methamphetamine Psychosis: Epidemiology and Management." *CNS Drugs* 28, no. 12 (2014), 1115–1126. doi:10.1007/s40263-014-0209-8.

Halkitis, Perry N., Preetika P. Mukherjee, and Joseph J. Palamar. "Longitudinal Modeling of Methamphetamine Use and Sexual Risk Behaviors in Gay and Bisexual Men." *AIDS Behav* 13, no. 4 (2008), 783–791. doi:10.1007/s10461-008-9432-y.

Harstad, Elizabeth, Sharon Levy, and Committee on Substance Abuse. "Attention Deficit/Hyperactivity Disorder and Substance Abuse." *Pediatrics* 134 (2014), e293–301.

Heekin, R. D., Daryl Shorter, and Thomas R. Kosten. "Current Status and Future Prospects for the Development of Substance Abuse Vaccines." *Expert Rev Vaccines* 16, no. 11 (2017), 1067–1077. doi:10.10 80/14760584.2017.1378577.

Huang, Ming-Chyi, Shu-Yu Yang, Shih-Ku Lin, Kuan-Yu Chen, Ying-Yeh Chen, Chian-Jue Kuo, and Yen-Ni Hung. "Risk of Cardiovascular Diseases and Stroke Events in Methamphetamine Users." *J Clin Psychiatry* 77, no. 10 (2016), 1396–1402. doi:10.4088/JCP.15m09872.

Hughes, Arthur, Matthew R. Williams, Rachel N. Lipari, and Struther Van Horn. "State Estimates of Past Year Cocaine Use Among Young Adults: 2014 and 2015—The CBHSQ Report." National Center for Biotechnology Information. Last modified December 20, 2016. https://www.ncbi.nlm.nih.gov/books/NBK424783/.

Karch, Steven B. *A Brief History of Cocaine*. Boca Raton, FL: CRC Press, 1998.

King, Samantha A., Marcel J. Casavant, Henry A. Spiller, Nichole L. Hodges, Thitphalak Chounthirath, and Gary A. Smith. "Pediatric ADHD Medication Exposures Reported to US Poison Control Centers." *Pediatrics* 141, no. 6 (2018). doi:10.1542/peds.2017-3872.

Kish, Stephen J. "Pharmacologic Mechanisms of Crystal Meth." *Can Med Assoc J* 178, no. 13 (2008), 1679–1682. doi:10.1503/cmaj.071675.

Kuo, Chian-Jue, Ya-Tang Liao, Wei J. Chen, Shang-Ying Tsai, Shih-Ku Lin, and Chiao-Chicy Chen. "Causes of Death of Patients with Methamphetamine Dependence: A Record-Linkage Study." *Drug Alcohol Rev* 30, no. 6 (2010), 621–628.

Lappin, Julia M., Shane Darke, and Michael Farrell. "Stroke and Methamphetamine Use in Young Adults: A Review." *J Neurol Neurosurg Psychiatry* 88, no. 12 (2017), 1079–1091.

Levin, Frances R., John J. Mariani, Sheila Specker, Marc Mooney, Amy Mahony, Daniel J. Brooks, David Babb, et al. "Extended-Release Mixed Amphetamine Salts vs Placebo for Comorbid Adult Attention-Deficit /Hyperactivity Disorder and Cocaine Use Disorder." *JAMA Psychiatry* 72, no. 6 (2015), 593–602. doi:10.1001/jamapsychiatry.2015.41.

Looby, Alison, Kyle P. De Young, Mitch Earleywine. "Challenging Expectancies to Prevent Nonmedical Prescription Stimulant Use: A Randomized, Controlled Trial." *Drug Alcohol Depend* 132, no. 1–2 (2013), 362–368. doi:10.1016/j.drugalcdep.2013.03.003.

McCabe, Sean E., Philip Veliz, Timothy E. Wilens, John E. Schulenberg. "Adolescents' Prescription Stimulant Use and Adult Functional Outcomes: A National Prospective Study." *J Am Acad Child Adolesc Psychiatry* 56, no. 3 (2017), 226–233.

Murphy, Fiona, Sheigla Murphy, Paloma Sales, Nicholas Lau. "Examining Social Supply among Nonmedical Prescription Stimulant Users in the San Francisco Bay Area." *Int J Drug Policy* 54 (2018), 68–76.

Nicosia, Nancy, Rosalie L. Pacula, Beau Kilmer, Russell Lundberg, and James Chiesa. "The Economic Cost of Methamphetamine Use in the United States." Santa Monica, CA: *Rand Corporation,* 2009. Accessed July 29, 2019. https://www.rand.org/pubs/monographs/MG829.html

Obert, Jeanne L., Michael J. McCann, Patricia Marinelli-Casey, Ahndrea Weiner, Sam Minsky, Paul Brethen, and Richard Rawson. "The Matrix Model of Outpatient Stimulant Abuse Treatment: History and Description." *J Psychoactive Drugs* 32, no. 2 (2000), 157–164. doi:10.1080/02791072.2000.10400224.

O'Brien, Megan S., and James C. Anthony. "Risk of Becoming Cocaine Dependent: Epidemiological Estimates for the United States, 2000-2001." *Neuropsychopharmacology* 30, no. 5 (2005), 1006–1018. doi:10.1038/sj.npp.1300681.

Partnership for Drug-Free Kids. "The Partnership Attitude Tracking Study: Teens and Parents." New York: Partnership for Drug-Free Kids, 2013.

Proebstl, Lisa, Felicia Kamp, Gabi Koller, and Michael Soyka. "Cognitive Deficits in Methamphetamine Users: How Strong is The Evidence?" *Pharmacopsychiatry* 51, no. 6 (2018), 243–250. doi:10.1055/s-0043-123471.

Rabiner, David L., Arthur D. Anastopoulos, E. Jane Costello, Rick H. Hoyle, Sean E. McCabe, and H. Scott Swartzwelder. "The Misuse and Diversion of Prescribed ADHD Medications by College Students." *J Atten Disord* 13, no. 2 (2009), 144–153.

Radfar, Sayed R., and Richard A. Rawson. "Current Research on Methamphetamine: Epidemiology, Medical and Psychiatric Effects, Treatment, and Harm Reduction Efforts." *Addict Health* 6, no. 3–4 (2014), 146–154. doi:10.1037/e636952009-001.

Renoux, Christel, Shin Ju-Young, Sophie Dell'Anniello, Emma Fergusson, and Sammy Suissa. "Prescribing Trends of Attention-deficit Hyperactivity Disorder (ADHD) Medications in UK Primary Care, 1995–2015." *Br J Clin Pharmacol* 82 (2016), 858–868.

Roche, Daniel J., Matthew J. Worley, Kelly E. Courtney, Spencer Bujarski, Edythe D. London, Steven Shoptaw, and Lara A. Ray. "Naltrexone Moderates the Relationship between Cue-Induced Craving and Subjective Response to Methamphetamine in Individuals with Methamphetamine Use Disorder." *Psychopharmacology* 234, no. 13 (2017), 1997–2007. doi:10.1007/s00213-017-4607-8.

Seth, Puja, Lawrence Scholl, Rose A. Rudd, and Sarah Bacon. "Overdose Deaths Involving Opioids, Cocaine, and Psychostimulants—United States, 2015–2016." *MMWR* 67, no. 12 (2018), 349–358. doi:10.15585/mmwr.mm6712a1.

Soyka, Michael, and Jochen Mutschler. "Treatment-Refractory Substance Use Disorder: Focus on Alcohol, Opioids, and Cocaine." *Prog NeuroPsychopharmacol Biol Psychiatry* 70 (2016), 148–161. doi:10.1016/j.pnpbp.2015.11.003.

Spencer, Thomas J., Joseph Biederman, Patrick E. Ciccone, Bertha K. Madras, Darin D. Dougherty, Ali A. Bonab, Elijahu Livni, Dolly A. Parasrampuria, and Alan J. Fischman. "PET Study Examining Pharmacokinetics, Detection, and Likeability, and Dopamine Transporter Receptor Occupancy of Short- and Long-acting Oral Methylphenidate." *Am J Psychiatry* 163 no. 3 (2006), 387–395.

Stoops, William, and Craig Rush. "Agonist Replacement for Stimulant Dependence: A Review of Clinical Research." *Curr Pharm Des* 19, no. 40 (2013), 7026–7035. doi:10.2174/13816128194013120914 2843.

Streatfield, Dominic. *Cocaine: An Unauthorized Biography*. New York: Picador, 2001.

Substance Abuse and Mental Health Services Administration. *Key Substance Use and Mental Health Indicators in the United States: Results from the 2017 National Survey on Drug Use and Health (HHS Publication No. SMA 18-5068, NSDUH Series H-53)*. Rockville, MD: Center for Behavioral Health Statistics and Quality, Substance Abuse and Mental Health Services Administration, 2018. Accessed July 29, 2019. http://www.samhsa.gov/data/.

Uchida, Mai, Thomas J. Spencer, Stephen V. Faraone, and Joseph Biederman. "Adult Outcome of ADHD: An Overview of Results from the MGH Longitudinal Family Studies of Pediatrically and Psychiatrically Referred Youth with and without ADHD of Both Sexes." *J Att Dis* 22, no. 6 (2015), 523–534.

Weisheit, Ralph A., and William L. White. *Methamphetamine: Its History, Pharmacology, and Treatment*. Center City, MN: Hazelden, 2009.

Weyandt, Lisa L., Danielle R. Oster, Marisa E. Marraccini, Berglijot G. Gudmundsdottir, Bailey A. Munro, Emma S. Rathkey, and Alison McCallum. "Prescription Stimulant Medication Misuse: Where are We and Where Do We Go from Here?" *Exp Clin Psychopharmacol* 24, no. 5 (2016), 400–414.

White, Barbara P., Kathyrn A. Becker-Blease, and Kathleen Grace-Bishop. "Stimulant Medication Use, Misuse, and Abuse in an Undergraduate and Graduate Student Sample." *J Am Coll Health* 54, no. 5 (2006), 261–268.

Wilens, Timothy E., Nicholas W. Carrellas, MaryKate Martelon, Amy M. Yule, Ronna Fried, Rayce Anselmo, and Sean E. McCabe. "Neuropsychological Functioning in College Students who Misuse Prescription Stimulants." *Am J Addict* 26 (2017), 379–387.

Wilens, Timothy E., Courtney Zulauf, MaryKate Martelon, Nicholas R. Morrison, Andrew Simon, Nicholas W. Carrellas, Amy Yule, and Rayce Anselmo. "Nonmedical Stimulant Use in College Students: Association with Attention-Deficit/Hyperactivity Disorder and Other Disorders." *J Clin Psychiatry* 77, no. 7 (2016), 940–947.

CHAPTER 9

Tobacco

Megan M. Kelly

Tobacco use is the leading preventable cause of death worldwide. The most commonly used form of tobacco is a cigarette, and cigarette smokers are more likely to die of a tobacco-related disease (e.g., cancer, chronic obstructive pulmonary disease, heart disease) than from any other cause and will lose about 10 years of their lives because of their tobacco use. Tobacco is a highly addictive substance because it contains the psychoactive drug nicotine; however, it is the other harmful chemicals in tobacco that are responsible for its deleterious health effects.

There are several other forms of tobacco use, including cigars and pipes, and the less familiar (in the United States) hookahs and smokeless tobacco products. Hookahs are single- or multi-stemmed instruments, also known as water pipes, used for vaporizing and smoking flavored tobacco; smoke passes through a water basin and is then inhaled. In general, the use of hookah is most prevalent among adults in the Eastern Mediterranean and youth in the Eastern Mediterranean and Europe (Jawad et al. 2018).

Smokeless tobacco includes any product that has a nonsmoking method of use, including chewing (e.g., chewing tobacco), sniffing (e.g., snuff), and placing the product between the teeth and the cheek (e.g., snus).

Another popular product is the e-cigarette, otherwise known as an electronic nicotine delivery system (ENDS). E-cigarettes are battery-operated devices designed to simulate the experience of using conventional cigarettes. These products heat an "e-liquid," which generally contains nicotine, other chemicals (such as glycerin and propylene glycol), and some flavorings. Once heated, the liquid generates an aerosol ("vapor"), which is then inhaled by the user. The act of inhaling vapor from an e-cigarette is called "vaping." There are divergent views about e-cigarettes—some experts consider them to be an important tool to help some tobacco users quit. Others are concerned about the potential health risks of these products and their use by adolescents.

Most of this chapter will be about addiction to smoking cigarettes.

Symptoms, Diagnosis, and Incidence

Symptoms

The symptoms of tobacco use disorder are in some ways subtler than the symptoms of other substance use disorders in that the effects on the person's mind are mild. There is no euphoria, intoxication, or hallucinations. The person enjoys the ritual and taste of the tobacco and feels less anxious and perhaps more able to concentrate. However, the person can develop a tobacco use disorder, or addiction, quickly.

Diagnosis

In the American Psychiatric Association's 2013 *Diagnostic and Statistical Manual of Mental Disorders* (DSM-5) (American Psychiatric Association 2013), tobacco addiction is diagnosed as a *tobacco use disorder*. Similar to other substance use disorders, the symptoms of tobacco use disorder involve tolerance (the person is able to smoke more cigarettes in a shorter span of time the longer he or she smokes) and withdrawal (the reason so many smokers cannot stop); smoking more tobacco or for longer stretches of time than the person at first wanted to; desire to cut down or stop using tobacco (often referred to as "quitting"); spending a lot of time using tobacco or on related activities, such as finding a smoking area or buying cigarettes both of which are becoming increasingly difficult to do; social and interpersonal problems related to tobacco use (for example, arguing with others or being asked not to smoke around them); use of tobacco in situations where it may be dangerous (for example, around oxygen or while feeling sleepy); smoking tobacco interfering with work (for example, having to take frequent smoke breaks); choosing smoking over other activities (for example, no longer going on long airplane trips or being in other places where one cannot smoke); and continued use in the face of medical problems such as lung disease or psychological problems that are exacerbated by tobacco use. *DSM-5* added the criterion of having a strong desire to use tobacco, which is also consistent with other substance use disorders. The person has a severe use disorder (sometimes still referred to as addiction) if he or she meets six or more criteria. In the *International Statistical Classification of Diseases and Related Health Problems-10* (*ICD-10*), the medical classification list developed by the World Health Organization, there are several diagnostic codes for tobacco use. However, the term used for tobacco addiction in *ICD-10* is *nicotine dependence* (World Health Organization 2016).

Incidence

There are about one billion cigarette smokers across the world, with a prevalence rate of about 30% in men and 7% in women. The countries that consume the most cigarettes in the world are China, Russia, United States, Japan, and Indonesia. In the United States, the prevalence of smoking has fallen from a high of 42% in 1965 to 15.5% in 2015 (Centers for Disease Control 2016). However, the rate of decline for the prevalence of smoking among the U.S. population has slowed over time. China has a high prevalence of smoking, particularly among men; smokers in this country consume more than 35% of all the cigarettes in the world, and about 47% of men are current smokers (World Health Organization 2018).

E-cigarettes are becoming increasingly popular in the United States. From 2014 to 2016, there was a significant increase in the prevalence of ever having used e-cigarettes among people in the United States, from 12.6% in 2014 to 15.3% in 2016, but current use of e-cigarettes decreased from 3.7% to 3.2% during the same time (Bao et al. 2018). Across the world, e-cigarette use among adults is still low. The prevalence of e-cigarette use among youth widely varies across the globe. Data from 13 countries during the period 2013–2015 showed that among youth, use was highest in Poland and lowest in Italy. E-cigarette use has increased in Poland, Korea, New Zealand, and the United States between 2008 and 2015; remained stable in the United Kingdom; and decreased in Italy and Canada (Yoong et al. 2018).

History

Native Americans began to cultivate the tobacco plant perhaps as early as 6000 BCE. They typically smoked it in pipes for medicinal purposes, spiritual ceremonies, or to seal a treaty or agreement. In 1492, Christopher Columbus observed tobacco smoking when he reached the Americas and then shared his discovery with Europe by bringing back tobacco leaves and seeds. In 1531, European settlers in Santo Domingo began to cultivate the tobacco plant. However, tobacco didn't gain much popularity in Europe until the 16th century. A French ambassador, Jean Nicot—for whom nicotine is named—sent tobacco leaves and seeds to Catherine de Médici in Paris (in the form of snuff) for her recurring headaches. In 1565, Sir John Hawkins likely introduced tobacco to England when he returned with the plant after he explored Florida. In 1570, tobacco was being referred to as *Nicotiana* by botanists. Tobacco also spread to other parts of the world; for example, Spanish and Portuguese sailors introduced tobacco to Japan in 1542 and to East Africa in 1560.

During the early years of tobacco use in Europe, physicians viewed tobacco as a medicine. But some people had some concerns about tobacco even then, including England's King James I, who wrote a pamphlet in 1604 on its dangers (see Sidebar 9.1).

Sidebar 9.1 The Royal Origins of the Earliest Anti-Tobacco Campaign

One of the earliest anti-tobacco efforts was led by King James I of England and might have been influenced by personal animosities and political concerns in addition to health concerns. King James loathed explorer, courtier, and poet Sir Walter Raleigh, who had contributed to the increased popularity of tobacco in England in the late 16th century. Although Raleigh was a favorite of Queen Elizabeth I, King James I, who was Elizabeth's cousin and successor, had a profound dislike of the man and was upset with him for introducing tobacco into the royal court. After Queen Elizabeth I died in 1603, King James had Raleigh arrested for treason and imprisoned in the Tower of London. In 1604, King James wrote "A Counterblaste to Tobacco," a treatise about his negative opinions regarding tobacco. He described tobacco as "a custome lothsome to the eye, hatefull to the nose, harmefull to the braine, dangerous to the lungs, and in the blacke stinking fume thereof, neerest resembling the horrible Stigian smoke of the pit that is bottomelesse" (James I 1604). It is not clear how much of this treatise was inspired by King James's genuine negative feelings toward tobacco, his aversion to Raleigh, or a combination of both. His dislike of tobacco was also probably due, in part, to the largely Spanish domination over tobacco cultivation at that time.

Raleigh was ultimately beheaded in 1618. After his execution, a small tobacco pouch was found in his prison cell. It contained the Latin inscription *Comes meus fuit in illo miserrimo tempore* ("It was my companion at that most miserable time").

Bibliography

James I. "A Counterblaste to Tobacco" (1604). Accessed April 8, 2018. https://www.laits.utexas.edu/poltheory/james/blaste/blaste.html.

In the early 1600s, English colonists started to cultivate tobacco to export overseas. John Rolfe, the husband of Pocahontas, grew the first successful crop. By 1614, about 7,000 English tobacco shops were selling Virginia tobacco. Tobacco became Virginia's largest export. It was so popular that it was even used as a form of currency in the colonies. By the 1700s, American tobacco was in demand in Europe, and the growth of tobacco as a lucrative cash crop increased the demand for slave labor in North America. At that time, tobacco use mainly consisted of pipe-smoking, chewing tobacco, and snuff. Cigars were not widely used until the 1800s, and cigarettes did not become popular in the United States until the late 1800s. The production of cigarettes increased with the invention of the automated cigarette-making machine, a device that could make 200 cigarettes per minute—about 60 times faster than hand-rolling.

In the early 20th century, cigarette consumption continued to increase because of several events: (1) the introduction of new blends and curing processes, which led to tobacco being milder and thus easier to inhale, (2) the mass production of cigarettes, (3) easier transportation and distribution of cigarettes, (4) the invention of the safety match, and (5) the increase in advertising to promote cigarettes. More women began to smoke due to direct marketing and social changes that encouraged the acceptability of smoking. World War I also contributed to the increasing popularity of cigarettes. Cigarettes were marketed to soldiers in the United States, and they also received a free weekly ration of 50 cigarettes.

By the middle of the 20th century, concerns about the health effects of smoking had started to accumulate. Four lines of evidence supported these concerns: (1) population studies, (2) animal experimentation, (3) cellular pathology, and (4) the identification of cancer-causing chemicals in cigarette smoke. During the 1920s and 1930s, the first early evidence of the link between smoking and lung cancer started to appear in the medical literature. Studies from the 1930s had shown that lung cancer was more prevalent in people who had smoked than in those who did not. Several large studies appeared in the early 1950s supporting these findings. Around the same time, research evidence from animal studies was growing, showing that tobacco was linked to cancer. In the 1950s, animal experiments showed that tumors were caused by exposing mice to chemicals from cigarette smoke. Other research showed that smoking caused pulmonary ciliastasis (the deadening of cilia, which are hairlike projections from the cells that clear the airways of dirt and mucus), and this effect could cause cigarette smoke to stay longer in the lungs, exposing smokers to a greater risk of cancer. Finally, in the 1950s and 1960s, studies revealed the numerous carcinogens (cancer-causing substances) contained in cigarette smoke, including polycyclic aromatic hydrocarbons, chromium, arsenic, and nickel.

In the 1950s, smokers were using unfiltered cigarettes. With the increase in awareness of the dangers of smoking, low-tar cigarettes were introduced and filters were added to reduce the amount of tar inhaled. However, smokers just inhaled more deeply, thus thwarting the goals of the redesigned cigarettes.

On January 11, 1964, the Surgeon General of the United States, Luther L. Terry, MD, released the first Surgeon General's report on smoking, *Smoking and Health: Report of the Advisory Committee of the Surgeon General of the Public Health Service*. It detailed the evidence for the negative health effects of smoking, concluding that smoking is a cause of lung and laryngeal cancer in men, a probable cause of lung cancer in women, and a cause of chronic bronchitis and emphysema. The incidence of cigarette smoking dropped shortly after the release of this report but rebounded by 1966.

The U.S. Congress adopted the Federal Cigarette Labeling and Advertising Act of 1965 and the Public Health Cigarette Smoking Act of 1969, which mandated an annual report on the health effects of smoking, banned advertising for cigarettes over broadcast media, and required a health warning on cigarette packaging. In September 1965, the U.S. Public Health Service (PHS) created the National Clearinghouse for Smoking and Health, the predecessor to the Centers for Disease Control and Prevention's Office on Smoking and Health. The PHS disseminated anti-smoking messages and research results related to tobacco use, as well as provided support to state and community programs to tackle tobacco use.

In the 1990s, several U.S. states sued major cigarette manufacturers to recover health-care costs incurred from treating cigarette smokers. The resulting Master Settlement Agreement (MSA) was reached in 1998 between the state attorneys general of 46 states, five U.S. territories, the District of Columbia, and the five largest cigarette manufacturers in the United States. The MSA required the tobacco industry to pay the settling states $12.75 billion in addition to annual payments in perpetuity to cover the health-care costs that states incur for treating cigarette smokers. It imposed prohibitions and restrictions on the sale of cigarettes, as well as tobacco advertising, marketing, and promotional programs by participating cigarette manufacturers. The MSA also provided resources to create a new foundation that had as one of its mandates the sponsorship of a national counter-advertising campaign. In 1999, the American Legacy Foundation was created for this purpose and has since spent about $100 million annually on a campaign that has been successful in developing awareness among adolescents and young adults about the dangers of tobacco use. Smoking rates have declined among this population because of this effort.

Most tobacco control efforts have concentrated on placing health warning labels on cigarette packages and educating the public about the negative health effects of smoking. Currently, most countries require some type of package warning label on cigarettes, although their content varies. Studies in countries that have pictorial health warnings on cigarette packs show that they lead to improved awareness of the negative health effects of smoking and are more effective than text-only warnings.

Development and Causes

Cigarette smoking is highly addictive because it quickly delivers high doses of the psychoactive drug nicotine to the brain. The nicotine enters the lungs and then travels rapidly to the brain via the blood circulation. Nicotine is similar in structure to the neurotransmitter acetylcholine and binds to nicotinic cholinergic receptors. When nicotine binds to these receptors in the ventral tegmental area of the midbrain, nerves that project to the nucleus accumbens fire at an increased rate. The nucleus accumbens is involved in processing rewarding and/or reinforcing stimuli like food, water, sex, exercise, and addictive drugs. Dopamine, another neurotransmitter, is released into the nucleus accumbens, providing a pleasurable experience to the person smoking and acting as a "teaching signal" that causes the brain to link certain situations, known as *cues*, with pleasure. For instance, common cues or triggers for smoking include driving, drinking alcohol or coffee, and the completion of a task. Associations between cues become *conditioned*, meaning that they are learned associations between the reinforcer (nicotine) and the situation in which the person smokes. After the situation and use of tobacco are paired many times, the cue triggers a strong impulse to use tobacco, which is often referred to as a *cue-driven smoking urge*.

Repeated exposure to nicotine leads to lower dopamine levels and lower neural activity in the ventral tegmental area and nucleus accumbens, which contribute to the development of tolerance to the effects of nicotine and withdrawal symptoms when an individual abstains from tobacco. As tolerance develops, the number of binding sites on the nicotinic cholinergic receptors in the brain increases, and more nicotine is needed to achieve the same pleasurable effect as before. Within a few hours without nicotine, withdrawal symptoms like anxiety, irritability, difficulty concentrating, and restlessness start to develop, indicating that the person has become physically dependent on nicotine. Many smokers report that smoking helps them manage stress and increases their attention and concentration, but this effect is likely due to the relief of nicotine withdrawal symptoms. The main factors leading to relapse appear to be cue-driven smoking urges and nicotine withdrawal.

Up Close—In Society

Tobacco use has become less socially acceptable over time. In the United States, for much of the 20th century, smoking was commonplace, acceptable, and at times, socially desirable. People smoked indoors, at work, and even in health-care settings. However, as the health dangers of tobacco use have become more widely known and publicized, the social acceptability of tobacco use has decreased. In response, the tobacco industry has engaged in many efforts to maintain the desirability of smoking, including targeting different demographic groups (such as adolescents, minorities, and veterans) to positively influence them to use tobacco, and seeking relationships with people in film, print media, and fashion to promote their products. These efforts have had a large effect on youth culture, since adolescents are more likely to learn and copy actions performed by role models if they are associated with desired outcomes such as increased social status, romance, power, and success. In addition, the portrayal of smoking in the media has also normalized smoking, which gives it a certain level of social acceptability among teens despite broader societal disapproval. The MSA and other legislative efforts that have restrained tobacco advertising have prompted the tobacco industry to look to other methods to promote tobacco use among adolescents, including offering flavored tobacco products, placing tobacco products strategically in shops and other retail outlets (such as near candy), and advertising heavily in retail areas near schools and playgrounds. The tobacco industry has also undertaken many efforts to undermine the science on the dangers of tobacco and secondhand smoke as well as policies concerning tobacco use.

Despite tobacco industry efforts to promote tobacco use in society, its use has become increasingly stigmatized. Nonsmokers and former smokers often hold negative beliefs about smokers, attributing tobacco addiction to individual characteristics such as "weak character" and even "bad genes." A large percentage of current and former smokers indicate that they would not hire a smoker to take care of their children and would be reluctant to date someone who smokes.

The level of stigma that smokers experience is related to their social environment: smokers who report that family and friends think that smoking is socially unacceptable are more likely to perceive high stigma than smokers who have family and friends that find smoking to be socially acceptable. There has also been an increasing aversion to secondhand smoke, and as a result, many smoke-free policies now prohibit smoking in public places in the United States and other countries.

Case Study

Joanne is a 60-year-old cigarette smoker. She began smoking when she was a teenager because her friends were doing it and she wanted to fit in. The more she smoked, the more addicted she became; she no longer smoked because of social reasons but because she wanted to avoid nicotine withdrawal symptoms and strong cravings worsened by stress. When she initially started working, she could smoke at her desk; however, as smoke-free regulations started to be passed, she was no longer able to do so. She was also used to smoking at her local bar with friends and at restaurants. As time went by, more laws were enacted, preventing her from smoking in these establishments as well. As smoking restrictions increased, she decided she was ready to quit. She was tired of having to leave movie theaters in the middle of a film to smoke, and she didn't like having to leave her office to smoke, especially in the winter. She also disliked the stigma she experienced as a result of smoking. Joanne set a quit date, received counseling and medication for quitting, and successfully quit smoking. She stated that she now has more free time, is no longer experiencing any social stigma because of smoking, and feels more freedom because of her abstinence from smoking. However, she has gained 10 pounds, as she has turned to eating instead of tobacco to manage stress.

Up Close—At Work

Tobacco has substantial costs to the economy, particularly to employers, because the health effects of smoking impact productivity and increase workplace absenteeism. In the United States, the total cost of smoking-related productivity losses each year is about $156 billion, including about $6 billion in lost productivity due to secondhand smoke exposure (Centers for Disease Control 2018b). Altogether, smokers cost employers about $6,000 more per year than nonsmokers.

Employers lose revenue when employees miss work because of smoking-related medical problems and when they take repeated smoke breaks throughout the workday. Individuals who smoke also have significantly higher absenteeism rates than former smokers or nonsmokers. In the United States, for example, people who smoke are absent from work for about seven more days per year than people who do not. Productivity for former smokers decreases shortly after quitting but is better than that of active smokers within two years.

There are other costs to both employers and employees for tobacco use. For instance, smoking increases the risk of both injuries and fires, which can lead to higher insurance costs. Employers are also less likely to hire or promote people who smoke. Some employers will not hire smokers. Twenty-one states have no laws protecting smokers from these hiring practices. In developed countries, more poor use tobacco than do people from a higher socioeconomic status, so such hiring practices likely hurt those who are already at a financial disadvantage.

Due to the negative impact smoking has on workplace productivity and the health of employees, many workplaces offer tobacco cessation support and treatment. A review of the evidence for these tobacco cessation programs indicates that group and individual counseling are more effective than no treatment or minimal interventions (Cahill and Lancaster 2014). Research also shows the same is true of nicotine replacement therapy and multiple interventions offered in the workplace. Self-help materials, relapse prevention, and social support appear to be less effective in helping employees quit.

Case Study

Lou is the head of engineering at a hospital. He is a long-time smoker with no interest in quitting. He smokes about one pack a day and takes frequent smokes breaks at work. Since smoking is prohibited at his hospital, Lou sneaks cigarettes at the back door of his building. He throws cigarette butts on the ground or into the water drainage grates around the hospital, which is problematic because this water goes out to the ocean, and tobacco is toxic to fish. The environmental safety officer at his hospital is on the hunt for the person or people responsible for the accumulation of cigarette butts. Lou's employees are aware that he smokes when he shouldn't, and so his other employees who smoke feel like they have permission to do the same and take repeated cigarette breaks. The nonsmoking employees resent this. The hospital police finally catch Lou smoking on hospital grounds; he is written up and notice is given to his supervisor. Lou's supervisor discussed this problem at Lou's performance evaluation and urged him to seek assistance from occupational health at his workplace to quit smoking.

Up Close—In Relationships

Tobacco use is intertwined with relationships. People who use tobacco tend to have coworkers, friends, and family who also smoke. Individuals who grew up in a household with a parent who smokes are more likely to smoke themselves. Research shows that a complete household ban on smoking and keeping cigarettes out of the home are effective preventive measures to keep adolescents from starting to use tobacco. Parents who talk to their adolescents respectfully and constructively about the importance of not smoking deter them from doing so.

People who use tobacco indicate that it eases some types of social interactions. It can help develop, maintain, and reinforce some relationships. For adolescents, a romantic partner who smokes makes it more difficult to quit, even if a best friend does not smoke. Particular patterns in romantic relationships are also associated with smoking, including a partner lighting up a cigarette for the other, sharing cigarettes, and smoking together during certain events and situations. However, tobacco can also be a deterrent for some people in friendships and relationships because of the stigma associated with its use. Smoking often makes a person's social sphere more limited. On the other hand, prolonged smoking abstinence is associated with improved physical and social functioning.

Tobacco use can be a concern for a person's nonsmoking family and friends who often implore individuals to quit because of tobacco-related health concerns. These pleas may motivate people to quit. People often report wanting to quit to be a good role model for children, allay the concerns of a partner, and decrease tension in relationships over concerns related to tobacco use.

Peers can be good sources of social support for quitting. Among individuals with serious mental illness, research has shown that having support from peers who have quit smoking helps the person quit. As a result, individuals with mental health disorders have become more involved in providing support and help for recovery from tobacco use among their peers over the past 20 years.

Case Study

Andrew is a U.S. military veteran who started smoking during his deployment to Iraq. When he came home, he married Sarah and started a family. Sarah was upset by his smoking—she didn't want him to expose her or their children to any secondhand smoke, and they had many arguments about his smoking. She prohibited him from smoking in the house, so Andrew started to hide his smoking from her and would only smoke in the car and with his veteran friends. This caused more friction with Sarah, because she still found evidence of his smoking—empty packs and cigarette ashes—in the car. As Andrew's children grew up, they became aware of his smoking and pleaded with him to quit. They even threw away his cigarettes or hid them from him. After several years of his family expressing these concerns, Andrew decided to quit. He bought nicotine patches to help him overcome the cravings to smoke. His family provided support and praised him every day that he remained abstinent. Andrew became proud of his effort and for being a role model for his children, showing them that with effort and dedication, challenging goals like quitting smoking can be achieved.

Effects and Costs

Health Effects

Despite a substantial reduction in smoking in some areas of the world, smoking continues to be the leading preventable cause of death worldwide. About 33%–45% of smokers will die from a tobacco-related disease, and on average, smokers die 10 years earlier than nonsmokers (Centers for Disease Control 2017). In 2016, tobacco use caused over 7.1 million deaths across the world (5.1 million in men, 2 million in women) (Eriksen, Mackay, and Ross 2013). Most were related to cigarette smoking, but 884,000 deaths were related to secondhand smoke. In the United States, smoking is responsible for 90% of lung cancer deaths and 30% of all other cancer deaths. Smoking increases the risk of developing lung cancer by 25 times and can be a causal factor in the development of cancer in virtually every part of the body, including the bladder, blood (acute myeloid leukemia), cervix, colon and rectum, esophagus, kidney, liver, pancreas, and stomach. For cancer patients and survivors, smoking substantially increases the risk of death. In fact, if no one smoked again, one out of every three cancer deaths in the United States would be eliminated (Centers for Disease Control 2017).

In addition, smoking is a significant risk factor for many serious medical conditions, including cardiovascular disease (i.e., heart attack, stroke) and peripheral vascular disease. It increases the risk of coronary heart disease and stroke by two to four times. Smoking damages blood vessels, causing them to become narrower and thicker, thereby increasing a person's pulse, blood pressure, and risk for clots. It is a causal factor in about 80% of deaths from chronic obstructive pulmonary disease (COPD), which includes chronic bronchitis and emphysema. People who smoke are 12 to 13 times more likely to die from COPD than people who do not. The risk of a smoker developing Type 2 diabetes is 30%–40% higher than that of a nonsmoker. In addition, smoking can trigger asthma attacks, cause tooth loss, increase the risk of cataracts and rheumatoid arthritis, and in general, increase inflammation throughout the body (Centers for Disease Control 2017).

People who quit tobacco reduce their risk of tobacco-related diseases and early death. Studies have shown that the benefits are greater for those who quit at an earlier age, and that improvements in health continue over time. In addition, smokers who quit demonstrate improved health even after the development of smoking-related diseases. Smoking cessation substantially improves the outcomes of cancer patients, and individuals with diabetes who quit smoking have better control over their blood sugar levels and lower their risk of heart and kidney disease, blindness, and amputations.

Other forms of tobacco can also cause significant health problems. At least 28 carcinogens have been found in smokeless tobacco. Among these are tobacco-specific N-nitrosamines, which have been linked to oral cancer and cancer of the esophagus, pancreas, stomach, lung, and bladder. Smokeless tobacco has also been associated with the development of heart disease, gum disease, and leukoplakia (precancerous white patches in the mouth).

The health effects of e-cigarettes are still being studied. While it is likely that the health effects are not as severe as conventional cigarettes because of the lower level and number of harmful chemicals in e-cigarette vapor compared to tobacco smoke, it is also unlikely that there are no negative health effects related to e-cigarette use. There is concern that these products will increase the risk of COPD, lung cancer, possibly cardiovascular disease, and other diseases after long-term use. The World Health Organization indicated that for e-cigarettes to have a population-wide positive health benefit, they should be at least three times "safer" than conventional cigarettes. There is also concern that e-cigarette use among adolescents can lead to the development of a tobacco addiction and then the use of conventional tobacco products. The evidence for a tobacco cessation benefit because of e-cigarettes is mixed, and more research is needed.

Financial Costs

The combined profits of the world's biggest tobacco companies were more than $62 billion in 2015, which is about $9,730 for the death of each smoker (Eriksen, Mackay, and Ross 2013). The health-care costs of smokers are 34% higher than nonsmokers (Leif Associates 2012).

Approximately 15% of all health-care expenditure in high-income countries is attributable to smoking. Smoking-related illness in the

United States costs more than $300 billion each year—this amount includes about $170 billion in direct medical care for adults and more than $156 billion in lost productivity (Xu et al. 2015). In the United States, the proportion of health-care expenditures related to smoking across different states ranges between 6% and 18% (Ekpu and Brown 2015). In 2009, the Institute of Medicine indicated that the tobacco-related disease burden was the most expensive health issue in the U.S. Veterans Health Administration, the largest health-care system in the United States (Institute of Medicine 2009). Quitting smoking could prevent approximately 70% of current smokers' excess medical care costs (Maciosek et al. 2015). In the United Kingdom, the direct costs of smoking to the National Health Service (NHS) are estimated at between £2.7–£5.2 billion, which is equivalent to around 5% of the total NHS budget each year (Ekpu and Brown 2015). The economic burden of smoking as estimated as a country's gross domestic product (GDP) indicates that smoking accounts for approximately 0.7% of China's GDP and approximately 1% of the United States' GDP (Ekpu and Brown 2015).

Theory and Research

Much of current tobacco theory and research focuses on tobacco use in vulnerable populations, such as pregnant women, adolescents, individuals with low socioeconomic status, the homeless, ethnic and racial minorities, the LGBT community, and individuals with mental health disorders. The effects of secondhand smoke exposure on individuals and the community have been studied. In this chapter we summarize the current research in these tobacco-related areas.

Pregnancy

Prenatal exposure to smoking has deleterious effects on pregnancy and fetal development (Drake, Driscoll, and Mathews 2018). Smoking affects epigenetic processes during the embryonic period of development and early pregnancy (i.e., by the second month). Maternal smoking in pregnancy increases the risk of the child having a low birth weight or being small for its gestational age. Maternal smoking is also a significant risk factor for sudden infant death syndrome (SIDS). Smoking increases the risk of pregnancy complications, including placental abruption, the premature separation of the placenta from the attachment site; premature rupture of membranes, when the amniotic sac prematurely ruptures and labor is induced early; and placenta previa, in which the placenta partially or totally covers the opening to the cervix. Placenta previa increases the risk of caesarian section deliveries and complications like a maternal hemorrhage (Cnattinguis 2004).

Tobacco cessation during smoking is important for prenatal health. Most studies, but not all, show that tobacco cessation interventions lead to a significant reduction in smoking in late pregnancy and up to the early postpartum period, but there is no evidence that these interventions retain their effectiveness at six months or more after birth. This may be because women who quit during pregnancy often think in terms of the unborn baby's health and resume smoking following the birth (Cooper et al. 2017, Lumley et al. 2009).

Adolescents

Tobacco use usually first occurs in adolescence. In 2018, the National Youth Tobacco Survey (NYTS) found that approximately 4.9 million middle and high school students used tobacco products during the past month. This survey also indicated that e-cigarettes were the most commonly used tobacco products among all middle and high school students (5% and 21%, respectively) (Gentzke et al. 2019). Research shows that the earlier someone begins to use tobacco, the less likely a person is to be able to quit.

Models of tobacco addiction indicate that behavioral, psychological, social, and environmental factors are important for the development and maintenance of addiction. For adolescents, these factors include having family and friends who smoke, exposure to advertising and films, overestimating the number of peers who smoke, underestimating how addictive tobacco products are, poor academic performance, lower socioeconomic status (discussed later in this chapter), sensation-seeking or rebelliousness, and intention to smoke in the future. In contrast, a high level of parental monitoring and higher self-esteem among adolescents are associated with a lower likelihood of the onset of smoking. How often an adolescent smokes is also an important factor in the development of a tobacco addiction. According to the sensitization-homeostasis model of tobacco addiction, even infrequent smoking by adolescents (e.g., on a monthly basis) increases the risk of becoming addicted to tobacco. This model holds that for beginning smokers, smoking one cigarette can suppress nicotine withdrawal for several weeks. But as tolerance develops as a result of repeated use, the time to nicotine withdrawal becomes shorter and the need to smoke occurs more frequently, leading to the development of a tobacco addiction (Wellman et al. 2016).

One study showed that monthly smoking multiplies by 10 the chances of an adolescent developing a tobacco addiction in the future (Doubeni, Reed, and Difranza 2010). It is not clear how to reduce adolescent tobacco smoking. Some limited evidence shows that group-based behavioral interventions are helpful, and some limited support for tobacco cessation medications exists; but overall, there is a lack of good research evidence for any type of intervention. More research is needed.

Low Socioeconomic Status

Socioeconomic status (SES) is a person's economic and social position in society, often measured by a combination of educational, occupational, and income factors. SES is substantially associated with tobacco use. In developed countries, including the United States, smoking rates are generally higher among individuals with lower SES (Centers for Disease Control 2018a). There is some evidence for a similar trend among less developed countries, but these results are not uniform.

Homelessness

The incidence of tobacco use is substantially higher among individuals who are homeless. In the United States, about three-quarters of homeless adults smoke, which is about four times higher than the general population. A number of factors contribute to this high rate of smoking. The homeless have higher rates of substance use and mental health disorders than others, and many people who are homeless live in environments where smoking is commonplace. In addition, the homeless often lack access to health care, which limits their access to tobacco cessation treatment (Baggett, Tobey, and Rigotti 2013).

Ethnic and Racial Minorities

In the United States, African Americans have a similar rate of smoking compared to Caucasians. Native Americans and multiracial individuals have higher rates of smoking than other racial and ethnic groups (Centers for Disease Control 2018a). Tobacco is not as heavily taxed in tribal lands and may have a different role in Native American culture (Centers for Disease Control 2018a). More tobacco retailers are found in areas with larger African American and Hispanic communities than in other communities. In addition, stores in predominantly African-American communities are much more likely to display tobacco ads both inside and outside their stores compared to stores in other communities. African Americans are also more likely to use menthol cigarettes, which are easier to smoke and harder to quit for unclear reasons. Cigarette companies market menthol cigarettes specifically to African Americans. Minority smokers are less likely to receive advice to stop smoking, to get help in so doing, or to quit. Limited access to health-care services, difficulties obtaining insurance coverage, and language barriers are all related to higher smoking morbidity and mortality among minority smokers.

LGBT Population

Tobacco use is high among lesbian, gay, bisexual, and transgender (LGBT) populations (Berger and Mooney-Somers 2017). In the United States, smoking rates in this community are double that of the general population. Reasons for the high prevalence of tobacco use among the LGBT population include low social support, stress because of discrimination, low SES, and internalized homophobia, which leads to increased depression and substance use. Access to LGBT resources and healthy habits such as diet and exercise may protect against tobacco use. More systemic factors associated with tobacco use among the LGBT population include smoking to appear or feel more masculine or feminine, perceived cultural and peer pressures to smoke, and the culture of bars and nightclubs. In addition, few tobacco cessation programs and health-care services are tailored for the LGBT population.

Mental Health Disorders and Co-morbid Substance Use

In the United States, 25% of the population has mental health and addictive disorders, and these individuals account for 40% of the cigarettes smoked (Centers for Disease Control 2019). Individuals with mental health disorders have less successful quit attempts, often directly related to their mental health symptoms and difficulty regulating emotions.

Smokers with mental health disorders frequently smoke in response to their psychiatric symptoms. These smokers often report that they smoke cigarettes to cope with emotional problems, to stabilize their mood, and to reduce stress. While smoking appears to temporarily reduce anxiety and improve mood, it is associated with deleterious long-term effects on mental health and worse mental-health treatment outcomes, including (1) increased psychiatric symptoms, (2) increased risk of suicidal behavior, and (3) an interference with mental health treatment. Both mental health disorders and smoking are also associated with poor life function-ing and more severe psychiatric symptoms.

Individuals with mental health disorders who also smoke spend a large percentage of their income on cigarettes rather than other needs, such as housing and transportation. Smoking also limits a person's social sphere because it is not socially acceptable and adds to the existing stigma expe-rienced by those with mental health conditions.

Tobacco treatment improves psychiatric symptoms, including depres-sion, anxiety, and stress. The reduction in psychiatric symptoms as a result of smoking cessation treatment is as large or larger than that achieved by antidepressant treatment for mood and anxiety disorders. Compared with those who continue to smoke, individuals who quit smoking report fewer continuous or recurrent drug use disorders (69% less), alcohol use disorders (36% less), and mood and anxiety disorders (30% less) after three years (Taylor et al. 2014).

Secondhand Smoke Exposure and Smoke-Free Policies

Secondhand smoke is a mixture of exhaled smoke and smoke from the burning end of a cigarette, pipe, or cigar. Secondhand smoke contains more than 50 chemicals that can cause cancer (U.S. Department of Health and Human Services 1986). According to the U.S. Surgeon General, there is no safe level of exposure to secondhand smoke. This finding has been supported by the National Health and Medical Research Council of Aus-tralia, the Scientific Committee on Tobacco and Health of the United Kingdom, and the International Agency for Research on Cancer. Second-hand smoke exposure causes 7,300 lung cancer deaths and 34,000 heart disease deaths in the United States each year (U.S. Department of Health and Human Services 2014). Even low levels of secondhand smoke expo-sure can exacerbate sensitive medical conditions (such as triggering an asthma attack). Secondhand tobacco smoke exposure is also a cause of many health problems in children, including asthma, wheezing, respira-tory illnesses, poor lung function, middle ear disease, and nasal irritation.

In 1972, the U.S. Surgeon General released a report on the dangers of inhaling tobacco smoke and indicated that secondhand smoke harmed nonsmokers. In 1981, a longitudinal study showed that nonsmoking wives of smokers and former smokers had significantly higher rates of lung cancer than wives of nonsmokers, demonstrating the effects of sec-ondhand smoke exposure (Hirayama 1981).

Due to the increasing scientific evidence that both smoking and sec-ondhand smoke are problematic for health, there has been an increase in smoking bans. In the 1970s, smoke-free initiatives started to take hold with increased petitions for nonsmoking sections in public areas. In 1975, Minnesota became the first state to pass a Clean Indoor Air Act, which banned smoking in most public areas. By 1981, 36 states had instituted some form of smoke-free policy. In 2015, 27 states had instituted comprehensive smoke-free laws prohibiting smoking in indoor areas of worksites, restaurants, and bars. As of 2012, 28 countries had national comprehensive smoke-free laws that prohibited smoking in bars, restaurants, and workplaces. There are many arguments for and against smoke-free policies. Those against these policies argue that compliance with these laws is difficult, that the hospitality industry could lose money, and that ventilation systems are sufficient for protecting the health of employees. Those in favor argue that most people want these policies to protect their health and that the potential benefits outweigh any decreased revenue to businesses. In addition, no good evidence has demonstrated that ventilation systems eliminate any health risks due to secondhand smoke exposure. Secondhand smoke is also elevated in hookah bars or places where hookah is used (Zhou et al. 2017).

Treatments

There are a variety of treatments for tobacco cessation, including pharmacotherapy, individual and group counseling, telephone counseling or quitlines, and internet-delivered tobacco cessation programs. Research demonstrates that the combination of pharmacotherapy and behavioral interventions is better than any type of treatment alone, and it has been shown to be more efficacious than single interventions at six months postquit.

Pharmacotherapy

In the United States, the first-line pharmacotherapies for tobacco cessation treatment include nicotine replacement therapy (NRT), such as the nicotine patch, nicotine gum, nicotine lozenge, nicotine nasal spray, and nicotine inhaler. The transdermal nicotine patch is applied to the skin and delivers a continuous dose of nicotine over 16–24 hours. People often start at the dose closest to their current level of smoking and then gradually "step down" to lower doses as their cravings for tobacco remit or become easier to manage. The nicotine gum and lozenge are administered orally. The nicotine gum is not used the same way as chewing gum—it is chewed a few times until some nicotine is released, leading to a tingling or peppery sensation, and then the gum is "parked" on the side of the mouth to allow the nicotine to be absorbed by the cheek.

Similarly, the nicotine lozenge is "parked" on the side of the cheek and slowly dissolves as the nicotine is absorbed. Both the gum and lozenge can be used several times during the day in response to cravings. The nasal spray delivers small doses of nicotine, which are absorbed through the lining of the nose. The inhaler consists of a thin plastic tube that often resembles a cigarette and a porous nicotine-filled plug located at base of the inhaler. Metered doses are delivered to users, and when inhaled, the nicotine vapor is absorbed in the lining of the mouth. (The nicotine vapor from e-cigarettes, in contrast, is absorbed in the lungs.)

Other treatments are the medications bupropion and varenicline. Bupropion is an atypical antidepressant that inhibits the reuptake of dopamine, serotonin, and noradrenaline in the central nervous system. It is also a noncompetitive nicotine receptor antagonist. How bupropion reduces craving in people who smoke is not yet clear, but inhibition of the reductions of dopamine and noradrenaline levels in the central nervous system associated with nicotine withdrawal could be involved. The mechanisms by which bupropion works as an antidepressant and a tobacco cessation medication do not appear to be related, as this medication is effective for smokers both with and without depression.

Varenicline has a unique dual mechanism of action, as a partial agonist and antagonist of nicotine acetylcholine receptors. When varenicline binds to these receptors, dopamine is released at about half the level as nicotine from cigarettes, thereby preventing a "high" from nicotine, but it is enough to relieve nicotine withdrawal symptoms and cravings. Smokers who use varenicline report that their urges to smoke are reduced, and in some cases, the thought or act of smoking is described as aversive. Varenicline is an effective aid to smoking cessation, with success rates similar to nicotine replacement (monotherapy) and bupropion.

All the aforementioned tobacco cessation medications have been found to improve tobacco cessation rates at six months postquit or longer. NRT has been found to increase cessation rates by 53%–68% compared with placebo or no NRT. The use of combination therapy is also efficacious. Combination therapy is the use of two types of nicotine replacement therapy, for example, the use of the nicotine patch and gum or lozenge, or the combination of bupropion and NRT.

Behavioral Interventions

Behavioral interventions for tobacco cessation are efficacious and highly recommended for individuals who use tobacco. One of the most effective elements in behavioral interventions is to identify tobacco cues and corresponding coping strategies for these triggers. Standard tobacco cessation treatments typically use a cognitive behavioral therapy (CBT) approach, which teaches people to avoid tobacco triggers, change routines that involve tobacco use, and alter thoughts about using tobacco (e.g., *I bet I could just have one cigarette without going back to smoking a pack a day*). Since stress and negative mood are often conceptualized as primary triggers for tobacco cravings, these treatments routinely discuss stress management and provide skills for managing negative mood, which might include exercises to alter a negative mood or thoughts about resuming smoking as well as relaxation techniques. Another effective element of behavioral interventions is to help individuals identify and develop a support network for quitting, such as friends and family willing to encourage people who use tobacco to quit.

One challenge to tobacco cessation interventions is lack of adequate access to care. Individuals who are most in need of behavioral interventions are often those who are poor and have difficulty accessing health-care services. In addition, there is a lack of supply of intensive behavioral counseling for tobacco cessation in health-care settings and the community. In order to provide greater access to tobacco cessation, national and state resources have focused on telephone quitlines for tobacco cessation, which are efficacious. One area of recent advancement is the dissemination of technology-based delivery methods for tobacco cessation, including smartphone apps, web-based interventions, and text messaging services.

Motivational Interviewing

Individuals who use tobacco are often ambivalent about quitting. Health-care providers can help their patients by recognizing this ambivalence and supporting the patient's autonomy in choosing to quit and increasing their motivation and to make a quit attempt. Motivational interviewing (MI) helps individuals voice their own perspectives and values with regard to making choices. Providers help support patient initiatives and choice regarding treatment, which differs from other approaches that use pressure based on the negative health effects of tobacco.

Alternative Tobacco Treatment Approaches

Not all people want to stop using tobacco or nicotine containing products. For those individuals, *harm reduction* can be considered. Harm reduction approaches include the use of e-cigarettes and snus to reduce tobacco smoking, the most dangerous form of tobacco/nicotine consumption, or encouragement to smoke fewer cigarettes. There have been few well-conducted studies of these approaches, so more research is necessary to better understand how efficacious they are (Lindson-Hawley et al. 2016).

Another approach to tobacco cessation is hypnotherapy. Professionals use hypnosis to try to weaken or remove one's desire for tobacco or improve one's ability to concentrate on quitting. Several studies have compared hypnotherapy to control conditions, including no treatment, advice, or psychological treatment. There was variability in the results of these trials, and there is no clear evidence that hypnotherapy is useful (Barnes et al. 2010).

Research has also been conducted on the use of other drugs for tobacco cessation. Alternative products being investigated include cytisine, a medication with a similar molecular structure to nicotine; nortriptyline, a tricyclic antidepressant; clonidine, an anxiolytic; selective serotonin reuptake inhibitors (SSRIs); and supplements such as St. John's wort (Beard et al. 2016). Much of this research is in the early stages, and clinical trials have not yet been conducted, so it is unclear whether these medications are efficacious for tobacco cessation.

In one study, psilocybin, a psychedelic substance, in combination with a structured treatment program, was found to be an effective aid for tobacco cessation (Johnson, Garcia-Romeu, and Griffiths 2017). More research is necessary to evaluate new and alternative approaches to tobacco cessation and the reduction of tobacco-related harm.

In summary, tobacco use is a serious and life-threatening addiction. Although the prevalence of its use is decreasing in some parts of the world, the overall mortality rate due to tobacco use across the globe is high. Vulnerable people, such as the poor and those with mental health disorders are most at risk for smoking and have the most difficulty quitting. Treatments such as pharmacotherapy and behavioral interventions are effective at helping individuals quit using tobacco, and more advancements in tobacco treatment, including the use of e-cigarettes as a harm reduction approach, require more research and evaluation.

Bibliography

American Psychiatric Association. *Diagnostic and Statistical Manual of Mental Disorders: Fifth Edition*. Arlington, VA: American Psychiatric Association, 2013.

Baggett, Travis P., Matthew L. Tobey, and Nancy A. Rigotti. "Tobacco Use among Homeless People—Addressing the Neglected Addiction." *New Engl J Med* 369 (2013), 201–204.

Bao, Wei, Guifeng Xu, Jiachun Lu, Linda Snetselaar, and Robert B. Wallace. "Changes in Electronic Cigarette Use among Adults in the United States, 2014–2016." *JAMA* 319 (2018), 2039–2041.

Barnes, Jo, Christine Y. Dong, Hayden McRobbie, Natalie Walker, Monaz Mehta, and Lindsay F. Stead. "Hypnotherapy for Smoking Cessation." *Cochrane Database Syst Rev* 10 (2010), 1–39.

Beard, Emma, Lion Shahab, Damian M. Cummings, Susan Michie and Robert West. "New Pharmacological Agents to Aid Smoking Cessation and Tobacco Harm Reduction: What Has Been Investigated, and What Is in the Pipeline?" *CNS Drugs* 30 (2016), 951–983.

Berger, Israel and Julie Mooney-Somers. "Smoking Cessation Programs for Lesbian, Gay, Bisexual, Transgender, and Intersex People: A Content-Based Systematic Review." *Nicotine Tob Res* 19 (2017), 1408–1417.

Cahill, Kate and Tim Lancaster. "Workplace Interventions for Smoking Cessation." *Cochrane Database Syst Rev* 2 (2014), 1–126.

Centers for Disease Control. "Burden of Tobacco Use in the U.S." (2018a). Accessed January 22, 2019. https://www.cdc.gov/tobacco /campaign/tips/resources/data/cigarette-smoking-in-united-states.html

Centers for Disease Control. "Current Cigarette Smoking Among Adults—United States, 2005–2015." *MMWR Morb Mortal Wkly Rep* 64 (2016), 1205–1211. Accessed April 20, 2018. https://www .cdc.gov/mmwr/volumes/65/wr/mm6544a2.htm?s_cid=mm6544a2_w

Centers for Disease Control. "Economic Trends in Tobacco" (2018b). Accessed May 10, 2018. https://www.cdc.gov/tobacco/data_statistics /fact_sheets/economics/econ_facts/index.htm

Centers for Disease Control. "Health Effects of Cigarette Smoking" (2017). Accessed March 20, 2018. https://www.cdc.gov/tobacco/data_statistics /fact_sheets/health_effects/effects_cig_smoking/index.htm

Centers for Disease Control. "Tobacco Use among Adults with Mental Illness and Substance Use Disorders" (2019). Accessed January 22, 2019. https://www.cdc.gov/tobacco/disparities/mental-illness-substance -use/index.htm

Cnattinguis, Sven. "The Epidemiology of Smoking during Pregnancy: Smoking Prevalence, Maternal Characteristics, and Pregnancy Outcomes." *Nicotine Tob Res* Supplement S (2004), 125–140.

Cooper, Sue, Sophie Orton, Jo Leonardi-Bee, Emma Brotherton, Laura Vanderbloemen, Katharine Bowker, Felix Naughton, et al. "Smoking and Quit Attempts during Pregnancy and Postpartum: A Longitudinal UK Cohort." *BMJ Open* 7 (2017), e018746. doi:10.1136/ bmjopen-2017-018746.

Doubeni, Chyke A., George Reed, and Joseph R. Difranza. "Early Course of Nicotine Dependence in Adolescent Smokers." *Pediatrics* 125 (2010), 1127–1133.

Drake, Patrick, Anne K. Driscoll, and T. J. Mathews. Cigarette Smoking during Pregnancy: United States, 2016. NCHS Data Brief, no 305. Hyattsville, MD: National Center for Health Statistics, 2018.

Ekpu, Victor U., and Abraham K. Brown. "The Economic Impact of Smoking and of Reducing Smoking Prevalence: Review of Evidence." *Tob Use Insights* 8 (2015), 1–35.

Eriksen, Michael, Judith Mackay, and Hana Ross. *The Tobacco Atlas, Fourth Edition.* Atlanta, GA: World Lung Association, 2013.

Gentzke, Andrea S., MeLisa Creamer, Karen A. Cullen, Bridget K. Ambrose, Gordon Willis, Ahmed Jamal, and Brian King. Vital Signs: Tobacco Product Use among Middle and High School Students—United States, 2011–2018. *MMWR* 68 (2019), 157–164. doi:10.15585/mmwr .mm6806e1.

Hirayama, T. "Non-Smoking Wives of Heavy Smokers Have a Higher Risk of Lung Cancer: A Study From Japan." *BMJ* 282 (1981), 183–185.

Institute of Medicine. "Combating Tobacco Use in Military and Veteran Populations." Washington, DC: National Academies Press, 2009.

James I. "A Counterblaste to Tobacco" (1604). Accessed April 8, 2018. https://www.laits.utexas.edu/poltheory/james/blaste/blaste.html

Jawad, Mohammed, Rana Charide, Reem Waziry, Andrea Darzi, Rami A. Ballout, and Elie A. Aki. "The Prevalence and Trends of Waterpipe Smoking: A Systematic Review." *PLoS One* 13, no. 2 (2018), e0192191. Accessed March 23, 2018. doi:10.1371/journal.pone.0192191.

Johnson, Matthew, Albert Garcia-Romeu, and Roland R. Griffiths. "Long-Term Follow-Up of Psilocybin-Facilitated Smoking Cessation." *Am J Drug Alcohol Abuse* 43, no. 1 (2017), 55–60. doi:10.3109/009 52990.2016.1170135.

Leif Associates. *The Business Case for Coverage of Tobacco Cessation: 2012 Update.* Denver, CO: Leif Associates, 2012.

Lindson-Hawley, Nicola, Jamie Hartmann-Boyce, Thomas R. Fanshawe, Rachna Begh, Amanda Farley, and Tim Lancaster. "Interventions to Reduce Harm From Continued Tobacco Use." *Cochrane Database Syst Rev* 10 (2016), 1–94.

Lumley, Judith, Catherine Chamberlain, Therese Dowswell, Sandy Oliver, Laura Oakley, and Lyndsey Watson. "Interventions for Promoting Smoking Cessation during Pregnancy." *Cochrane Database Syst Rev* 3 (2009), CD001055. doi:10.1002/14651858.CD001055.pub3.

Maciosek, Michael V., Xin Xu, Amy L. Butani, and Terry F. Pechacek. "Smoking-Attributable Medical Expenditures by Age, Sex, and

Smoking Status Estimated using a Relative Risk Approach." *Prev Med* 77 (2015), 162–167.

Taylor, Gemma, Ann McNeill, Alan Girling, Amanda Farley, Nicola Lindson-Hawley, and Paul Aveyard. "Change in Mental Health After Smoking Cessation: Systematic Review and Meta-Analysis." *BMJ* 348 (2014), g1151.

U.S. Department of Health and Human Services. "The Health Consequences of Involuntary Smoking: A Report of the Surgeon General." Rockville, MD: U.S. Department of Health and Human Services, Public Health Service, Centers for Disease Control, Center for Health Promotion and Education, Office on Smoking and Health, 1986.

U.S. Department of Health and Human Services. "The Health Consequences of Smoking—50 Years of Progress: A Report of the Surgeon General, 2014." Atlanta, GA: U.S. Department of Health and Human Services, Centers for Disease Control and Prevention, National Center for Chronic Disease Prevention and Health Promotion, Office on Smoking and Health, 2014.

Wellman, Robert J., Erika N. Dugas, Hartley Dutczak, Erin K. O'Loughlin, Geetanjali D. Datta, Beatrice Lauzon, and Jennifer O'Loughlin. "Predictors of the Onset of Cigarette Smoking: A Systematic Review of Longitudinal Population-Based Studies in Youth." *Am J Prev Med* 51 (2016), 767–778.

World Health Organization. "International Statistical Classification of Diseases and Related Health Problems, 10th Revision" (2016). Accessed April 13, 2018. http://apps.who.int/classifications/icd10/browse/2016/en

World Health Organization. *WHO Global Report on Trends in Prevalence of Tobacco Smoking 2000–2025, Second Edition.* Geneva: World Health Organization, 2018.

Xu, Xin, Ellen Bishop, Sara Kennedy, Sean Simpson, and Terry Pechacek. "Annual Healthcare Spending Attributable to Cigarette Smoking." *Am J Prev Med* 38 (2015), 326–333.

Yoong, Sze Lin, Emily Stockings, Li Kheng Chai, Flora Tzelepis, John Wiggers, Christopher Oldmeadow, Christine Paul, et al. "Prevalence of Electronic Nicotine Delivery systems (ENDS) among Youth Globally: A Systematic Review and Meta-Analysis of Country Level Data." *Aust N Z J Public Health* (2018). Accessed May 1, 2018. doi:10.1111/1753-6405.12777.

Zhou, Sherry, Leili Behrooz, Michael Weitzman, Grace Pan, Ruzmyn Vilcassim, Jaime E. Mirowsy, Patrick Breysee, et al. "Secondhand Hookah Smoke: An Occupational Hazard for Hookah Bar Employees." *Tob Control* 26, no. 1 (2017), 40–45. doi:10.1136/tobaccocontrol-2015-052505.

Glossary

AA (Alcoholics Anonymous)

a mutual-aid group in which people with an **alcohol use disorder** support each other.

Abstinence

the practice of not engaging in **addictive** behaviors or using substances that may lead to **substance use disorder.**

Abuse

misuse of **drugs.** Term perceived by some as derogatory because it connotes violence and anger and is not relevant to **substance use disorder.**

Addict

person with an **addiction.** Term often avoided; some perceive it as derogatory because it seems to imply that person is nothing but their **addiction.**

Addiction

compulsive or out-of-control substance use or involvement in activity despite adverse consequences, involving **craving, dependence, tolerance,** and **withdrawal.** Some prefer the phrase **substance use disorder.**

Addictive

description of substance or activity that may lead to **addiction.**

Adrenaline

hormone produced in adrenal gland, related to stress, sometimes known as epinephrine.

Agonist

ligand or **drug** that activates **receptor**.

Alcohol

ethanol, or ethyl alcohol; molecule containing two carbon atoms, six hydrogen atoms, and one oxygen atom. Liquid at room temperature. Common substance of **misuse**.

Alkaloid

bitter-tasting, nitrogen-containing compound of plant origin; has physiological actions on humans, e.g., atropine, caffeine, **cocaine**, **morphine**, quinine, and strychnine.

Amphetamine

addictive stimulant drug, used in treatment of **attention deficit hyperactivity disorder**.

Amygdala

part of **limbic system** to do with emotions and memory.

Analgesia

relief of pain.

Anandamide

endocannabinoid molecule produced in the body, acts at **cannabinoid CB1 receptors**.

Anesthesia, general

unconsciousness caused by anesthetic substance, purpose is to allow painless surgery; some general anesthetic agents are **chloroform**, **ether**, **ketamine**, and **nitrous oxide**.

Anesthesia, local

unawareness of sensation, particularly pain in one area of the body; has no effects on consciousness, purpose is to allow painless surgery. **Cocaine** is sometimes still used as topical local anesthetic in ear, nose, and throat surgery.

Antagonist

substance that binds to but does not activate **receptor**, blocking effects of another substance.

Anticholinergic

blocking actions of **acetylcholine**; leads to dry mouth, constipation, and sometimes confusion.

Aromatic hydrocarbon

cyclic compound with benzene ring, used as industrial **solvent**, e.g., benzene, toluene, xylene. Characteristic smell, can be **misused**. See **inhalant**.

Associative learning

process of learning in which a response is associated with a particular stimulus. Offers way of understanding **addiction** and **relapse**. See **conditioned response**.

Attention deficit hyperactivity disorder (ADHD)

psychiatric disorder marked by impulsivity, hyperactivity, and difficulty sustaining attention.

Ayahuasca

also known as yage, beverage made from the shrub chacruna (*Psychotria viridis*), which contains the **hallucinogenic** indole **alkaloid dimethyltryptamine (DMT)**, and the ayahuasca vine (*Banisteriopsis caapi*), which contains a monoamine oxidase inhibitor that prevents the body's breakdown of **DMT**. Used for treatment of post–traumatic stress disorder and **addictions**. Causes violent vomiting and **hallucinations**.

Bagging

method of inhaling gases or **vapors** from bag placed over the mouth, mouth and nose, or head. See **inhalants.**

Benzedrine

first pharmaceutical **drug** containing **amphetamines**; marketed as decongestant inhaler, bronchodilator, and appetite suppressant; sold in pill form to treat obesity and narcolepsy and to increase wakefulness; known as "bennies," **addictive.**

Benzodiazepine

class of **psychoactive** drugs formed by benzene and diazepine rings. Widely prescribed to treat anxiety, can be **addictive.**

Binge

short period of extreme use of drug or involvement in activity.

Binge drinking

excessive **alcohol** use, or drinking enough **alcohol** to have **blood alcohol level** of over 0.08%, or drinking four or more **alcoholic** drinks at one time for women and five or more for men, associated with harm.

Blood alcohol level

amount of **alcohol** in blood, sometimes referred to as "blood alcohol concentration," measured in grams of alcohol per 100 ml of blood; expressed as percent of blood volume; a breathalyzer approximates blood alcohol level. Levels of over 0.08% indicate level of **intoxication** that impairs driving.

Buprenorphine

semisynthetic partial **mu-opioid agonist,** used in treatment of **opioid addiction.**

Burn

chemical reaction, combustion, rapid combination of fuel with oxygen that changes the nature of the fuel and produces energy. **Tobacco,** cocaine powder, and **cannabis** are burned. Burned **tobacco** releases several thousand chemicals, some toxic and/or carcinogenic. See, in contrast, **vapor** and **e-cigarette**.

Cannabidiol (CBD)

nonpsychoactive phytocannabinoid with medical uses. Does not bind strongly to CB1 or CB2 **cannabinoid receptors**; seems to act as **antagonist** with respect to other **cannabinoids**.

Cannabinoid

substance active at cannabinoid **receptors**. Three types exist: **phytocannabinoids**, endogenous cannabinoids, also known as **endocannabinoids**, and **synthetic cannabinoids**.

Cannabinoid receptors

receptors located in nervous system; CB1 **receptors** are found primarily in brain, CB2 **receptors** in immune system.

Cannabis

genus of annual weedy plant; female plant produces resin containing **phytocannabinoids** and **terpenoids**, also produces fiber (**hemp**); term sometimes used to refer to resinous and **psychoactive** product of leaves and flowering tops of female plant, sometimes known as buds. See **marijuana**.

Cannabis indica

species of *Cannabis*, short bushy plant with wide leaves, native to Asian mountainous regions, frost tolerant.

Cannabis sativa

species of *Cannabis*, tall plant with narrow leaves, native to warm or equatorial climates.

Chloroform

$CHCl_3$, produced by some seaweed and fungi, can be synthesized in laboratory; liquid, easily **vaporized**; its **vapors** were used as **general anesthetic** agent; can be drunk or sniffed; **addictive**.

Cigarette

small, convenient, and easily transportable paper cylinder from which burning **tobacco** or **cannabis** can be **smoked.**

Coca

shrub growing in the Andes, *Erythroxylon* (or *Erythroxylum*) *coca;* leaves contain the **alkaloid cocaine.**

Cocaine

addictive drug; alkaloid produced by **coca** shrub; in brain it leads to **dopamine** increase by disabling protein that removes **dopamine** from **synapses.**

Codependence

term describing relationship in which one person has an **addiction** and another (the "codependent" person) seems to be controlled by or feel responsible for that person; closely related to **enabling.**

Comorbid

presence of two or more related medical disorders.

Compulsion

a difficult-to-control impulse to repeat a behavior; in the past, **gambling** was considered a compulsion.

Conditioned response

response that becomes associated with a stimulus after this stimulus is paired with another stimulus that normally yields the response, sometimes considered as a part of learning. See **relapse** and **associative learning.**

Contingency management

method of treating **substance use disorder** in which reinforcement is used to encourage selected behaviors, e.g., giving someone a voucher or money if they attend a **meeting** or provide a urine sample.

Controlled substance

government-regulated substance thought to be dangerous.

Controlled Substances Act

in 1970, Congress passed the Comprehensive Drug Abuse Prevention and Controlled Act. Title II of this federal legislation, commonly known as the Controlled Substances Act, established five groups or "schedules" of controlled substances or drugs. Schedule I drugs are thought to have no medical use and to be highly addictive. Some examples are cannabis, DMT, heroin, MDMA (ecstasy), and peyote. Schedule II drugs have some medical use and include cocaine, methadone, methamphetamine, and methylphenidate. Schedule III drugs are less addictive and include acetaminophen with codeine, anabolic steroids, and testosterone. Schedule IV drugs include many benzodiazepines. Schedule V drugs include drugs with very low quantities of codeine, diphenoxylate with atropine, and pregabalin.

Co-occurring

presence of two or more unrelated medical disorders

Crack cocaine

rock-like form of free-base cocaine prepared with baking soda (sodium bicarbonate) and cocaine powder; vaporizes at 89°C. Can be smoked and enters brain within 10 seconds, where it creates intensely pleasurable and reinforcing effects. Called crack because the "rock" crackles when heated.

Craving

powerful desire for substance or activity, an addition to *DSM-5* criteria for substance use disorder.

DEA (Drug Enforcement Administration)

created by President Richard Nixon in 1973 to enforce the Controlled Substances Act and to oversee scheduling of drugs. The DEA ensures security and storage as required by the Controlled Substances Act. The DEA also works with state and local law enforcement to prevent drug trafficking and drug-related violence.

Default mode network

theoretical brain network that is active during daydreaming and thinking about self, others, the past, and the future.

Denial

refusal or inability to recognize painful truths.

Dependence

hallmark of **addiction**; can be physiological, meaning that there are changes in the **reward system**, and that the person has become **tolerant** of the dose or activity and/or goes through **withdrawal** without the **drug** or activity. Dependence can also be psychological, meaning that the person feels that he or she must continue **drug** or activity.

Detoxification

process through which a person with a **substance use disorder** passes after deciding to stop substance use (rather than just reduce it), commonly called "detox."

Disease model

theory that **addiction** is a disease or medical condition rather than a social or psychological issue or choice.

Dissociative drugs

drugs that make people feel disconnected from their body and environment; a subgroup of **hallucinogenic drugs**; e.g., **ketamine, phencyclidine,** *Salvia divinorum.*

Distillation

process whereby the alcoholic content of **alcoholic** beverages is increased.

DMT (dimethyltryptamine)

hallucinogen found in a number of Amazonian plants, active ingredient in **ayahuasca**; can also be synthesized. **Smoked** in pipe or drunk.

Dopamine

neurotransmitter; many, perhaps all, **addictions** involve a rapid but not sustained increase of dopamine at the **nucleus accumbens** in the **reward system**; dopamine is motivating and connected with anticipation and **associative learning**; also a **hormone**; precursor to **adrenaline** and **noradrenaline**.

Double-blind study

clinical trial in which researchers and subjects do not know which treatment the subject is receiving. See **open-label study**.

Dronabinol

synthetic **THC**; used to decrease nausea and vomiting and to increase appetite.

Drug

substance prescribed by a health-care provider or bought over the counter that is used in the treatment or prevention of disease; also known as medicine or medication, e.g., antibiotics or aspirin; or a substance used to enhance physical or mental well-being that may be illegal to sell, e.g., **heroin**.

DSM (Diagnostic and Statistical Manual of Mental Disorders)

manual prepared by the American Psychiatric Association containing descriptions, symptoms, and other criteria for diagnosing mental disorders; most recent version is fifth, *DSM-5*, published in 2013.

E-cigarette

electronic **nicotine** delivery system in which liquid **nicotine** is **vaporized**. Thought to be safer than **burning tobacco,** which produces carcinogenic substances.

Enabling

helping an **addicted** person maintain their **addiction** but not necessarily in a deliberate manner, e.g., bailing out family members to protect them from legal consequences of their **addiction**; closely related to **codependence**.

Endocannabinoid

endogenous cannabinoid; short-lived molecule in nervous and immune systems of animals (including humans) that is active at **cannabinoid receptor**. See **retrograde transmitters**.

Endogenous

within or from the organism or system, usually the brain.

Endorphin

neurotransmitter produced by brain (*endogenous* m*orphine*); vigorous activity leads to endorphin production; endorphins activate **opioid receptors**, producing **analgesia**, decreasing anxiety, and improving mood.

Ether

volatile flammable liquid, used in "ether frolics" in the 19th century, **addictive**; ether **vapor** was used as **general anesthetic**. See **inhalant**.

Evidence-based treatment

treatment based on scientific research, often meaning randomized **double-blind studies** that are peer reviewed.

Executive functioning

brain activities including impulse inhibition, task initiation, planning, and self-monitoring; and capabilities such as working memory and cognitive flexibility.

Fentanyl

potent synthetic **opioid**; used in patch form as a topical medication for safe and effective pain relief; also made illegally and the cause of many **opioid** overuse deaths.

Fetal alcohol syndrome

consequences to fetus of mother who drank **alcohol** while pregnant, including characteristic facial features, birth defects, and developmental delays.

Free-base

basic form of amine, usually an **alkaloid**. Free-base **cocaine** is heated, **vaporized**, and **smoked**. Crack **cocaine** is a form of free-base **cocaine**.

GABA (gamma-aminobutyric acid)

amino acid, chief inhibitory **neurotransmitter** in brain.

Gambling

playing a game of chance with uncertain outcome for a prize of some sort; involves varying amounts of skill, knowledge, and luck. Understood now as a behavioral **addiction** because it shares characteristics with **substance use disorders**.

Glutamate

amino acid, chief excitatory **neurotransmitter** in brain, connected with **addiction** and **dopamine**. Glutamate pathways modify **dopaminergic** pathways.

G-protein-coupled receptors

protein in cell membrane that in response to extracellular substances transmits signal to a G protein (guanine nucleotide-binding protein), a molecule within a cell that activates enzymes.

Hallucination

seeing, hearing, touching, tasting, or smelling something that is not there; visual hallucinations are associated with **hallucinogens**.

Hallucinogen

drug causing **hallucinations**, usually visual, and distortions in emotion and judgment; includes **dissociative drugs**.

Harm reduction

decrease of adverse consequences caused by risky activities without eliminating activity; e.g., helmets, seat belts, and sunscreen; with respect to **addiction** an example is supplying clean needles to **heroin addicts**.

Hashish

strong **drug** produced by drying resin from *Cannabis* plant, can be **smoked** or ingested orally.

Hemp

fiber of stem of *Cannabis* plant, used in the past to make rope, fabrics, sails, and paper; sometimes used to refer to variety of plant or to its psychoactive products.

Heroin

morphine with two acetyl groups added to it. It is lipid soluble and enters the brain easily where it is metabolized into the active **drug morphine**. It can be injected, **smoked**, **snorted**, or sniffed.

Hippocampus

part of **limbic system** and **reward system** where emotions and memories are processed.

Hormone

molecule produced by a gland that reaches its target organ via circulation.

Huffing

inhaling vapors from a material saturated with a **solvent** that is placed near mouth or nose, or, more generally, inhaling fumes, usually through the mouth. See **inhalants**.

Hypnotic

sleep-inducing or calming medication; similar to **sedatives** and **tranquilizers**, but more often refers to the sleep-inducing activity of a **drug**.

Incidence

risk of having certain condition or number of new cases of disorder. Compare to **prevalence**.

Inhalants

large group of substances intended for a variety of purposes that some people **inhale** for their intoxicating effects, e.g., gasoline, glue, **nitrous oxide**, paint thinner.

Inhale

to breathe in, particularly with respect to **volatile** substances not intended for that purpose.

Intoxication

state in which a person has **volatile** emotions, is uncoordinated, has slurred speech, impaired judgment, sedation, or excitement. Caused by many substances, particularly **alcohol**.

Kappa-opioid receptor

opioid-receptor subtype, involved in **misuse** of *Salvia divinorum*.

Ketamine

anesthetic drug, **snorted** as a recreational **drug** ("special K") because of its **dissociative** effects; being explored as a rapidly acting antidepressant medication that may "reset" the **default mode network**.

Ligand

molecule that binds to a **receptor**.

Limbic system

brain network associated with emotions and drives such as fear, anger, pleasure, hunger, and sex; contains the **reward system**.

LSD (d-lysergic acid diethylamide)

classic **hallucinogen**. Synthesized by Albert Hofmann in 1938 from lysergic acid, an **alkaloid** produced by an ergot fungus that grows on rye.

Marijuana

popular name for **cannabis**; may come from Mexican word *mariguana* although this is far from clear; can refer to plant or just the **psychoactive** dried flowers and leaves; can be **smoked**, **vaped**, or ingested orally.

MAT (medication-assisted treatment)

use of medication to treat **substance use disorders**.

MDMA (3,4-methylenedioxy-methamphetamine)

a synthetic **hallucinogen** and/or **stimulant**, also known by its street names, ecstasy or Molly. May be **addictive**.

Medical marijuana

marijuana used for medical purposes, not for its **psychoactive** properties.

Medical model

See **disease model**.

Meeting

important part of **AA**; a group of people who get together to discuss their **alcohol** use; often part of treatment approach to other disorders as well. Sometimes called 12-step meeting.

Mescaline

hallucinogenic drug found in **peyote** and San Pedro cacti, can be chemically synthesized.

Mesocorticolimbic dopamine pathway

meso refers to **ventral tegmental area** and **nucleus accumbens**, which are located in **midbrain**, also known as *mesencephalon; cortico* refers to **prefrontal cortex;** *limbic* refers to **limbic system**. Sometimes referred to as mesolimbic pathway. Brain pathway implicated in **substance use disorders**. See **reward system**.

MET (motivational enhancement therapy)

therapeutic technique used to help people with **addictions**; encourages them to realize ways in which **addiction** is harming them, involves **MI**, and includes personalized assessment, feedback, and plans for how to change.

Methadone

synthetic **opioid**, full **agonist** at **mu-opioid receptor**, treats pain and opioid addiction.

Methylphenidate

stimulant used for treatment of **attention deficit hyperactivity disorder.**

MI (motivational interviewing)

talking to people with **addictions** in a nonconfrontational and nonjudgmental way; helping them address ambivalence and realize how **addiction** is harming them or interfering with their other values or goals, inquiring about their readiness to change and eliciting that person's motivation for change.

Midbrain

also known as *mesencephalon*, sits at top of brain stem, where **ventral tegmental area** and **nucleus accumbens** are located.

Misuse

preferred word for **abuse** with respect to **drugs;** using drug or activity in a way that was not originally intended and that causes problems.

Morphine

active ingredient of **opium;** precursor to **heroin; analgesic** and **addicting,** acts at **mu-opioid receptor.**

Mu-opioid receptor

opioid-receptor subtype, involved in **addiction,** responsible for pleasurable and **analgesic** effects of **opioids,** also leads to lower blood pressure, itching, nausea, decreased respiration, constricted pupils, constipation.

Naloxone

opioid antagonist, reverses **opioid** overdoses.

Naltrexone

opioid antagonist, used to block **cravings** for **opioids, alcohol,** and **addictive** activities; long-acting intramuscular form may be more effective than pill.

Narcotic

opioid. In the past, also referred to other mind-altering or **addictive** drugs, including **cocaine**. Sometimes refers to any **drug** that reduces pain and leads to sleep or stupor.

Neuron

nerve cell, fundamental unit of the brain, main purpose is transmission of information.

Neurotransmitter

chemical substance; messenger that is released from a **neuron**, diffuses across a **synapse** or junction, and causes activity in another **neuron**, a muscle fiber, or some other structure.

Nicotine

alkaloid produced in leaves of **tobacco** plant, *Nicotinia*. Acts at **acetylcholine receptors** to excite **dopaminergic neurons** in **reward system**; increases levels of other **neurotransmitters**; highly **addictive**.

Nitrite inhalants

amyl, butyl, isobutyl nitrites, **inhaled** to enhance sexual pleasure. May lead to mild euphoria. See **inhalant**.

Nitrous oxide

N_2O; colorless, mildly **intoxicating** gas now used as **anesthetic** agent in dentistry and obstetrics and gynecology; known as "laughing gas"; also **drug** of **misuse**. See **inhalant**.

NMDA (N-methyl-D-aspartate) receptor

receptor activated by **glutamate**, inhibited by **alcohol**; increased activity during **alcohol withdrawal** can lead to seizures and death. Also involved with learning and memory.

Noradrenaline

hormone and **neurotransmitter**, sometimes known as norepinephrine.

Nucleus accumbens

group of **neurons** in **limbic system**, part of **reward system**; "tags" some activities as needing to be repeated, receives **dopaminergic** input from **ventral tegmental area.**

Open-label study

clinical trial in which researchers and subjects know which treatment the subject is receiving. See **double-blind study.**

Opiate

related to **opium,** and natural substances related to it, such as morphine and codeine. See **opioid.**

Opioid

natural, synthetic, or semisynthetic substance acting at **opioid receptor.** More inclusive word than **opiate.**

Opioid epidemic

rapid increase in use of **opioid drugs** in the early 21st century that has led to many deaths.

Opioid receptors

group of inhibitory **G-protein-coupled receptors;** delta, kappa, and mu; activated by **endorphins** produced by brain or by exogenous opioids.

Opium

drug produced by unripe seed capsule of opium poppy, *Papaver somniferum.*

Organic solvent

carbon-based **solvent** that dissolves fatty or nonpolarized substances, or lipids, e.g., dry-cleaning fluid, gasoline. Can be **misused.** See **inhalants.**

Papaver somniferum

poppy plant that produces **opium** in its unripe seed capsules.

Paranoia

Undue suspiciousness, associated with **misuse** of many **drugs**, particularly **stimulants**.

Partial agonist

substance that binds to a **receptor** but does not fully activate it.

Peyote

Lophophora williamsii; small, spineless cactus growing in northern Mexico and Texas, produces **psychoactive alkaloids**, particularly **mescaline**; used in some Native American rituals.

Phencyclidine (Phenyl-cyclohexyl piperidine, or PCP)

anesthetic drug (in the past), **snorted, smoked,** injected, or swallowed, misused as **dissociative drug;** possibly **addictive**.

Phytocannabinoid

one of over 100 closely related compounds, active at **cannabinoid receptor,** produced by **cannabis;** most important are **cannabidiol** and THC.

Postsynaptic neuron

neuron receiving message (via **neurotransmitters**) from **presynaptic neuron**. (But see **retrograde transmitters**.)

Prefrontal cortex

part of brain just behind forehead where we plan, organize, and entertain abstract thoughts.

Presynaptic neuron

neuron sending message (via **neurotransmitters**) to **postsynaptic neuron**. (But see **retrograde transmitters**.)

Prevalence

number of people having certain disorder. Compare to **incidence**.

Prohibition

banning of substance or activity; when capitalized refers to banning of **alcohol** from 1920 to 1933 in the United States.

Psilocybin ([3-(2-Dimethylaminoethyl)-1*H*-indol-4-yl] dihydrogen phosphate)

hallucinogen, found in "magic mushrooms." Eaten raw or brewed into tea. Can be synthesized.

Psychedelic drug

hallucinogenic drug, from Greek for "mind-altering," coined by Humphry Osmond in 1956 with respect to **LSD** and **psilocybin.**

Psychoactive drug

drug that changes thinking and feeling.

Psychological dependence

emotional or cognitive need to take **drugs** or to continue in **addictive** activity.

Psychosis

mental health disorder involving some combination of hallucinations, delusions (fixed false beliefs), paranoia, and poor insight.

Psychotropic drug

psychoactive drug.

Receptor

protein in cell membrane that responds to specific molecules from outside of cell; similar to a lock that opens with a specific key. **Opioids** and **cannabinoids** have specific receptors.

Recidivism

return to undesirable behavior.

Recovery

stopping substance **misuse** and returning to normal state of health, mind, or strength; can be a slow, back and forth, and painful process.

Recovery model

approach to mental illness or substance **misuse** emphasizing hope, optimism, connection with others, and personal growth by increasing coping and problem-solving skills.

Recreational use

use of **drug** or activity for pleasure, without medical need, and without being **addicted**.

Relapse

recurrence of **addictive drug** use or activity. May happen in response to trigger, e.g., person or place associated with **misuse**. See **conditioned response**.

Remission

state when person with a **substance use disorder** no longer meets *DSM-5* criteria with exception of **craving**; several types exist early (3 to 12 months); sustained (over 12 months); in maintenance therapy (taking medications; see **MAT**); or in a controlled environment, such as prison or hospital, where there is no access to substances.

Retrograde transmitters

neurotransmitters that diffuse *backward* from **postsynaptic neurons** across **synapses** to **presynaptic** terminals where they bind to specific **G-protein-coupled receptors** and inhibit **neurotransmitter** release for a few seconds; e.g., **endocannabinoids**.

Reward system

circuit within brain; from **ventral tegmental area** to **nucleus accumbens** (where rapidly increasing **dopamine** levels play a role in **addiction**), **amygdala**, **hippocampus** and **prefrontal cortex**. Involved whenever we are engaged in activity likely to prolong our life or lead to reproduction.

System is "hijacked" by **drugs** or **addictive** activities, which lead to supranormal surges of **dopamine** in the **nucleus accumbens**. Over time, these **dopamine** surges decrease, so pleasure decreases, and **dopamine** also decreases during **withdrawal**, leading to misery.

Salvia divinorum

plant growing in cloud forests in Mexico (especially Oaxaca), Central America, and South America; can be chewed or **smoked**; leaves contain a **dissociative drug**; also known as diviner's sage or seer's sage.

Schedule

See **controlled substances**.

Sedatives

sleep-inducing or calming medication.

Serotonin (5-hydroxytryptamine, 5-HT)

neurotransmitter; at least 14 different **receptors** exist; classic **psychedelic** or **hallucinogenic drugs** may act at 5-HT2A **receptor**.

Smoke

to inhale gases released by **burning** or **vaporizing** substances such as **cannabis** (burns, vaporizes), free-base cocaine (vaporizes), heroin (vaporizes), nicotine (vaporizes), or tobacco (burns).

Sniffing

inhaling through nose, less powerful than **snorting**, lower down in nose; refers to use of **inhalants**; substance is absorbed through lungs, not nose. Sometimes used as synonym for **snorting**.

Snorting

inhaling **cocaine powder, heroin,** or **tobacco** through nose, more powerful than **sniffing**, higher up in nose, often done with a straw, tube, or rolled up currency bill; substance is absorbed into the blood stream through the nasal cavity blood vessels. Sometimes used as synonym for **sniffing**.

Solvent

substance capable of dissolving or dispersing one or more other substances. Water is the "universal solvent" and dissolves polar substances, as opposed to **organic solvents**, which dissolve nonpolar substances.

Speedball

mixture of **heroin** and **cocaine** (or similar substances); associated with many deaths, especially when used intravenously.

Stimulant

substance that increases physical and emotional energy; e.g., **amphetamine**, caffeine, **cocaine**.

Substance use disorder (SUD)

in *DSM-5*, describes pattern of **substance misuse** that adversely affects one's life and involves **craving, dependence, tolerance, and withdrawal**; some prefer this phrase to **abuse** and **addictions**.

Synapse

junction between two **neurons**, or a **neuron** and a muscle, or a **neuron** and a gland.

Synthetic cannabinoid

confusing term that refers to legal medical molecules such as **dronabinol**, or to illegal **addictive drugs** such as K2 or spice.

Terpenes

volatile compounds with flavor and fragrance; non**cannabinoid** plant components of *Cannabis*; may be synergistic with **THC**.

THC (delta-9-tetrahydrocannabinol)

phytocannabinoid, main psychoactive component in *Cannabis* plants.

Tobacco

plant in genus *Nicotinia* or product of leaf itself, contains **addictive alkaloid nicotine. Smoking burning** (sometimes called combustible) tobacco exposes person to thousands of carcinogenic substances.

Tolerance

the need for increasing amounts of a **drug** or activity to get same effect, as the brain learns to lower **dopamine** surge produced by the **addicting drug** or activity.

Tranquilizer

medication that lowers tension or anxiety. Similar to **hypnotic** and **sedative**. (But note that in the past *major tranquilizer* referred to medication used to treat **psychosis**.)

Vapor

gas resulting from heating of liquid or solid matter; structure of molecule does not change as a result of this process. **Cannabis** vaporizes at lower temperature than it **burns** and is thought to be purer, less toxic, and more potent than **burned cannabis**. **Alcohol** vaporizes to a small extent. **Solvents** vaporize. **Crack cocaine** (which is **free-base cocaine**) and **opium** are **smoked** as vapors. Vaporized **nicotine** is used in **e-cigarettes** and is thought to be safer than **burning tobacco**.

Ventral tegmental area (VTA)

a group of **neurons** in **midbrain**, origin of **dopaminergic** cell bodies of **mesocorticolimbic dopamine** system and other **dopamine** pathways; part of **reward system**; other **neurons** from VTA project to other parts of the brain, including **prefrontal cortex**.

Volatile

description of liquid that evaporates rapidly at room temperature; also used to describe state in which a person has rapidly changing emotions.

Whippit (or whippet)

small metal cartridge that contains compressed **nitrous oxide**; used as propellant for whipped cream, sometimes bought for the purpose of **inhaling nitrous oxide**.

Withdrawal

distress, or physical and psychological unease, insomnia, tremors, and malaise that occurs when someone **addicted** to a substance stops taking the **drug**. Hallmark of **addiction**. **Alcohol withdrawal** involves increased **NMDA** activity and may cause seizures; can be lethal.

For Further Reading

Alexander, Michelle. *The New Jim Crow: Mass Incarceration in the Age of Colorblindness*. New York: The New Press, 2012.

Brandt, Allan J. *The Cigarette Century: The Rise, Fall, and Deadly Persistence of the Product that Defined America*. New York: Basic Books, 2007.

Courtwright, David T. *Dark Paradise*. Cambridge: Harvard University Press, 2009a.

Courtwright, David T. *Forces of Habit*. Cambridge: Harvard University Press, 2009b.

Edwards, Griffith. *Alcohol: The World's Favorite Drug*. London: Thomas Dunne Books, 2003.

Frankenburg, Frances R. *Brain-Robbers: How Alcohol, Cocaine, Nicotine, and Opiates Have Changed Human History*. Santa Barbara: ABC-CLIO, 2014.

Heyman, Gene M. *Addiction: A Disorder of Choice*. Cambridge: Harvard University Press, 2010.

Markel, Howard. *An Anatomy of Addiction: Sigmund Freud, William Halsted, and the Miracle Drug Cocaine*. New York: Vintage Books, 2012.

Pert, Candace B., and Solomon H. Snyder. "Opiate Receptor: Demonstration in Nervous Tissue." *Science* 179, no. 4077 (January 1973), 1011–1014. doi:10.1126/science.179.4077.1011.

Pollan, Michael. *How to Change Your Mind: What the New Science of Psychedelics Teaches Us About Consciousness, Dying, Addiction, Depression, and Transcendence*. New York: Penguin Press, 2018.

Proctor, Robert N. *Golden Holocaust: Origins of the Cigarette Catastrophe and the Case for Abolition*. Berkeley: University of California Press, 2011.

Schultes, Richard Evans, Albert Hofmann, and Christian Rätsch. *Plants of the Gods: Their Sacred, Healing and Hallucinogenic Powers*. Rochester, VT: Healing Arts Press, 2001.

Schwartz, David G. *Roll the Bones: The History of Gambling*. London: Penguin, 2006.

Spinella, Marcello. *The Psychopharmacology of Herbal Medicine: Plant Drugs That Alter Mind, Brain, and Behavior*. Cambridge: MIT Press, 2001.

Streatfield, Dominic. *Cocaine: An Unauthorized Biography*. New York: Picador, 2001.

Tone, Andrea. *The Age of Anxiety: A History of America's Turbulent Affair with Tranquilizers*. New York: Basic Books, 2008.

Vaillant, George E. *The Natural History of Alcoholism*. Cambridge: Harvard University Press, 1985.

Volkow, Nora D., George F. Koob, and A. T. McLellan. "Neurobiologic Advances from the Brain Disease Model of Addiction." *New Engl J Med* 374, no. 4 (2016), 363–371.

About the Editor and Contributors

Editor

Frances R. Frankenburg, MD, obtained her medical degree at the University of Toronto where she completed a psychiatry residency. She was awarded a two-year fellowship at McLean Hospital in Belmont, Massachusetts, associated with Harvard Medical School. A clinician and educator, she has written over 120 academic journal articles and 3 books. She is a psychiatrist at the Edith Nourse Rogers Memorial Veterans Administration Medical Center (VAMC) in Bedford, MA. Dr. Frankenburg is professor of psychiatry at the Boston University School of Medicine.

Contributors

Caroline A. Arout, PhD, is an assistant professor of clinical neurobiology (in psychiatry) at Columbia University Irving Medical Center, and a research scientist at the New York State Psychiatric Institute. Her current research focuses on opioid and cannabis use disorders.

Jennifer Grant, MA, is a doctoral student in the clinical psychology program at Bowling Green State University. Her research focuses on addictions, particularly gambling disorder.

Joshua B. Grubbs, PhD, is an assistant professor in the Clinical Psychology Doctoral Program at Bowling Green State University. His research focuses primarily on morality, self-perception, and addiction, with a particular focus on behavioral addictions, such as gambling and compulsive sexual behavior.

Megan M. Kelly, PhD, is an associate professor of psychiatry at the University of Massachusetts Medical School. She is developing tobacco cessation treatments for those with mental health disorders as well as tobacco use and is also involved in research and implementation of organizational change for addressing tobacco use in mental health settings.

Shane W. Kraus, PhD, works in the areas of psychopathology, trauma, substance abuse, gambling disorder, and compulsive sexual behavior. He is an assistant professor of Clinical Psychology at University of Nevada, Las Vegas. He has published over 50 articles or chapters concerning addiction and psychopathology.

Anna Terajewicz LaRose, MD, completed her addiction psychiatry training at Boston University Medical Center. She has coauthored chapters on topics including alcohol and opioid use disorders. She is currently a staff psychiatrist at the Albany Stratton VAMC and clinical assistant professor in psychiatry at Albany Medical College.

Mehmet Sofuoglu, MD, PhD, is a professor of psychiatry at Yale University School of Medicine with expertise in the development of novel pharmacological and behavioral treatments for addictive disorders. He has served as principal investigator for five National Institutes of Health/National Institute on Drug Abuse funded grants on nicotine, cocaine, or opioid addiction.

Amanda U. von Horn, MD, is chief resident of psychiatry at Boston University School of Medicine. She will be an addiction psychiatry fellow at Boston University beginning in July 2019. Her current research focuses on involuntary commitment for substance abuse disorders in Massachusetts.

Amy Yule, MD, is board certified in adult, child, and addiction psychiatry. She is the medical director of the Addiction Recovery Management Service at Massachusetts General Hospital, where she works with young people with substance use disorders.

Index